A special gift
to

.... Irene ....

Love from

.... Iris ....

xxx

Solly Ozrovech

On Wings of Faith

*. . . but those who hope in the LORD
will renew their strength.
They will soar on wings like eagles . . .*
ISAIAH 40:31

Lux Verbi

Originally published by Lux Verbi
under the title OP VLERKE VAN GELOOF

Translated by Monica de Vries

Copyright © 1997 Lux Verbi
P.O. Box 1822, Cape Town

All rights reserved
Set in 12.5 on 15 pt Quorum
Printed and bound by
National Book Printers
Drukkery Street, Goodwood, Western Cape

First edition, first printing 1997
ISBN 0 86997 640 0

All Scripture quotations in this publication are from
The New International Version
Copyright © 1978
New York International Bible Society

AUTHOR'S NOTE

❖ ❖

In terms of history a quarter-century is very short, but in terms of one's life, it is a considerable period of time.

When I think back on this period, one word sums it up: "Grace!" and the song of praise in my heart is therefore, "Soli Deo gloria!"

A word of sincere thanks to Lux Verbi for their valued recognition in the form of this edition. Many images and faces come to mind when I recall the past years:

The well established "NG Kerk-Uitgewers" which was relaunched as the vibrant publishing company Lux Verbi.

The Head Office in the DRC Synod building was moved to Waterkant Street.

During the years there were some very special people who gave valuable input:

— Miss Elize Muller who inspired me to take the first cautious steps;
— Miss Berta Smit who further fired inspiration;
— Dr Willem van Zijl, the competent Christian businessman and planner;
— Mrs Hester Venter with whom I have had an open and meaning-ful relationship over many years;
— Rev Stefan Spies who personifies a new, contemporary, dynamic style ;
— all the friendly and accommodating staff members at Lux Verbi;
— all the known and unknown readers who form part of our ministry.

And Louise, my wife; the tender, quiet, caring influence; my sound-ing-board, honest critic, loved one and faithful companion.

How shall I ever be able to thank God for the past quarter-century?

"Give thanks to the LORD, for he is good; his love endures for ever!" (Ps 106:1).

Solly Ozrovech and his family

Solly Ozrovech, the sportsman

A young Solly Ozrovech with his legitimation in 1951

"Oom Solly" today

PUBLISHER'S NOTE

✦✦✦✦✦✦✦✦✦✦✦✦✦✦✦✦✦✦✦✦✦✦✦✦✦

Solly Ozrovech is undoubtedly one of the most popular Afrikaans authors of our time. Over the past 25 years more than a million of his books were sold at LUX VERBI and year after year they remain top sellers.

People often ask us as a publisher where the secret of Solly Ozrovech's success as an author lies. For those of us who are privileged to know "Oom Solly", as we call him, a number of reasons come to mind:

Solly Ozrovech is a devout Christian who practises what he preaches. Like Paul, he believes that nobody who believes in Jesus Christ will be disappointed. This faith is the basis of his characteristic *joie de vivre*, his humbleness and friendliness.

He is, above all, a man who loves people. He penetrates into the hearts of his readers and has great compassion for their suffering – a characteristic which is prominent in all his books. Whenever Solly Ozrovech writes about suffering and the comfort which God offers, he speaks from his own experience, because he is familiar with the dark side of life.

ON WINGS OF FAITH is our tribute to Solly Ozrovech who, for the past 25 years, has pursued his spiritual ministry through the written word.

To introduce each new month of this special devotional, twelve pictures of beautiful birds were selected. The bird theme was chosen because they symbolise God's care for us:

'Look at the birds of the air; they do not sow or reap or store away in barns, and yet your heavenly Father feeds them. Are you not much more valuable than they?"
— MATTHEW 6:26

There is also a symbolic link between the title ON WINGS OF FAITH and the motto of the book, Isaiah 40:31.

In all of this the message for us is: God will protect us; under his wings we are safe. We can trust in God. He will give us strength and through him we shall soar like eagles on wings of faith.

I NDEX TO SUBJECTS

❖ ❖

I f you are looking for a specific daily reading which best corresponds with your emotions or circumstances, or if you wish to read more about a specific subject, consult this index to subjects for the key word which best describes your situation or the subject and read the daily reading(s) indicated.

INDEX TO SUBJECTS

INDEX TO SUBJECTS

INDEX TO SUBJECTS

JANUARY

FEBRUARY

1
2
3
4
5
6
7
8
9
10
11
12
13
14
15
16
17
18
19
20
21
22
23
24
25
26
27
28
29
30
31

MARCH

APRIL

	1
	2
	3
	4
	5
	6
	7
	8
	9
	10
	11
	12
	13
	14
	15
	16
	17
	18
	19
	20
	21
	22
	23
	24
	25
	26
	27
	28
	29
	30
	31

MAY

JUNE

	1	
	2	
	3	
	4	
	5	
	6	
	7	
	8	
	9	
	10	
	11	
	12	
	13	
	14	
	15	
	16	
	17	
	18	
	19	
	20	
	21	
	22	
	23	
	24	
	25	
	26	
	27	
	28	
	29	
	30	
	31	

JULY

OCTO

BER

AUGUST

	1	
	2	
	3	
	4	
	5	
	6	
	7	
	8	
	9	
	10	
	11	
	12	
	13	
	14	
	15	
	16	
	17	
	18	
	19	
	20	
	21	
	22	
	23	
	24	
	25	
	26	
	27	
	28	
	29	
	30	
	31	

SEPTEMBER

OCTOBER

1
2
3
4
5
6
7
8
9
10
11
12
13
14
15
16
17
18
19
20
21
22
23
24
25
26
27
28
29
30
31

NOVEMBER

DECEMBER

	1
	2
	3
	4
	5
	6
	7
	8
	9
	10
	11
	12
	13
	14
	15
	16
	17
	18
	19
	20
	21
	22
	23
	24
	25
	26
	27
	28
	29
	30
	31

JANUARY

PRAYER

❖❖❖❖❖❖❖❖❖❖❖❖❖❖❖❖❖❖❖❖❖❖❖

*H*eavenly Father

At the beginning of a new year we come to you, our almighty and omniscient Father, the one who is able to see not only the beginning but also the end.

Before we venture onto a new, unknown road, we must confess that we shall be safe only if our hand is in yours with each step we take.

Though the road that lies ahead may seem dark, grant us the courage to proceed by the light of our faith alone. If our eyes are unable to see your hidden truths, help us to remain faithful to the truths you have made known to us and to which our eyes have been opened. Although we do not always know our destination, may we be thankful for each small step you reveal to us.

Though we may not understand your godly nature, help us to rely on your promises in a childlike way. Should our faith fail us from time to time, help us never to abandon the love and hope you have kindled in our hearts, and strenghthen us in our struggle against our lack of faith. Should we fail to understand what you have in store for us in life, keep us from questioning your will in a spirit of disobedience.

Should we be successful in the year to come, keep us grateful, humble and meek. Help us not to despair when disappointment or failure might come our way. Whether our dreams and ambitions are fulfilled, or whether our dreams should turn to ashes in our hands, embrace us with your love and teach us that in everything that happens to us you have a plan for our lives.

Let us rejoice in you throughout this year.

This we pray in the name of him who, through his death, has made it possible for us to choose life everlasting – Jesus Christ, our Lord and Saviour, who lives now and for evermore.

*A*men

Read JOHN 10:1-17

YES! That is my answer to life

A new year lies ahead of you. You have unlimited opportunities to do good and to live life to the full.

Though your past may have been filled with frustration and bitterness and you have no incentive to tackle anything new, simply because it seems to be to no avail; though you may have little reason to feel confident about the present or the future, never forget that the future lies in your hands. The choice of whether you approach the future with a constructive or destructive, a positive or negative attitude, is always yours.

God has a specific purpose for your life. You can experience life to the fullest

> *I have come that they may have life, and have it to the full.*
> JN 10:10

and feel satisfied only if you fulfil this purpose. Fulfilling this purpose depends entirely on your relationship with Jesus Christ. If your life has a spiritual foundation, it will also have a deeper purpose. In accepting this truth as it is made evident in your everyday life, you will experience joy and satisfaction. Then a resounding YES! will be your answer to life in all its fullness and richness.

Fullness of life is a gift from God. He grants it abundantly to all who are willing to receive it and use it to his glory. This is not merely your privilege but also your responsibility.

*S*ource of all life, I wish to live joyfully in your abundance and grace for the rest of my life. I gratefully accept this gift
of true life.

Do not loose yourself in the distant future. Seize the day,
because it belongs to you – *SCHILLER.*

2 JANUARY

Read 1 THESSALONIANS 5:12-18

The ministry of encouragement

The slogan most often heard in the world today is, "To each his own!" However, the Gospel teaches us the opposite: We are called upon to encourage and to help one another and to be patient with everyone. This is no small challenge in a selfish world where people seem neither committed to spending time in serving their fellowmen, nor do they seem willing to open their hearts or eyes to the needs of others.

> . . . *encourage the timid,*
> *help the weak,*
> *be patient with everyone.*
> 1 THESS 5:14

This heartless world desparately needs encouragement. Those who have fallen by the wayside deeply yearn for a friendly word, a warm handshake or a spontaneous smile!

God grants us so many opportunities to practise this ministry. Yet we allow these opportunities to slip through our fingers. Consider the disastrous consequences had the Good Samaritan also "passed by on the other side"!

Many people on the battlefield of life long for a drink of cold water, a friendly gesture to bring some light into lives filled with darkness. The Master was willing to touch a leper in a loving way and to heal him. We, as his disciples, dare not do less!

Lord of mercy and grace, teach me by your example to encourage others through the power of the Holy Spirit.

Encouragement is the oxygen of the soul – *GEORGE M ADAMS.*

Christff, our model

Christians often underestimate the inherent power of prayer. We are inclined to see it as a burden instead of a dynamic driving force in our lives. However, Christ teaches us what a potent force prayer can be. He often prayed to his Father, particularly before each crisis or decision in his life. Filled with an inner calmness and self-assurance he would return from this fortifying communion. God's perfect plan for his life was revealed to him through prayer.

If Christ deemed it necessary to maintain a close relationship with his Father, surely we have a far greater need for a closer walk with him. Prayer is the cornerstone of our spiritual life. Your faith could never be undermined if your prayer life is strengthened continually. It is impossible to stumble on the road of faith while you are on your knees, praying to the Lord!

> *One of those days Jesus went out to a mountainside to pray, and spent the night praying to God.*
> LK 6:12

Wisdom to cope with life in accordance with the will of God will be granted to you if you earnestly ask this of the Lord in prayer. Without prayer it is impossible to experience the power and guidance of the Lord. Prayer must therefore not be regarded as an end in itself. It forms part of an ongoing process that is carried out from day to day.

Lord Jesus, please help me to put prayer just as high on my list of priorities as you were prepared to do, so that your will for my life can always be clearly seen.

What the church needs today, is . . . people who can be used by the Holy Spirit – PEOPLE WHO PRAY! The Holy Spirit does not flow through structures but through people who pray! – E M BOUNDS.

God: the Light of life

There is no escape from the heartbreaking grief that we experience when a loved one dies. We live in a world filled with pain, suffering, misfortune, tribulations and death. At such times the one person who is capable of bringing light in the darkness, of healing a heart torn by tribulation, of bringing inner peace and of calming the wounded heart is God our Father.

Job and Paul and an untold number of people through the ages have experienced this peace and he wants to give it to you as well.

> *Speak tenderly to Jerusalem, and proclaim to her that her hard service has been completed.*
> IS 40:2

God does not say that you will be exempted from grief of any kind. But he does promise his loving comfort and the power to face all earthly struggles. Faith is not a magic charm which will make life easier for us, but it channels grace to strengthen us for the challenges that await us. Faith does not relieve us of the burden, it merely gives us the power to bear the burden.

The cross of Jesus Christ shows us that even the innocent have to face suffering on earth; furthermore it assures us that we can do everything, thanks to God's comfort which strengthens us to triumph over our losses. This knowledge gives us the strength to carry our own cross in silent obedience and to follow in the footsteps of the perfect Sufferer without ever complaining.

Holy Father, we turn to you, the refuge of peace and the giver of strength to all your troubled children, asking you to comfort those passing through the valley of shadows.

We shall never reach the dawn, unless we are prepared to walk along the road of darkness – *KAHLIL GIBRAN.*

God will not forsake you

Loneliness is completely different from solitude. Sometimes a person has the desire to be alone, but being lonely is a very painful experience. At times all of us feel that nobody understands us or cares about what happens to us. When overcome by such feelings, it seems as though even God is far away and that he has lost interest in you. Self-pity overwhelms you.

Loneliness often drives us to despair and threatens our spiritual life. It is then that you should put your trust in the loving and Almighty God and become aware of his presence. Gradually your faith will be strengthened and you will be assured that he is always with you wherever you go and whatever you may do.

> *The eternal God is your refuge, and underneath are the everlasting arms.*
> DEUT 33:27

Sometimes it might look as if God is no longer present in your life. But take heart: He will never desert you. He loves with an unfailing and everlasting love. He has faith in you even when you have lost faith in yourself. His everlasting arms always embrace you. When Josua feared the unknown road on which he was sent, God gave him this promise, "I will never leave you nor forsake you" (Jos 1:5). Claim this promise for yourself.

*H*oly God, I praise you that I may rejoice in the knowledge that your presence in my life does not depend on an emotional awareness, but is rooted in your unfailing love which daily bears my burdens and embraces me with everlasting arms.

God does not guarantee us a life without suffering, but he guarantees that he will never forsake us — *HELMUT THIELICKE.*

Faith in the face of the storms of life

A young boy was sitting in his father's cabin, playing peacefully with his toys, while a storm was raging outside and tilted the ship dangerously. Someone asked him how he could stay so calm while everybody feared for their lives. With the faith of a child he replied, "My father is the captain of this ship. Why should I be afraid?" Amidst the storms we have to face in life we must keep the same kind of faith that this young boy displayed.

> *He said to his disciples, "Why are you so afraid? Do you still have no faith?"*
> MK 4:40

Where Christ is present, life's hurricanes will recede. When the icy winds of grief howl in our lives, we can find peace and comfort in the sure knowledge that he is with us. Amidst every storm which shakes us, he allows us to share in his peace – something which no storm on earth can rob from us.

Christ gives tranquility when our problems shake our faith or drive us to despair. He tells us about a Father who lovingly takes our hands in his so that we shall never stray from his protection. Grasp this truth and be saved, or allow yourself to be carried away in the storm.

O, master of the tempests, thank you for holding my hand in yours. Please lead me beside quiet waters where I shall find peace.

Our trust in Christ does not make us lazy, careless or reckless. On the contrary, it inspires us, pushes us forward, and encourages us to live a righteous and good life – ULRICH ZWINGLI.

Spiritual growth

Every Christian must have the desire to grow spiritually, because without growth there will be stagnation and death. The ways in which we are spiritually stimulated are therefore of the utmost importance.

People who desire to grow spiritually often resort to mysticism. This is a dangerous thing to do. People like these mislead themselves by thinking that they have earned their progress through their own ingenuity. Christ does not approve of any form of mystic spirituality and none of them can be linked with his name or doctrine.

The challenge for us is to be conformed to the likeness of our Master through the power of the Holy Spirit who lives within us. To be possessed by the Spirit of God does not require any hidden or mysterious rites. God gives you his Spirit freely and as a sign

> *. . . speaking the truth in love, we will in all things grow up into him who is the Head, that is, Christ.*
> EPH 4:15

of your gratitude you reveal him through your deeds and through the way you live.

When the Holy Spirit is a living presence in your life, you will radiate this fact through the practical and loving way in which you serve the Lord and others. The more you allow the Spirit to work in your life, the more you will become aware of his presence and the closer you will grow towards Christ.

Lord, you have unconditionally endowed me with your Spirit. I pray that the sole purpose of my growth will be to reflect your glory to all the world.

Where you find yourself right now, is not relevant. What really matters, is your destination – OLIVER HOLMES.

Spiritual barrenness

However sincerely you might desire to experience the presence of Christ in your life, you will undoubtedly experience times of spiritual barrenness too. At times God will seem far away and we will sigh like Job: "If only I knew where to find him; If only I could go to his dwelling!"

If this is what you are experiencing at the moment, remember that times like these could lead to spiritual growth and maturity. These are the times when you should hold on to your faith in God; the time when you should not allow your emotions to destroy your spiritual depth. Reflect on the words of Psalm 42:8, "By day the Lord directs his love, at night his song is with me – a prayer to the God of my life."

> *If only I knew where to find him; if only I could go to his dwelling!*
>
> JOB 23:3

Spiritual barrennness could also be the result of your unwillingness to accept God's will for your life. Should you persist in doing something against the will of God, you are in fact accumulating debt and building a wall of sin around you, thereby separating him from you. Confess your sins before God. If spiritual barrenness, accompanied by loneliness is present in your life, find solace in the knowledge that God is with you. He will give you his power, forgive your sins and prepare you for a fuller and richer life ahead.

Heavenly Father, whatever the cause of the spiritual barrenness in my life might be, I affirm my love for and dependence on you.

Some people have just enough religion to make them unhappy
— JOHN WESLEY.

Read ISAIAH 41:8-10

How God comforts us

W hen a loved one dies, it always comes as a shock. You feel completely overcome by the loss and you realise that you will have to make difficult decisions and changes in the future.

Though you might experience your loss as very painful and almost unbearable, always hold onto God's promise of help and comfort, "As a mother comforts her child, so will I comfort you . . ." (Is 66:13).

When you are trying to come to terms with pain after the death of a loved one, you are sure to be comforted by the Word of God and the accounts of others with a similar experience. A wise man once said to a grieving friend, "I have not come to comfort you – God alone can do that. I have merely come to tell you how deeply and sincerely I share in your loss." God uses people who reveal genuine concern for others to channel his comfort to those who are grieving.

Trust God from day to day. His comfort will be a refreshing spring shower in the barren dessert. If you trusted him when the tree of your life was covered with spring blossoms, you can trust him when grief has you in its icy grip.

> *So do not fear, for I am with you; do not be dismayed, for I am your God.*
> *I will strengthen you and help you; I will uphold you with my righteous right hand.*
>
> IS 41:10

/ plead with you, dear Lord, to grant me your comfort because you alone can give it. Heal the wound in my heart torn by grief, and grant that I shall be able to see the rainbow of hope through my tears.

Grief is a fruit which God only allows to grow on branches which are strong enough to bear them – VICTOR HUGO.

10 JANUARY

Read PSALM 149

Praise the Lord

Have you ever experienced how thankfulness and praise can set you free?

Human beings have an irresistible tendency to grumble and complain. Such an attitude could have a destructive effect on a person's life. Complaining can become a way of life and can have a negative influence on everybody with whom you come into contact.

Throughout the Bible and especially in the Psalms, we are urged to, "Give thanks to the LORD"; "Praise the LORD, o my soul!"

When we praise and thank the Lord we are exalted into a new level of awareness. When your heart is brimming with praise and you rejoice in the goodness of God, you become aware of a revitalising power that flows through your body. This power enables you to come to terms with your problems and to overcome your difficulties. Don't expect them to disappear completely, but when you praise the Lord you will be uplifted with a song in your heart, even when the night is at its darkest.

> Sing to the LORD a new song, his praise in the assembly of the saints.
> PS 149:1

Heavenly Father, when I look around me, I become aware of so much beauty for which I want to thank and praise you that there is no time left for complaining. Help me always to sing your praise, even in the darkest night.

***Do not be afraid when you hear the sound of a song – bad people don't sing!** – A MUSICIAN.*

Growing older

I t is a painful thought that your youth is slipping away forever. Moreover, most of the time old age is accompanied by loneliness beyond description: fellow-travellers pass away, things around you change, your surroundings are no longer the same as those in which you grew up and worked. Your physical strength diminishes rapidly and it is difficult to accept that, "when you were younger you dressed yourself and went where you wanted; but when you are old you will stretch out your hands, and someone else will dress you and lead you where you do not want to go" (Jn 21:18).

Nevertheless, it is comforting for any elderly Christian to know that God is also a God of old age and that he provides amply. Indeed, he compensates for the damaging effects of age. Physical strength is replaced by increased spiritual strength. Outward strength gives way to inner strength. It is then that we begin to understand the Word of God that says, " 'Not by might nor by power, but by my Spirit,' says the LORD Almighty" (Zech 4:6).

> *Remember your Creator in the days of your youth, before . . . the years approach when you will say, "I find no pleasure in them".*
> ECC 12:1

H oly Father, thank you that I shall not be on the losing side as the years go by. On the contrary, I shall gain so much more because I am your child and can put my faith in you completely, trusting that you will uphold me even in the mature years of my life.

If you grow old with God as your friend, you will find that life in the more mature years is definitely not a downhill road –
KOBUS ANTHONISSEN.

12 JANUARY

Read JOHN 14:15-31

The peace of Christ

C hrist left us his peace because he knew that the search for peace would form part of our lives. We keep on trying to find peace because we know that the peace which this world offers us, is but a poor reflection of the peace God promises us.

To claim the peace of Christ, we must first of all become children of God by accepting him in true faith (Jn 1:12). We must long for him to be Lord of our lives. We must accept his forgiveness and be cleansed from all unrighteousness. Our motto should be: *The Lord is with us.* We must then seek his will for our lives; we must accept and obey his will. Following the example of Christ we must strive to please God and allow his will to rule our lives.

> *Peace I leave with you;*
> *my peace I give you.*
> *I do not give to you*
> *as the world gives.*
> JN 14:27

Christ offers us the most wonderful kind of peace: the peace of God. This peace is unique and different; it is perfect and constant, universal and genuine. To share in this peace we must have a steadfast faith in Jesus Christ, the source of peace. The relationship between us and God must be a healthy one and we must live in peace with ourselves and others.

L oving Father, thank you that I may claim your peace because Jesus Christ has paved the way to you .

Lord . . . help us to accept the truth of your promise that
NOTHING can rob us of the peace you have accomplished
for us – S KIERKEGAARD.

Each day is a gift from God

"Today" is an unequalled gift from God to you. This does not mean that you will always be prosperous or that you will not be tempted. But if you accept this gift with a greatful heart, you will become aware of God's grace in your life.

You can count your years by *number* or by the *quality* thereof. A long life which lacks faith and love, which does not witness God's grace, is very short when measured by God's standards. A short life, how-ever, filled with joy, faith, work and love, could be long when blessed by God's grace. How you occupy your-self each moment of each day will determine the quality of your life.

> *This is the day the Lord has made; let us rejoice and be glad in it.*
> PS 118:24

In his immeasurable grace God leaves it to us to decide what this day will be like. Perhaps you have already anxiously wondered what kind of misfortune could befall you. Maybe you are feeling dejected and depressed before the day has even started. Thoughts of this kind are counter-productive and cause unnecessary unhappiness.

If you try to make others happy, you will guarantee your own happiness. The happiness of others will be yours and boundless joy will bring warmth into each new morning.

Lord our Creator, I worship you as the giver of this day. Thank you for the privilege to glorify your name on this day and to share your glory with others.

The more I study the wonders of nature, the more I stand in awe of the Creator – *LOUIS PASTEUR.*

14 JANUARY

Read 2 CORINTHIANS 4:7-15

God is greater than any problem

Often tragic events and problems come our way unexpectedly. When this happens we become confused and often even rebellious. We demand an answer as to why we of all people have to suffer and sometimes we even dare to call God to account.

If we are really committed to finding a solution, we must ask the Holy Spirit to help us to discover who we really are. This is a real challenge, but at the same time a liberating experience. If our self-examination convinces us to repair the broken relationship between us and the Lord, we learn something about his love, grace and forgiveness. Our faith will be strengthened and once again God will have revealed himself to us as an almighty and loving God; moreover, we shall be blessed when we realise that God is greater than any disaster that might come our way.

> *We are hard pressed on each side, but not crushed; perplexed, but not in despair; persecuted . . . but not destroyed.*
> 2 COR 4:8-9

Go to your heavenly Father with your problem today. Live your life in the conviction that God is the answer to your problem and be prepared to submit to his will for your life. You will experience his all-embracing comfort!

*H*eavenly Father, whenever my problems seem to get me down, teach me through your Holy Spirit who I really am. Strengthen my faith that you, dear Lord, are the answer to all my problems through Jesus Christ our Saviour.

If you have no problems, go onto your knees and pray, "What is wrong, dear Lord? Don't you trust me with a problem?"
— NORMAN VINCENT PEALE.

Compassion: born out of Christ's love

F aith which is not demonstrated through deeds of loving-kindness, is fruitless and useless. Your faith must lead you to a more intimate relationship with God, the source of all true love. Only a continuous relationship with the Lord will make it possible for your faith to express itself in deeds of compassion.

> *The only thing that counts is faith expressing itself through love.*
> GAL 5:6

When you love the Lord in such a way that his presence becomes a reality in your life it will inspire you to deeds of love and will be reflected in acts of true Christian compassion. Faith can be alive and meaningful only if it is rooted in love. Without the foundation of true Christian love, our faith will never reach the height, the depth, the length or the breadth which has been made possible through Christ Jesus, our Lord.

The love of Christ needs to be the continued inspiration for our practical deeds of loving-kindness to others. When you take the focus off yourself and your problems, you will see a world in distress. You will hear cries for help and realise how big a task you have to fulfil. If you practise your faith it will no longer be mere pious words; it will become love at work!

H oly Father, you taught us to serve others in love. Kindle our faith so that we will be able to follow your loving example. Help us in our struggle against our lack of faith.

Man is never nearer to his Creator than in those moments when genuine compassion is revealed — JOSEF HERTZ.

Read ISAIAH 59:1-8

Productive prayer

M any children of God regard prayer and meditation as something that is practised only if time allows it; almost like an insurance against disaster and accidents.

However, the purpose of prayer is not for us to try and bend the will of God to fit in with our plans. Prayer is God's means of allowing us to discover his will for our lives.

Before we can share in the blessings of prayer, we must master the technique of prayer and practise the art of prayer diligently.

> *Surely the arm of the Lord is not too short to save, nor his ear too dull to hear.*
> IS 59:1

Time spent with God in our quiet time forms the basis of true prayer. Waiting upon the Lord can have the most astounding effect on your life. If we seek him early in the morning it will add a lively, sparkling quality to our day.

After you have spent time with the Lord, you will feel calm and composed, able to face the day as a well-balanced person. Your choices regarding moral issues will be clearly defined and God's guidance will be more pronounced. You will develop confidence to cope with the problems of the day. You will feel cheerful, your thoughts will be purified, your actions will be unwavering, your eyes will sparkle and you will be a far more productive person who lives to the glory of God!

D ear Lord, hear my prayer; do not allow anything to rob me of the valuable time I can spend alone with you.

Prayer is not a magic formula trying to manipulate God into granting us our requests; it is the only way to become what God intended us to be – STUDDERT KENNEDY.

God of hope

When death enters into a family circle, it causes immense grief. We are sad because we have suffered loss. We feel alone, insecure and anxious. It is then that God's free gift of grace fills our hearts with hope. Our anxiety is replaced by trust, our sadness by joy, our doubt by faith and our loneliness is converted into holy communion with the God of faith. Hope fills our hearts and we are able to rejoice in the Lord and to trust his eternal goodness.

Hope is one of the three gifts of grace which will remain forever, Faith being on the left-hand side, Hope in the middle and Love on the right-hand side (1 Cor 13:13).

Without Hope, Faith has no depth and Love no meaning. Hope is the anchor for our souls (Heb 6:19).

Hope fosters in us an unconquerable spirit. If Hope is alive, all other things will survive.

Hope assures us that this life is only the preface to life eternal.

> *For in this hope we were saved. But hope that is seen is no hope at all. Who hopes for what he already has? But if we hope for what we do not have, we wait for it patiently.*
> ROM 8:24-25

Should the world ask, "Are you afraid?", Hope will answer, "No, because my Lord is near!" Hope fills us with composure and secures a safe haven for us.

Eternal God, we praise you for your Word which never fails to bring hope when we are threatened by despair.
Strengthen us daily in he inextinguishable Hope
which we share as your children.

Before long you will hear that D L Moody has died. Please do not believe it. At that very moment I will be far more alive than now
— DWIGHT L MOODY.

18 JANUARY

Read 1 THESSALONIANS 5:12-22

The power of prayer

To pray is a way of life, not an emergency button. Many people think that prayer is only meant for those who lack the courage to accept the challenges of everyday life. They think that prayer is a formula by means of which God does things for you which you could and actually should do yourself.

However, prayer offered to God in truth is far more than a call in distress when all other efforts have failed and we stand with our backs against the wall. Prayer has unlimited advantages for those who make it part of their lives. Its positive power can bring us true peace and can restore the balance in our lives.

Being quiet in the presence of God enables us to see life in perspective. Whenever we pray to God and wait upon him for guidance we shall be led, provided we are willing to do our share. James tells us, "If any of you lacks wisdom, he should ask God, who gives generously to all without finding fault; and it will be given him" (Jas 1:5).

> *Pray continually.*
> 1 THESS 5:17

God also desires to speak to us through prayer. All we have to do, is to allow him to speak. Through meditation before God he will lead us in his Spirit. Prayer assures us of God's omnipotence and presence in our lives. Through prayer we will truly experience real life.

*H*oly Lord, thank you that the light of your holiness lights my path and enables me to bear fruit to your honour and glory.

Perhaps true prayer means to be so attuned to God that you are not even aware of the fact that you are praying
— *ST FRANCIS DE SAËL.*

An Immanuel faith

Through his son Jesus, God came to live among us with a glorious purpose. He assumed the image of a servant so that ordinary people could have a better understanding of him and could enter into a new relationship with him.

We have an inborn hunger to live in a close relationship with our Creator and this urges us to keep searching for God. In Christ God offered himself to each of us in a very special way. The surprising aspect of this gift of God was the simplicity of it all: a baby in a crib; a carpenter's son; a man dying on a cross. Although everything appeared to be so simple

> *She will give birth to a son, and you are to give him the name Jesus, because he will save his people from their sins.*
> MT 1:21

many found it difficult to understand the greatness and uniqueness of it all and could not surrender to the Lord in faith.

God still lives amongst us. To those who love him and serve him, who remain in him as the branch in the vine, he promises his everlasting presence through the Holy Spirit. If you are filled with the Spirit you will always feel safe within the Lord . You will never be alone. You will never fear the challenges of life because you have an Immanuel faith!

Eternal God, I thank you that you are my Father through Christ and that I can treasure your promises. Grant that I may always be near you.

It is not how long you have lived, but how that is important
— P J BAILEY.

Amazing grace

The grace of God is the only remedy for all misunderstandings, hatred and bitterness in this world. Unfortunately many Christians claim this grace only for themselves. This often has a negative effect on the task to which the church on earth has been called, that of proclaiming this amazing grace of God. Instead of churches being unified, they are divided and torn apart and their true calling is obscured.

There are people who could make large financial contributions or have the ability to take the lead in church matters, but they insist on being afforded recognition and getting preferential treatment. This results in jealousy among members of the congregation – something that is not worthy of a Christian church.

> *He saved us, not because of righteous things we had done, but because of his mercy.*
>
> TIT 3:5

Every Christian disciple should be aware of one all-important truth: we have been saved through God's mercy alone, and not because we deserve it. If we accept this truth with a thankful heart, we shall reflect the humbleness and the love which featured so clearly in the life of Christ. In fact, this should be characteristic of all Christians and it should bind us all together to form the true body of Christ on earth.

Redeemer, through your amazing grace and mercy I have been saved. Help me to convey this truth to all who may pass my way and grant that I shall forever reflect your image.

Only God can cast the first stone, but he never does
– XHOSA LAY PREACHER.

How God makes his will known

God has various ways of making his will known to us. When Elijah had lost courage, the Lord wanted to reveal himself to Elijah to restore his strength and to encourage him. First a great wind tore the mountains apart; after the wind there was an earthquake; after the earthquake came a fire – but the Lord was not in any of these. "And after the fire came a gentle whisper" (12). When God speaks to us in a gentle whisper he makes it possible for us to know his will, to experience his guidance, his healing power and his love in a concrete manner.

> *After the earthquake came a fire, but the Lord was not in the fire. And after the fire came a gentle whisper.*
> 1 KINGS 19:12

In our hectic life it is a comforting thought, however, that God sometimes speaks to us in the whirlwind and in the hurricane too, as he did to Job, "Then the Lord spoke to Job out of the storm . . ." (40:6).

He is not only a God of gentle whispers, but also a God who shouts out out names amidst our hectic lives. God can guide you through the storms of life if only you were willing to listen to his voice and to obey him. A busy life should never interfere with our relationship with God. We just need to have the desire to know him. You will find that he is already waiting for you.

Thank you, Lord, that I need not be separated from you, despite my busy life. Please grant me your everlasting peace.

Every step closer to Christ means death to yet another doubt
— *THEODORE CUYLER.*

The light that shines in the darkness

Sometimes life presents its darker side when one encounters problems or grief. You feel insecure and find it extremely difficult to deal with life's crises; to such an extent that you feel incompetent to make appropriate use of the aids God has put at your disposal.

Some people manage to overcome this situation in a triumphant way because Christ enables them to proceed from the darkness into the light. Jesus is the true light which lights the way of man (cf Jh 1:9). When the road ahead seems unfamiliar and you have to make difficult decisions, Christ will lead you out of your darkness of grief and confusion into his wonderful light.

> *In him was life, and that life was the light of men. The light shines in the darkness, and the darkness has not overcome it.*
>
> JN 1:4-5

The light of God's love enfolds you; he will protect you from dangers of which you may be unaware. In times of grief and affliction he lovingly watches over you. Turn your face towards the Light in times of distress. In Christ lies triumph and joy and through him we grow blessedly in the full light of God's immeasurable love.

*H*elp me, dear Lord, to venture upon life's way, filled with the courage and understanding that your light allows me.
I place my hand in yours – guide me in your light.

The darkness affords us no choices – only in the light are differences revealed to us. Christ alone is the giver of this light
– C T WHITMELL.

Follow God's guidance

G od guides those who put their trust in him. This knowledge helps us to start every demanding day and to face every unknown night with confidence.

When we joyfully acknowledge the Lord as our guide, we are not merely engaging in intellectual gymnastics but we know that the Lord truly guides us in all real-life situations, the kind of guidance which all people who have pledged their lives to his service experience.

In order to experience God's guidance clearly, total and complete surrender to Him is advisable. Nobody would ever choose to follow a leader without trusting him completely.

This must be followed by continuous communcation with God. We must become sensitive to his guidance. However, you will have to do your share as well. God will unlock the door, but you still have to turn the knob.

> *I will instruct you and teach you in the way that you should go;*
> *I will counsel you and watch over you.*
> PS 32:8

It requires real courage to follow the Lord unwaveringly and faithfully. Following him step by step without being able to see the destination, requires a courageous spirit. To remain convinced that he knows the way and that he will guide you in accordance with his will, requires an equally strong faith. But don't hesitate to take the risk – you will be surprised to see how his holy will unfolds in your life.

L ord, you are our refuge and our fortress. In distress you have always proved yourself faithful. Make me sensitive to recognise your will in my life and grant me the grace to be guided continually by your will for my life.

Life is my journey, Jesus is my guide and faith is my staff.

24 JANUARY

Read HEBREWS 13:7-19

God our fortress

I n this rapidly changing world and the accompanying challenges which make more and more demands upon us, we keep searching for a steadfast anchor on which we can rely. God is this anchor in our lives.

Change is part of our earthly existence. Circumstances change inexorably from moment to moment: the peace and the storms of life, the sunshine and the clouds, health and sickness, life and death. Jesus Christ, our Redeemer, however, never changes. In him we have a fortress which will remain steadfast for ever.

> *Jesus Christ is the same yesterday and today and for ever.*
> HEB 13:8

The bewildering changes affecting our lives may have caused us to suffer various losses, but if our losses have brought us closer to the Lord, and have stripped us of all outward trappings, we have gained infinitely more than we could ever have lost.

God sometimes allows storms in our lives. He wants us to be bereft of all possible earthly assistance so that we can seek refuge in him – the fortress who will never fail us.

M y Lord and God, I thank you that I can say: My times are in your hands. You are my fortress in which I seek refuge; you put my heart at rest amidst all the changes of the world around us.

There is no need to lift up your hands to heaven: God is near you, with you, in you – SENECA.

Read LUKE 24:36-49

Let the peace of God fill your heart

L ife is stressful. Bad experiences make us anxious and we become tense, moody and disgruntled – because our peace have been disturbed. In situations where tension seems to be mounting it is essential that you build up some reserves from which you can draw your strength. The most important source of power in such times is the peace which Jesus Christ grants everyone who loves him and who lives in a close relationship with him.

What a wonderful comfort to know that this peace is available to every person who is prepared to follow Christ.

> *While they were still talking about this, Jesus himself stood among them and said to them, "Peace be with you."*
> LK 24:36

Whenever tensions build, consciously fight against letting yourself be engulfed by it. Guard against moodiness and irritability. Don't become part of the hectic life of the masses around you. Force yourself to relax and keep calm. Withdraw and seek the face of Christ; it might be only for a few minutes, but do it. Reaffirm your dependence on him, believe that his peace is at your disposal and accept it with all your heart.

You will soon find that your tired, rushed spirit will come to rest and the peace of Christ will refresh your life. You will experience peace and nothing or nobody will be able to take it away from you. You will hear the Master say, "Peace be with you!"

H oly God, bring me beside quiet waters amidst the rush and tension of life.

Peace is not agreed upon in council chambers or by means of agreements; peace comes from within the hearts of men
— HERBERT HOOVER.

A new life in Christ

We live in a world broken and burdened by sin. Dangers and temptations are forever threatening our lives. We are constantly prone to depression and are caught in the web of sin. However, there is a way out of this suffering: through Jesus Christ.

If you have come to Christ and have confessed your sins, forget the failures and disappointments of the past and reach out towards the new life in Christ Jesus. Put your shame behind you and accept that you are a child of the King of kings. Forget defeat and follow Christ on the path of triumph. Fix your eyes on Jesus, the author and perfecter of your faith.

> *Then I acknowledged my sin to you, and did not cover up my iniquity.*
> *I said, "I will confess my transgressions to the Lord"*
> *– and you forgave the guilt of my sin.*
> PS 32:5

God is merciful and his grace is sufficient for you under all circumstances. If you take your stand against sin in the powerful name of the Lord and arm yourself with the shield of faith, you will be triumphant. Full of courage you will step towards the future, despite all dangers which might come your way because you have been set free from your sins.

What a wonderous thought that you can set me free, Lord and Redeemer! I thank you that I can confess my sins and needs at your feet as a prelude to singing songs of triumph.

Whenever sinful thoughts enter into your mind, shatter them against the Rock of Ages, Jesus Christ – BENEDICTUS.

Christ is with us

L oneliness and the feeling of being forsaken by God is one of the most powerful weapons used by Satan. Through this he delivers us to despondency and depression. If we wait upon the Lord we can resist this kind of attack by Satan. Through Jesus Christ God relieves our distress and through his eternal Word God assures us that he cares.

Loneliness has many faces. There is the loneliness within marriage; the loneliness of being isolated; of increasing age; of change; and eventually the final loneliness – the loneliness of death.

The solution to all the faces of loneliness can be found in Christ, who also knew loneliness intimately. He once had to cry out that he was forsaken by God so that he can say to you and to me, "I am with you al-

> *The Lord is the everlasting God . . . He gives strength to the weary and increases the power of the weak . . . those who hope in the LORD will renew their strength.*
> IS 40:28-31

ways, to the very end of time. Never will I leave you; never will I for-sake you." If Christ has entered your life, your loneliness will not only be tempered; your heart will learn to rejoice!

T hank you, heavenly Father, that you never forsake me; that you are always the same. Thank you that all things are known to you, that you care and that you are able to do immeasurably more than we can ask or imagine .

When Christ came to the world, we celebrated peace; when he left this earth, peace was left behind as our heritage
— FRANCIS BACON.

---

28 JANUARY

Read ISAIAH 30:8-18

In quietness and trust

H ow must we deal with a building up of tension?
    Start with the past. Don't allow the heavy burden of your past to drag you down. After all, Christ promised to make everthing "new". He casts your sinful past into the depths of the ocean.

Don't try to hide your resentment. Discuss your problems in a mature way with your marriage partner, a trusted friend, or a pastoral counsellor.

Go somewhere quiet and be at peace with yourself – possibly at a place where you can be alone with your Creator to regain your perspective on life. You will feel the tension drain from you.

> *In repentance and rest is your salvation, in quietness and trust is your strength . . .*
>
> IS 30:15

Hold onto God's wonderful promises. When we have reached the end of our tether, God still knows best and he will restore our strength.

Don't succumb to despondency, but rather do something constructive. Go out into the world and become aware of the distress of others.

Be honest with yourself and accept your limitations. Talk to God in prayer. Share everything with him and you will find peace of mind.

/ thank you Lord, that I may know for sure that I can find a place of quiet with you, when the pressure of the world becomes unbearable.

Where there is peace, there is God! *– GEORGE HERBERT.*

Learn to listen

It is not easy to listen to God, because he does not speak to us in an audible voice as in the days of Samuel. Today we must use other ways and means to listen to him.

The first and most important prerequisite is that we must make contact with him. This is possible only if we really believe in him and trust him. Talk to your heavenly Father frankly and remember that he knows you far better than you know yourself. Confide in him and share even the most seemingly insignificant aspect of your life with him.

If you persevere in prayer you are sure to experience rewarding moments. Conversation will no longer be necessary because you will marvel at the mere presence of God. In

> *Speak, for your servant is listening.*
> 1 SAM 3:10

these amazing moments of silence your needs and demands disappear and you remain content to be like the branch clinging to the Vine for support.

During these holy moment he who answers your prayers can make his holy will known to you. Suddenly a thought might strike you so clearly that you cannot doubt that it is God's way of conveying his message to you.

God will bless you abundantly if you wait upon him with a sensitive ear!

Heavenly Father, teach me to listen in such a manner that I shall be able to echo the words of Samuel: Speak, your servant is listening! Thank you that Jesus had made it possible for me.

If prayer does not drive away sin in your life, sin will drive away prayer – SPURGEON.

God comforts those who stay behind

T he person who stays behind after a spouse has passed away, is intensely lonely because a partner, a companion, a confidante is no longer there. The loneliness becomes even more intense because nobody really understands this feeling of desolation. You have to face the storms on your own, you have to make decisions on you own; on festive occasions you are alone, often you are left to deal with your grief, illness and distress all by yourself.

> *When I said,*
> *"My foot is slipping,"*
> *your love, O LORD,*
> *supported me.*
>
> PS 94:18

Who will now be willing to listen to your complaints? With whom could you share your joys and daily experiences? Suddenly tomorrow holds no excitement at all. At night you involuntarily put out your hand to touch your loved one, but his or her place is empty.

The solution to this loneliness lies in your relationship with God. Blessed is he or she who is able to say, "When anxiety was great within me, your consolation brought joy to my soul" (19).

Pass your loneliness over to God and trust him with your future. He will provide. Make a contribution to life wherever possible. You can help to build God's kingdom around you and at the same time support others who are also distressed and grieving. This will help you to overcome your hour of crisis.

L ord of the lonely, you taught us that we would find strength in quietness and trust. Fill me with that strength in these dark moments.

You cannot prevent the birds of grief from flying over your head, but you can prevent them from nesting in you hair
— CHINESE SAYING.

Obey the Lord

O bedience is better than sacrifice. This was the lesson which king Saul as well as Jonah had to learn before they could be of service to the Lord. "The word of the LORD came to Jonah . . . 'Go to the great city of Nineveh'. . . . But Jonah ran away from the LORD . . . and headed for Tarshish . . ." (Jon 1:1-3).

Today many people still do exactly what Jonah did. They know what God expects of them and what his will is for their lives, but they try to escape his plan.

Sometimes the road the Lord wishes us to follow is clearly laid out; but unfortunately there are also times when it is difficult to accept or understand God's way. Perhaps you don't feel like following where God leads you, because you lack the confidence or because you fear what could happen to you on that road.

> *To obey is better than sacrifice and to heed is better than the fat of rams.*
>
> 1 SAM 15:22

However, obedience to God requires absolute trust in him. Remember, wherever God may send you, in Christ Jesus he will also be there. No matter how difficult the way may be, obey unconditionally and you will experience the joy in which all those share who follow the way in submission to the guidance of the Spirit.

I thank you, heavenly Father, that I need only follow in true obedience wherever you lead me. Guide my every step.

Prayer is not a fruitless effort to try and change the will of God; it is a childlike desire to get to know God's will and to obey it
— GEORGE A BUTTRICK.

Notes

_____

FEBRUARY

PRAYER

❖ ❖

Loving Father
A mere thirty one days of this year have passed
    and with shame I have to confess before you
    that already so many of my good intentions for this new year
    have come to grief.
    I have wasted so many valuable hours.
    I could have spent much more time with you in prayer
    – time to talk to you, to listen to you.
    I could have treasured and sought your Word more often
    so that my life would reflect your abundant mercy.
    I have neglected to seek your will
    and to put it obediently into practice.
Lord, thank you that you do not only forgive,
    but that through the Holy Spirit you kindle in my heart
    the desire to live a triumphant life, to love you more,
    to follow you conscientiously and to be more faithful in
    living according to your will.
Thank you that through Jesus Christ
    the old has gone and we are a new creation.
Guide me through this month by the grace of your Holy Spirit
    and for Jesus' sake.

Amen

Blessed assurance

God did not save us or call us to his service because we are such good people. On the contrary, he saved us in spite of our sinfulness and shortcomings. He found us mired in sin; but through this he would demonstrate his power. He is concerned about smouldering wicks and bruised reeds (cf Is 42:3).

The moment we confess that we are weak and sinful, we take the first step towards being filled with power. If we as poor sinners depend on his almighty strength, he will empower our empty lives. "My grace is sufficient for you, for my power is made perfect in weakness" (2 Cor 12:9).

Surrender in faith, allow the Holy Spirit to enter into the most intimate sanctuaries of your life and your entire existence will be inspired by Christ's living presence.

> *The Spirit himself testifies with our spirit that we are God's children. Now if we are children, then we are heirs.*
> ROM 8:16

A continuous relationship with the Lord is essential. Out of this a blessed assurance will grow that you are forever his child who will never be alienated from him and that you are an heir to his power and love. The moment this testimony materialises in your life through the workings of the Holy Spirit, God will become an unfailing reality – and you will live from him, through him and unto him!

Lord, thank you that through your Holy Spirit I can rejoice, "Blessed assurance, Jesus is mine, o what a foretaste of glory divine!" I praise and thank you for this blessing .

A Christian has been united with Jesus Christ into a nobler, more intimate and more perfect union that that of the limbs with the head – JOHN EUDES.

2 FEBRUARY

Read PSALM 106:1-12

Never underestimate God's love

We so often take God's unlimited goodness and love for granted. We adopt a familiar attitude towards Jesus Christ which borders on disrespect. We begin to accept the blessings of the Lord as a right rather than a privilege; and we seldom thank the Lord for his numerous blessings and mercy.

You and I may never underestimate the importance of God's forgiving love. That is the reason why Jesus Christ sacrificed his life to save us. No love on earth can equal such a great love. Moreover, this great love is continuously being poured out over you, regardless of who you are or what you do.

> *Give thanks to the Lord, for he is good; his love endures for ever.*
> PS 106:1

The indescribable majesty of God's love is of such magnitude that we shall never be worthy of it. Yet he always offers it to you, even though you might have strayed from him for some reason or other. Therefore, live your life in such a way that you will show your gratitude for this great love.

I bow before you in humbleness, o Lord. A love so godly, so magnificent claims all: body, soul and spirit.

That God pours out his love to people who realise that they possess nothing save their sins, is a miracle. It is an even bigger miracle that he offers his abundant LIFE to people who still think that their many possessions is life – H DRUMMOND.

Overcome depression

There are definite measures you can take in faith when trying to overcome depression. You must simply be willing to put them to the test.

First of all you must believe that God is greater than your circumstances and problems. Know that you will be triumphant in his name and commit all your stress and problems into the hands of your heavenly Father in prayer. List each problem you have to face in life.

Believe firmly that God has a purpose with this dark period in your life (28a). Do not resist when God desires to shape your life by trying you in a particular way.

> *. . . in all these things we are more than conquerors through him who loved us.*
> ROM 8:37

Realise that you cannot have your way all the time. If you willingly accept your circumstances you accept God's will for your life. Frustration and worry will never solve any problems. Find something for which you can thank God and live a life of grateful praise.

Confess and renounce sinful deeds and thoughts. Study the Word of God. Think and act as a child of God should think and act. Surely it is a privilege to be a child of the King of kings! Take the focus off yourself and open your eyes to the world around you. Be alert, see God's purpose in all your surroundings and develop a joyful spirit.

My soul thirsts for you, o God. Thank you for never leaving me, not even in my darkest moments. Thank you for the example of Jesus Christ in Gethsemane. Grant me the grace to follow in his footsteps.

A life without rejoicing is like a long road without any accommodation en route – DEMOCRITUS.

4 FEBRUARY

Read PSALM 37:1-11

Whom can I trust in my sorrow?

T he heavier the burden you have to carry, the greater your need for someone whom you can trust unreservedly. Only the Almighty can meet this high requirement. If you trust God with all your heart you can accomplish anything.

God is filled with compassion for you. He can fully sympathise with you and never lets go of you – not even in your deepest despair. His will for you is the best; he alone can change evil into good, grief into joy, tears into laughter. The mere fact that you don't know how he will do it, does not mean that you cannot trust him. God never errs. Every event in your life forms part of his blueprint for your life.

> *Commit your way to the LORD; trust in him and he will . . . make your righteousness shine like the dawn.*
>
> PS 37:5

One aspect that is underlined by grief and loss, is your inability to understand what is happening to you and what the future has in store for you. Trusting God under such circumstances brings peace of mind and peace beyond all understanding. He will carry out his plan with your life and in the end you will marvel at it all and call out, "He did it well!"

L ord, I commit my whole life to you, my grief and my confusion, praying in quiet trust and faith that your will be done in my life.

Trusting God is the only key to understanding God's dealings with us. The real meaning of our existence, the answers to all the questions which determine our peace of mind and our happiness can only be discovered by trusting God with all our heart – THOMAS MERTON.

Read PSALM 4

With the Lord you are safe

How does one overcome fear? At some stage or other we are all troubled by this question. You may even be looking for an anwer to that question at this very moment.

Fear can have so many faces: it can be the fear of a little child going to school for the first time; the fear of a young person who starts his or her first job; the fear of the adult who is faced with a crisis in his or her life; the older person's fear of the degenerating signs of approaching old age.

If you are faced with any or these situations there is a wonderful message in Psalm 4:8. Even if the entire world succumbed to destructive fear, as God's child you can remain relaxed and composed because you have put your trust in him. You can

> *I will lie down and sleep in peace,*
> *for you alone, O LORD,*
> *make me dwell in safety.*
> PS 4:8

be convinced that God cares for you and you can trust God that he works for the good of those who believe in him.

Whatever your circumstances, never forget for a moment that you have a heavenly Father. Never allow a nagging fear to overshadow this truth. Rather approach life with confidence, filled with the peace of God which transcends all understanding.

*O*nce again I thank you, heavenly Father, for your presence which helps me to overcome my fear. Thank you that I can face every day with confidence which is granted me through Jesus Christ my Lord.

Without God: not a single step. With him: to the ends of the earth – *DAVID LIVINGSTONE.*

Doubt

When life's circumstances are bewildering it is so easy to allow doubt to creep up upon us. The sad truth is that we allow it to happen. However, whenever this happens, these words that describe Abraham, the hero of faith, can strengthen us in our faith, "Yet he did not waver through unbelief regarding the promise of God, but was strengthened in his faith and gave glory to God, being fully persuaded that God had power to do what he had promised. This is why it was credited to him as righteousness" (Rom 4:20-22).

> *Because you have seen me, you have believed; blessed are those who have not seen and yet have believed.*
>
> JN 20:29

We are inclined to measure God by the same standards by which we measure ourselves. If we find a situation impossible to handle, we so easily forget that God will not fail to deal with it. Therefore, whenever you are confronted with a seemingly unsolvable problem, or when you have to carry a heavy burden where relief seems improbable, ask yourself: From whose perspective do I see my problem, my burden? From my own perspective or from God's perspective?

Remember and accept: You are serving a Lord whose majesty and omnipotence surpass all you can ever desire or hope for.

Heavenly and almighty Father, I thank you once again for the blessed assurance that for you all things are possible. I commit all my problems and burdens to you in the conviction that you will have the solution.

God is the answer to every question – INAYAT KHAN.

Shalom! Peace be with you!

"Shalom" means to be what God has meant you to be – filled with peace. And what you are, is far more important than what you possess. A shalom person experiences inner peace, harmony and fulfilment.

"Shalom" is the kind of relationship which should prevail among people. This is exactly what Paul had in mind when he encouraged the Christians in Rome to do whatever would lead to peace (Rom 14:19).

This harmony and peace should also be a feature of the family circle. How tragic that so often the home is the battlefield of conflict among members of the family. If the family cannot live together in peace, how will the world ever be safe from conflict?

> *May the LORD turn his face towards you and give you peace.*
> NUM 6:20

If you have no love, inner peace will also be lacking in your life. This sick world of ours lacks love, therefore true peace is also lacking. However, God grants us his peace and he expects us to pass it on to a peace-starved world. We are not only committed to this duty by virtue of our Christian faith – it is also part of the mission with which God has entrusted us into the world: to bring about peaceful relationships so that God can rule this world through his peace.

*T*hank you, Father of grace, that I may inherit your peace. Strengthen my will so that I can share your peace with all with whom I come into contact.

Hatred can never bring an end to hatred; hatred is overcome by love alone – BUDDHA.

Trust in the Lord

S ometimes we find a particular situation in life totally unfamiliar and it fills us with fear and anxiety. Perhaps you have to consult a specialist; you might have to go to hospital where everything is unfamiliar and all the people are complete strangers; you are wheeled into the operating theatre on your own . . . or what do you do when you see your once happy marriage going to pieces right before your eyes.

> *Wait for the LORD;*
> *be strong and take heart*
> *and wait for the LORD.*
>
> PS 27:14

Where can you find comfort in such distress? Who will relieve your anxiety, your worries, your grief, fear and depression? "Wait for the LORD, and he will deliver you" (Prov 20:22).

This "waiting" for the Lord means that you put your trust in the almighty God even in the most desperate situation and through a living faith allow him to take complete control over your thoughts and your life.

Confirm your religious conviction by singing a song of praise, a joyful hymn to his honour in the words of Psalm 13: 5-6, "I trust in your unfailing love; my heart rejoices in your salvation. I will sing to the LORD, for he has been good to me."

J esus Christ, teach me that the hours I spend waiting for you are never wasted hours; those are the times when God reveals himself through the marvellous ways in which he works in my life.

What could be more uplifting and ennobling than a heart trusting so completely that it is willing to forfeit everything for the sake of fulfilling God's will? – *JOHN HENRY NEWMAN.*

Read JOB 42:9-17

God is good

G rief often unexpectedly steals upon us and throws our entire life out of gear. In times like these we feel like echoing Job when his misery made him say, "My eyes have grown dim with grief; my whole frame is but a shadow" (Job 17:7).

Whatever the nature of your grief or sorrow may be, you should approach it with the right attitude. To be embittered by your grief would be to allow it to rule your life, with detrimental and dangerous results.

The first and foremost requirement when trying to cope with grief is to have a strong and living faith in a loving God. This will help you to stay in control of your emotions and will protect you against self-destruction.

> *The LORD blessed the latter part of Job's life more than the first.*
>
> JOB 42:12

Having faith in the eternal goodness of God will enable you to accept grief as an ingredient of life, without allowing you to wallow in bitterness or self-pity. If you believe in life eternal the death of a loved one will become bearable. If your ideals in life have been shattered, your faith will fill you with the power to live a new life, triumphant in the Lord.

L ord, only you can free our hearts and minds from anxious emotions. Thank you for that blessing and thank you that we can be triumphant through the power of your Spirit who lives within us.

Faith is the power of life – *LEO TOLSTOI.*

Read REVELATION 21:1-8

Failure need not be final

To experience failure in life is very depressing. Ideals are shattered, hope dies and dreams become nightmares. In addition your self-image suffers a serious blow.

In times like these the future seems dark and without any prospects. You pity yourself or put the blame for your failure on others or your circumstances. However, it is far more beneficial to judge your life and deeds honestly and objectively. Try to determine the reason for your failure and deal with these causes firmly.

> He who was seated on the throne said. "I am making everything new!"
> REV 21:5

Don't regard your failure as final. It might be necessary to confess that you are guilty. Perhaps you need to be forgiven. You may need to form new resolutions. Remember that you will only be a failure for as long as you accept yourself as such.

We all experience failure and disappointments in life. However, as a Christian you have the power of Christ at your disposal. He gives it liberally to all who love and serve him. If you have faith and trust in him, he will make you triumphant. Put your failures behind you. Face the future with faith and put your trust in your Redeemer, for he has called you to triumph over all that has gone wrong in your life.

Risen Lord, if you fill my life, I will be able to triumph over every failure. Make me a new person every day.

Failure can sometimes broaden your mind. It forces you to rely on God and on others – CHARLES H COOLEY.

Effective intercession

To uphold an effective prayer life it is essential that our relationship with God must be pure and sincere.

It is not difficult to pray daily for those who are dear to you, to commit each aspect of their lives to the Father. But much as you love them, you might not know what is best for them. That is why you need the guidance of the Holy Spirit when you pray for others. The Spirit of God will guide and help you to intercede on their behalf according to the will of God.

Always pray in a spirit of expectation. Believe that God will answer your prayers in his own good time and in his own way. You will then experience how his will is revealed in your own life and in the lives of those for whom you pray. Keep the channels open between yourself and God and those persons whose needs you pass on to God. His holy will shall be done, because God is almighty and because you have prayed in faith and in obedience to his will. This you may firmly believe.

> In the same way, the Spirit *helps us in our weakness. We do not know what we ought to pray for, but the Spirit himself intercedes for us with groans that words cannot express.*
> ROM 8:26

Lord, you have called us to the ministry of intercession. Please make me sincere, faithful and obedient to your holy will. Thank you for this wonderful privilege which Jesus Christ has made possible for us.

Prayer is releasing the energy of God, because prayer is to ask God to do what seems impossible to us – *CHARLES TRUMBULL.*

Read REVELATION 21:1-5

Turn to God

We often comfort people who have lost a loved one by saying, "You have many happy memories which can warm your heart when your longing becomes unbearable." Memories can indeed console us, but they can also bring more grief.

Each day brings its share of unforgettable memories: a song on the radio which you used to enjoy together; the scent of wild flowers; a breathtaking sunset – memories which can brutally recall the past and cause intense emotional distress. Give vent to your sorrow. Tears are a liberating mechanism given you by God. A trusted friend's company can also be comforting. Make time for these things.

> *God himself will be with them and be their God. He will wipe every tear from their eyes.*
>
> REV 21:3-4

Most of all, turn to God, because you cannot brave these dark depths alone. He will lead you beside quiet waters and will restore your restless and pained soul.

You are needed in life and you need life. There are so many things to which you can dedicate your life and which will bring you comfort. Stay close to the Lord, for in him you will find peace and quiet. You may be alone at times, but you will never be lonely.

Even though I walk through the valley of the shadow of death, I will not fear, for you are with me. Hold my hand and ensure me of your loving presence all the days of my life.

Life never treats us too good to not have any fear and never too badly to not have hope and trust – TURKISH SAYING.

Read 1 PETER 4:12-19

Get rid of self-pity

Some people cause their own grief. They are constantly bemoaning their fate and see only the shortcomings of others. The slightest problem is blown up out of proportion and all they can talk about is their disappointments, their hardships and lost opportunities.

To avoid this pitfall you need to make peace with yourself and remember that your attitude towards life is of the utmost importance. You might well be passing through difficult and dark times and feel that you have been left on your own and that God has forgotten you.

However, if you rid yourself of self-pity and ask God to make his will clear to you in these dark circumstances, the light will break through the dark.

Believe with conviction that God has a plan for your life and that everything which comes your way is part of that plan. Trust in him every day

> *But rejoice that you participate*
> *in the sufferings of Christ,*
> *so that you may be overjoyed*
> *when his glory is revealed.*
> 1 PET 4:13

of your life for every step you take. Then you will experience peace and security. Through this you will become a co-worker of God, working at your own happiness and turning your suffering into joy.

Lord, I don't always understand your ways. Please help me to be a joyful person who follows you in obedience wherever you may lead.

To bear every setback with courage and dignity; to see the good in everything – that is the essence of a steadfast character
– ARISTOTLE.

14 FEBRUARY

Read PSALM 146

Praising the Lord in faith

Through the ages men have done many noble deeds. Deeds at which we marvel because they reflect sacrifice and unselfishness and speak of the grace and love of the persons concerned. Yet, the noblest and most uplifting deed a human being can perform, is to sing the praise of the almighty God, "I will praise the LORD all my life; I will sing praise to my God as long as I live" (Ps 146:2).

It is a pity, however, that we often neglect praising God in our daily devotions. When we refer to praise and worship, we tend to picture a formal devotional service; hymns in church; reading the Holy Scriptures; corporate prayer. Granted, these things are important, but praising the Lord in faith implies much more than a formal religious ceremony. It is an attitude towards life which is inspired by our faith in Christ.

> *I will praise the LORD*
> *all my life;*
> *I will sing praise to my God*
> *as long as I live.*
>
> PS 146:2

Praise should fill our lives every hour of every day. Praising God is a powerful force which sanctifies the mundane things in life, for the simple reason that God is central to our lives and has a powerful influence on all the areas of our human existence. We pay homage to God and sing his praises each time we perform a noble deed in his name.

I want to praise you, Lord, with every fraction of my being I want to praise your holy name.

Praising God is the product of a rejoicing heart. The inmost being reacts to the goodness of God and to the beauty of his creation – BASIL HUME.

"Chicken" or "Eagle" Christian?

B oth chickens and eagles have feathers and wings; that is where the resemblance ends, however. Chickens scratch around in the soil; they cannot fly; they eat and lay eggs for the person who owns and feeds them. Eagles, on the other hand, fly high in the sky which is their hunting ground; they are in nobody's service. Chickens are inclined to be overweight and rather weak on account of the abundance of food they are fed. Eagles, however, are lean and tough because they hunt for their food themselves.

> *But those who hope in the LORD*
> *will renew their strength.*
> *They will soar*
> *on wings like eagles.*
>
> IS 40:31

Many Christians display the characteristics of chickens. Their eyes are constantly on the ground instead of on the horizon. They are spiritually overweight as a result of worldly ambitions and possessions and are therefore too weak to rise from the ground or to fly on wings of faith.

However, there are Christians who develop the characteristics of eagles through the grace of God. They undertake flights on wings of faith. Flights that put their faith to the test and make them stronger in faith. They put all their trust in the Lord and have complete faith in his care. Thus they are truly free and can reach for the stars.

From time to time a "chicken" might see an "eagle" flashing by, without realising that in Christ he or she has also been given the "eagles flight" of faith. In contrast the "eagle" is carried up high by the winds of faith and cleaves the air, reaching towards the open spaces of God's grace and protection.

T o you, o Lord, who is able to do immeasurably more than what we can pray for or imagine, to you be all honour and glory.

To have faith is to have wings – *J M BARRIE.*

Read ISAIAH 61:1-11

God holds your hand

S ome of life's truths can only be learned through grief. For this reason we cannot experience only joy in our lives. We also need to taste the bitterness of grief, for it makes us reach out to God. When we suffer grief we get to know God as never before. When grief threatens to cast us into the depths of depression, God himself comforts us. "Comfort, comfort my people, says your God. Speak tenderly to Jerusalem, and proclaim to her that her hard service has been completed" (Is 40:1-2).

> *I delight greatly in the LORD; my soul rejoices in my God. For he has clothed me with garments of salvation.*
> IS 61:10

Christ sometimes tells us what he told his disciples in Mark 6:31, "Come with me by yourselves to a quiet place and get some rest." Our grief can be such a quiet place. In our moments of sorrow we are alone with the Lord and we discover how utterly dependent we are on him. However, in every dark moment we must remember: God holds our hand, ". . . to comfort all who mourn, and provide for those who grieve in Zion – to bestow on them . . .the oil of gladness instead of mourning, and a garment of praise instead of a spirit of despair" (Is 61:2-3).

C omforter of our souls, help me when trials and tribulations assail me. Thank you that it never gets so dark in my life that I cannot see your light, and that you do this all for the sake of Jesus Christ.

God is not an idea or a definition which we have created in our minds. He is a loving presence which we can experience within our hearts – LOUIS EVELEY.

Comfort in the knowledge that promises are fulfilled

W e have the firm promise that God will never forsake or leave us. And he is the God who fulfils his promises, even though we may deem it impossible.

He promised Jacob, "I am with you and will watch over you wherever you go" (Gen 28:15). In his wonderful way God made this promise come true!

Joshua received the encouraging promise, "I will never leave you nor forsake you" (Josh 1:5), and Joshua experienced the presence of God every day of his life.

Before David died, he encouraged his son Solomon with these words, "Do not be afraid or discouraged, for the LORD God, my God, is with you" (1 Chron 28:20).

> So we say with confidence, "The Lord is my helper; I will not be afraid. What can man do to me?"
> HEB 13:6

The book Hebrews assures us that these promises include all those who believe in Jesus Christ and trust in him (Heb 13:5b-8). We need God's promises so desperately. Amidst our loneliness he assures us that we are never alone, because he is there, with us and whatever he promises us, he can and will fulfil!

L ord God, in Christ Jesus you are my Father. Thank you that I can rely on your promises through the merit of my Redeemer, Jesus Christ.

Gratefulness is not only the memories of the heart; it is also the sacrifice of the heart. This we offer God for his immeasurable goodness — NATHANIEL PARKER WILLIS.

18 FEBRUARY

Read ISAIAH 55:1-13

God will answer

When we turn to God and call upon him for help, we should allow him the opportunity to answer our prayers. So often we turn away from him in despair, simply because we lack the faith to wait patiently upon the Lord's answer.

We must be willing to wait – because God's time is different from ours. We must be prepared to be guided by the Lord – because he never errs. We must have the steadfast faith in our hearts that he knows what to do and when to do it.

> *"For my thoughts are not your thoughts, neither are your ways my ways,"* declares the LORD.
>
> IS 55:8

Such faith will bring peace to your restless spirit. You will experience that God, through his perfect timing, always opens up new prospects for you if you remain steadfast in your faith.

The thoughts of the Lord are not our thoughts and his ways are not our ways; nevertheless we will discover that God lovingly cares for each and everyone of us. It is not always easy to walk the road God has planned for you; to sacrifice your own ways for those of the Lord, but obedience in his service reaps you incalculable spiritual riches.

Lord my God, I thank you that each day with you is an exiting new adventure. Save me from becoming impatient. Grant me your mercy so that I can wait upon you quietly and can follow you in obedience.

I kept on searching for God until he found me – BLAISE PASCAL.

Suffering: How do I cope?

Sickness and suffering are part of our lives. As Christians we are not excluded from the mystery of suffering. How are we expected to understand it and how must we come to terms with it? Be assured: With Jesus Christ as the author and perfecter of our faith, suffering in itself can be an opportunity to learn.

In his gospel, Mark relates how Jesus healed a sick man. It reads, ". . . he took him aside, away from the crowd" (7:33). God sometimes wants to share something with us, but our busy lives do not allow us the time to listen to him, or perhaps we don't really understand him. He then takes us aside so that he can talk to us in person and in silence.

> *For my yoke is easy and my burden is light.*
> MT 11:30

Have you ever heard God's voice through a particular situation? Did you really understand his message? He speaks to you of a number of things when he takes you aside: He speaks to you of peace wrought for you through the blood of Jesus Christ who took our weaknesses upon himself; he speaks of redemption, of support, of healing, of his love which is stronger than sickness, suffering or death.

May God grant that you may hear what he wishes to convey to you in your quiet time and may his words lead you to rejoice in him.

Dear Lord, you fill my heart with joy and gratefulness. You bless me, comfort me and support me by your grace. Thank you that I may know that you uphold me when I am sad. Help me to hear your voice and grant that I may understand the message you want to share with me.

Suffering opens us up to the suffering of others and makes us willing to commit ourselves to a life of serving others
— D LOUW.

20 FEBRUARY

Read EPHESIANS 2:11-22

Eiréne – peace with God

C hrist is the One who can bring us peace! When he reconciled us with God, he made it possible for us to share true peace. Christ brings us *eiréne*: in the place of "old" resentful people he creates "new" peace-loving people. Instead of enmity between us and God he puts us into a relationship where peace reigns. This he has brought about by reconciling us with God through his death.

> *He came and preached peace to you who were far away and peace to those who were near.*
>
> EPH 2:17

This peace enables us to live in peace with others, to make every effort to do what leads to peace and to mutual edification (Rom 14:19). This peace also affects a marriage (1 Cor 7:15). It is capable of bringing joy and happiness into a family because of its meaningful influence. This peace grows in us as fruit of the Holy Spirit (Gal 5:22-23) and creates a spiritual unity which maintains the bond of peace (Eph 4:3). We all have a responsibility to be peacemakers. This particular kind of peace forms a significant part of the Christian's character (Jas 3:17,18). The final outcome is an inner joyfulness, simply because our inner lives are "in order". When this happens, we have a foretaste of the heavenly peace and joy which is the spiritual fruit of eiréne – peace with God!

L ord, teach me that my salvation lies within you and that my future is in your hand. May that knowledge be my joy, my serenity, my redemption and my hope.

"Reconciliation" sounds like an impressive theological term; however, it merely means that we have come to our senses, that we are prepared to get up and go to our Father
– JOHN OMAR.

God cares

L ife does not always treat you the way you would like. Sometimes everything you attempt, comes to nothing. You believe yourself to be a failure, you feel disappointed and miserable and begin to despair of ever leading a triumphant spiritual life.

Setbacks and problems become formidable enemies when you try to triumph over them in your own strength or try to find a solution on your own. You get spiritually and physically worn-out and eventually you feel you have reached breaking-point.

When your spirit is so despondent and your powers of recovery are no longer as strong as they used to be,

> *Cast all your anxiety on him because he cares for you.*
> 1 PET 5:7

you need a real experience with God – so real that you will be willing to share your life with him completely. When you share your concerns and burdens with him, you are brought into contact with a source of strength which will enable you to remain firm in faith, even when you believe the foundations of your life to be crumbling.

God is aware of all your circumstances. He cares and wants to help you. If you know him, particularly when you encounter dark times in your life, every small worry or every burden will become an opportunity to get to know your Father better and to learn to trust him fully.

L ord, thank you that you are the unfailing Provider. Thank you that you know everything and that you care. Grant that this conviction may be my strength and inspiration every day of my life. Grant me your peace, particularly during the stormy times in life.

We do not really know whether God has a hand in our pain, but what we know for sure, is that his hands are around us whenever we suffer – D LOUW.

I am sorry

"I am sorry" or "I am also guilty", are certainly some of the most difficult words to utter.

"I am sorry" can, however, bridge the abyss of estrangement between friends; a relationship which is threatening to disintegrate, can be put right again by these words; likewise they can drive away grief and bitterness. However, whenever we try to utter these words, many reasons come to mind why we shouldn't say it. We try to convince ourselves that we have done nothing wrong, with thoughts such as, "People will think that I am a weakling. I shall have to sacrifice my dignity. The other person will just get his own way." When Satan subtly prompts these excuses, we listen to them – with the result that we never get round to confessing openly. Consequently we never experience the liberating effect of admitting our guilt openly. We miss the riches of a merciful Father, and bitterness and misunderstandings will accumulate in our lives.

> I confess my iniquity;
> I am troubled by my sin.
> PS 38:18

A troubled relationship can only be repaired by a confession of guilt. This applies not only to our relationship with God, but also to our relationship with others. We cannot afford to be too proud or haughty to admit that we are guilty. Ask God to grant you the courage to say that you are sorry. The results will surprise and uplift you.

Lord Jesus, help me to follow your example of forgiveness. I want to mend broken relationships in my life by confessing my guilt. You can make all things new and I wait upon you, trusting you in faith.

Mistakes are almost always forgiven if only people would have the courage to confess – LA ROUCHEFOUCOULD.

The glory of compassion

Perhaps there was a time when you felt true compassion for the needs of the less privileged and you did something constructive to relieve their distress. Right now, however, you are no longer touched by their plight. Your conscience has become hardened to the ever increasing poverty which surrounds us. If this is true of you, you have allowed an important part of your spiritual life to be broken down.

> *Be kind and compassionate to one another, forgiving each other, just as in Christ God forgave you.*
> EPH 4:32

If you go through life without caring about the needs of others, you make it practically impossible for the Holy Spirit to work through you. Remember that God uses sensitive and obedient people to do his work on earth.

A sensitive conscience does not make life easy for you, because you become totally involved with the pain and distress of others. However, it will make you a more understanding person, you will have a clear conscience and God will be able to let his grace enter into your life. You will be at peace with both Christ and your fellow-men and you will realise how merciful and sympathetic God is in his dealings with you when you are in need. Then you will reflect a Christ-like attitude, you will be filled with compassion towards others and be sympathetic and warm-hearted towards all people who are, just like you, trying to keep up with the demands of life.

Lord, keep me sensitive and grant me sufficient understanding so that I shall be able to deal compassionately with others, by the powerful workings of your Holy Spirit.

We must not merely give of what we have; we must also give of ourselves – *JOSEPH MERCIER.*

The abundant blessing of solitude

People thrive on company and often do things in a group which they would not dream of doing when on their own. The truth is that many people fear loneliness. They cannot face their own company and are afraid of their own thoughts. To enjoy good company is refreshing and beneficial, but a person's true character is revealed when he is alone. The riches or the poverty of a person's soul becomes evident when left alone.

We must nurture the free gift of being content with our own company. We should learn to control our thoughts in a constructive manner and focus on a continuous communion with our Lord. If we succeed, we have discovered the secret of a productive approach to dealing with our loneliness.

> *After he had dismissed them, he went up on a mountainside by himself to pray. When evening came, he was there alone.*
>
> MT 14:23

If you make time to be alone with the Lord, his power will flow through to you, your judgement will be sound, you will act in a more balanced way and will be able to make wise decisions.

Quiet time spent with the Lord will enrich your spirit. You will become a direct blessing to others as Christ demonstrated in many instances.

*D*ear Lord, thank you for the times of solitude during which you strengthen me. Grant that I may never complain about my loneliness but use it as an opportunity to spend time in communion with you and to serve others.

The secret of prayer is prayer in secret – D L MOODY.

God the unchangeable

C hange is part of our lives here on earth. Since early childhood and even into our old age we experience endless changes which sometimes disrupt our lives.

God, however, is unchangeable. In our desperation he comforts us by promising, "Never will I leave you; never will I forsake you" (Heb 13:5). "Jesus Christ is the same yesterday and today and for ever" (Heb 13:8); and this is our guarantee that there are treasures which are everlasting.

> *And now these three remain:*
> *faith, hope and love.*
> *But the greatest of these is love.*
> 1 COR 13:13

FAITH IS EVERLASTING. Have faith in God who works for the good of those who love him. Have faith in Christ who is with us all the days of our lives. Have faith in the Holy Spirit who is our comforter. And have faith in the Word of God which is full of comforting promises.

HOPE IS EVERLASTING. Cherish the hope for an eternal life with God. Hope that tomorrow will be a better day because God will be there.

LOVE IS EVERLASTING. Cherish God's love for us and our love for one another; both will remain for ever. We draw our strength from this love.

Faith, Hope and Love will remain our guiding stars amidst all change and herald the dawn of a new day for us.

G od of Faith, Hope and Love, thank you that you, the Unchangeable is the guiding star of my life. Strengthen my faith; intensify my hope and purify my love through the workings of your Son.

Others expect a hopeless end. However, those who believe in God, have endless hope – *GILBERT BEEKEN.*

Read EPHESIANS 5:6-20

Give thanks to God

G iving thanks to God is a Christian virtue which lends a unique quality to our lives. Every child of God has abundant reasons for giving thanks to God.

The secret of giving thanks to God is to *live* greatfully.

Give thanks to God for the gift of life by living a positive and triumphant life.

Give thanks for your opportunities. Regard them as challenges to prove how you can be used successfully in the service of the Lord .

> *Always giving thanks to God the Father for everything, in the name of our Lord Jesus Christ.*
>
> EPH 5:20

Give thanks for your happiness and prove your thankfulness by striving to make others happy.

Give thanks for the beauty of God's creation and try to enrich your surroundings.

Give thanks for your health and strength by taking care of your physical health and by using it to serve the Lord and others.

Finally, support your prayers of thanksgiving by *living* a life of thankfulness.

C reator God, recreate my life so that it will be a life of total dedicated thankfulness for your love and grace which I receive in abundance. Help me to lead a life of thankfulness all the days of my life.

If you wish to give thanks for all the blessings you have received, you need to bring some kind of sacrifice in your life for the sake of others — ALBERT SCHWEITZER.

Grief tempered by faith

During our lifetime most of us will experience intense grief. We are powerless to avoid it. The moment grief strikes you become so confused that you can only much later evaluate to what extent it has affected your life.

Grief can lead to self-pity which delays your recovery. It can affect your attitude towards life and you can feel bitter, because you, of all people, have had to suffer. The only way out of the quagmire is the way to God. By believing firmly that he loves you and cares for you, you will be delivered from bondage. You will discover new dimensions in life. You can be enriched by acquiring a better knowledge of God, something which you might previously have lacked. Your relationship with the Lord can become more intense because "Godly sorrow brings repentance that leads to salvation and leaves no regret" (2 Cor 7:10).

> He will wipe every tear from their eyes.
> There will be no more death or mourning
> or crying or pain, for the old order of things
> has passed away.
> He who was seated on the throne said,
> "I am making everything new !"
>
> REV 21:4-5

God will grant you the wisdom and the power to stand firm in your faith when grief assails you. With God by your side you will triumph over grief.

Lord God, you comfort me in the darkness of my grief. Thank you that I can sing your praises despite my grief, because through Jesus Christ I am bound to you with everlasting bonds.

It is through those who have suffered that there is progress in this world — LEO TOLSTOI.

28 FEBRUARY

Read JOHN 14:15-31

He is with us to the end of time

O f all the things that people fear most, loneliness is probably the worst. There can be many reasons for being lonely: you may have been removed from familiar surroundings to a new situation in life and you may find it difficult to adjust; you may have problems which you cannot share with anybody and which prey upon your mind; you may have been separated from your friends and your loved ones because of all the demands made upon you; it could even be the cruel separation which death has brought. These experiences could leave us feeling lonely and despondent, even in the midst of a crowd. What should we do in such circumstances?

> *I will ask the Father, and he will give you another Counsellor to be with you for ever.*
> JN 14:16

The Word of God guides us in every crisis in life. Although we might feel like a stray child, completely lost, we shall never be forsaken by God. Because Jesus once had to cry out in lonely agony on a Godforsaken cross, God will now always be with us through his Holy Spirit. We shall never be forsaken. Our loneliness will therefore never mean abandonment because we can hear him say, "And surely I am with you always, to the very end of the age" (Mt 28:20).

*H*eavenly Father, thank you that your love also embraces my loneliness. Thank you, Holy Spirit, for comforting me and for assuring me of your presence which will never fail me.

Whether or not a person is a believer, his or her loneliness is essentially a longing for God — HUBERT VAN ZELLER.

Heavenly consolation

If only we could have some impression of the heavenly glory we would not mourn the death of our loved ones. God's perfect provision for those who believe in him is so indescribable that they will only experience joy and fulfilment in his presence.

The book Revelation repeatedly gives us glimpses of this heavenly glory: those who live there are no longer subject to earthly suffering but are protected by the Lord who is seated on the throne and who consoles them in a merciful and loving way. Their hunger is stilled in green pastures and their thirst is quenched at the fountains of living water. God himself wipes away every tear from their eyes (cf Rev 7:16-17).

> *No eye has seen,*
> *no ear has heard,*
> *no mind has conceived*
> *what God has prepared for*
> *those who love him.*
> 1 COR 2:9

The mere thought that our deceased loved ones are privileged to share God's living presence compels us to glory in God's abundant mercy. It gives us the courage to continue our disrupted lives in renewed faith. Whoever lacks this consolation is exposed to despair. However, if our hearts are filled with the knowledge that God is our comforter, our courage will never fail us, even in the face of the deepest grief.

*H*eavenly Father, comfort through your grace and through your Holy Spirit all those who are grieving and strengthen them so that they will be able to face the challenges of a new phase in life.

To believe in a God who is in heaven does not imply fleeing from real life; but facing life in the name of the Lord – J BLINCO.

Notes

MARCH

PRAYER

❖❖❖❖❖❖❖❖❖❖❖❖❖❖❖❖❖❖❖❖❖❖

*I*t is autumn, Lord
   and an abundance of colours have ripened into maturity.
Thank you for spiritual growth
   which culminates in peace and fulfilment.
Man of Sorrows, it is also the time of year when we
   follow you in the spirit on your road to Calvary.
You suffered for the world –
   but also for me –
   all your suffering, the insults, the grief,
   every word spoken on the cross –
   even being forsaken by God –
   was suffered for my sake.
You gave your life for me,
   though I could never deserve it.
In renewed gratitude
   I now dedicate my
   body and soul to you.
Make me your disciple and fearless witness.
Grant that through the cross I may see
   how doomed I have been through my sin,
   and grant that I may be saved.
Allow me to see your love through Jesus Christ
   and let me find my refuge in you.
Lead me for evermore
   in the light of your beautiful countenance.

*A*men

We are under God's care

I t is encouraging to know that God is not only our Creator but also the faithful God who maintains his creation.

Not only does God know all there is to know about us, he also cares for us from day to day. We must therefore never be under the wrong impession that he leaves us on our own to battle with the problems of life. Worry does not solve any problems; on the contrary, worry has a paralysing effect and it only serves to trouble us.

> *Cast all your anxiety on him because he cares for you.*
> 1 PET 5:7

Why should we worry and be anxious if we know that we have an almighty God who cares for us and supports us, who loves us and takes an interest in us? Worry does not honour God; more often than not it is simply a symptom of lack of faith in him, "He who did not spare his own Son, but gave him up for us all – how will he not also, along with him, graciously give us all things?" (Rom 8:32).

He gave us his most precious, his utmost – his Son. Surely he will give us all those things which we need on our journey through life: grace to face every trial, strength to face every affliction and daily bread according to our needs.

E ternal Lord and Redeemer of my life, I praise you as the author and perfecter of my faith. Trusting in your love and loyalty I now surrender myself to you unconditionally.

To trust God is to start every day as if nothing at all has been done before – *C S LEWIS.*

2 MARCH

Read 1 JOHN 4:7- 21

God is love

W e could easily lapse into an existence of absolute selfishness and self-centredness. It is possible to lead a life completely lacking in love; a life which consists of complaining and of making demands; a life filled with discontent and even bitterness about an alleged injustice we have suffered. This happens particularly when life has laid a heavy burden upon us and we complain as we shoulder the weight.

> *Dear friends, let us love one another, for love comes from God. Everyone who loves has been born of God and knows God. Whoever does not love does not know God, because God is love.*
>
> 1 JN 4:7-8

How does one overcome this negative attitude towards life? In Jesus Christ God demonstrated the perfect solution : serving through love. Demonstrating love is the most balanced, sober, practical and fulfilling way to live your life. If you love God and you broaden the circle of your loving service to include all those around you, you are a new creation in Christ and a blessing to others.

Through your love you commit yourself to God in full surrender, because God is love!

H eavenly Father, grant me the grace to look away from myself and to see Christ and the needs of others. Grant me the grace to share my love so liberally that Jesus will be revealed through my life.

There is no comfort stronger than the certainty that the love of God will embrace you in all your distressing circumstances
— J CALVIN.

Peacemakers for God

M any believe that an abundance of possessions or victorious war will bring them peace. Neither of these groups will ever find the kind of peace they are searching for, for true peace has to do with people and righteousness, not with possessions or war.

Peacemakers have a mission assigned to them by God himself. This mission requires positive and dynamic action. Peacemakers don't shirk responsibilities. They grapple with problems until they have found a solution.

Are you searching for peace? You will find it in God. You will then be able to pray even for your enemies. Peace with God is your point of departure when trying to fulfil your task and to obey your calling as a peacemaker. Peace is not a personal

> *Blessed are the peacemakers, for they will be called sons of God.*
>
> MT 5:9

possession but should be shared with others. After all, those who try to be peacemakers will be blessed, not those who already have peace.

When there is no peace among people, the cause lies in a broken relationship between them and the Lord. Christ came to this world to reconcile the world with God. As his witness you should persuade the world to accept God's peace. You will then experience the greatest fulfilment because you have contributed to bringing about peace in this world.

D ear Lord, reveal your love in us and so inspire us to love one another and thereby find true peace in you.

Peace does not lie in the absence of war; it is a virtue, a state of mind, an attitude of reconciliation: trust and righteousness
– SPINOZA.

Read 1 JOHN 4:7-21

Let peace take the place of fear

I t is impossible to put all your trust in God and still live in fear. If you allow fear to rule your life, trusting God will eventually be completely out of the question. The decision is yours alone. God wants you to say, "I will lie down and sleep in peace, for you alone, O LORD, make me dwell in safety" (Ps 4:9).

You can only trust God fully if a conviction of the living, risen God fills your entire life. Only then will fear be dealt the final blow.

When God is present in your life, an indescribable peace will fill your life. This peace is not selfish. It will have a ripple effect to bring blessings to all those with whom you come into contact. You can be the channel through which God's perfect peace can flow to others so that they may conquer all worldy fears.

> *There is no fear in love. But perfect love drives out fear.*
> 1 JN 4:18

Only love will equip us for this task. Perfect love drives out fear so completely that it will never ever rule our lives again. Then we shall finally claim the inheritance which Christ promised us when he said, "Peace I leave with you; my peace I give you" (Jn 14:27).

*G*od of love and mercy, thank you that your Son also took away our fear. Grant that our love for you will drive out all fear from our lives because we put all our trust in you.

Peace, like all other rare and valuable possessions, does not automatically come to you. You have to go out and search for it
— FAITH FORSYTHE.

Jesus – the power in your life

When we are confronted with failure in our lives it is essential to handle it in a positive and creative manner. As God's children we must not allow failure to overwhelm us. We are expected to meet the challenges of life in the spirit of the joyfulness which Paul describes to us in 1 Corinthians 15:57.

Many people live in constant fear of failure and would therefore not dare to try their hand at anything new. Through this fear their initiative is destroyed and they limit their prospects. Remember, you are only a failure if you have decided that you are one. Many people have tried again after initial failure and have come out on top.

> But thanks be to God! He give us the victory through our Lord Jesus Christ.
> 1 COR 15:57

If you have failed, remember: God never writes off a person. Jesus Christ is the power in your life and can make everything new again. He understands your heart and knows how you feel. If you have complete faith in him, you will be victorious in the end. Face life with its numerous demands confidently, trust God unconditionally and you can be sure that you will be victorious!

Heavenly Father, so often I do not have the strength to fight life's battles, but I thank you that through your grace I will be triumphant in life – particularly over sin and failure.

Man must be ruled by God, otherwise he will be destroyed by his tyrannical self – WILLIAM PENN.

Christian hope

I n the Tate gallery in London there is a striking picture painted by Frederick Watts. Its title is "Hope". An extremely beautiful woman is sitting on a globe. She is blindfolded and has a lute in her hands. All the strings of the lute have been broken, except for one. Her hand touches that particular string and while she bows her head over the lute, she listens to that string attentively. She waits anxiously to hear what kind of sound might spring forth from that one string. She has hope – she hopes for the best in spite of the worst of cirumstances.

> *Brothers, we do not want you to . . .*
> *grieve like the rest of men, who have no hope.*
> 1 THESS 4:13

As long as hope is kept alive in our hearts we shall not succumb to any form of grief or problems. Should tragedy come our way, we have this consolation: where Christian hope is alive the night will never be too dark. Hope is optimism, based on God's capability of allowing the best to come from the worst. This unshakeable hope regarding the future fills our hearts with joy. Hope is our steadfast trust in the eternal goodness of God and it kindles in us an unconquerable spirit. That is why Paul is capable of saying, "Christ (is) in you, the hope of glory" (Col 1:27).

E ternal God, we praise you for your Word which always brings renewed hope whenever despair comes knocking at our door. Please strengthen us daily with your inextinguishable hope.

HOPE is the word which God has engraved on the forehead of every person – VICTOR HUGO.

Prayer in the valley of darkness

I n the life of every child of God there are times when you find it difficult to pray, when you feel that you are losing your grip on the only anchor in life: the awareness that God is a living presence in your life. God, the one who has always been a reality in your life, suddenly feels distant and unreal.

Most people do not recognise the potential for spiritual growth afforded by these dark times. They draw the wrong conclusion that God no longer cares. These are the times when you must not doubt the living presence of God in your life; such times should add a more intimate dimension to your relationship with God. We need to learn to hold God's hand when our burden is light, but also when the valley of shadows darkens our lives. Then he will become a living presence in our lives and we shall be able to rejoice in spite of difficulties.

> *He will respond to the prayer of the destitute; he will not despise their plea.*
>
> PS 102:17

The dark hours will pass. Do not rebel against your inability to pray. Rather try to determine what lessons you can learn from this experience. Cling to the truth that God's love for you will never change.

L oving God, help me to take the focus off myself and my problems and to seek you with greater dedication. Help me to live according to your will until you have transformed the darkness into light.

Let us move forward on our knees — NEESIMA.

Read JOHN 12:20-36

Death is no more!

On Calvary Jesus Christ triumphed over death! Physical death is therefore no longer a tragedy for us Christians. This is the essence of our Christian faith .

Viewed from an eternal perspective it is not *physical death which is tragic, but* spiritual death when a person does not take the kingdom of God seriously and is unwillling to surrender to Christ.

Life is not about what you possess, but lies essentially in the quality of your spiritual life. The Christian dies only so that he or she can rise from the dead. He triumphs over death. We shall not know what true life means unless we have died. In Christ who has conquered death we have true life because he has transformed death into the potential of life everlasting.

> *I tell you the truth, unless an ear of wheat falls to the ground and dies, it remains only a single seed.*
> *But if it dies, it produces many seeds.*
> JN 12:24

Let us therefore no longer be afraid of the powers which afflict the body. Let us rather be on the lookout for the powers of this dark world which try to destroy our spirit. For we as believers have the guarantee that life everlasting has the final say over our lives and the lives of our loved ones.

*H*eavenly Father, grant that I may live every day in view of life eternal. Thank you, Jesus, that you have died for me and have conquered death.

To die is no art; the most wicked can succeed in doing it. To live is an art; the most virtuous cannot do it successfully
— C J LANGENHOVEN.

What do you give to God?

Have you ever honestly and earnestly asked yourself: What do I give to God? In church, without realising what we really mean, we often sing these words, "Take my life and let it be, consecrated Lord to thee." And after that we go out into the world and adapt our pretended dedication to suit our selfish comfort. If we examine our lives honestly, it is disturbing to discover that the sum total of what we are really prepared to sacrifice for the Lord, is often alarmingly little.

It is impossible to dedicate your possessions to God without dedicating yourself to him. You might confess that all you possess really belongs to God, yet you have inherited one gift from God which you can choose to keep to yourself or to give away: the gift of love.

Whatever your offering to God, it will be of no value if it is not given with genuine love. Only the gift of

> *Live a life of love, just as Christ loved us and gave himself up for us as a fragrant offering and sacrifice to God.*
>
> EPH 5:2

love makes all other offerings acceptable in God's sight, for genuine love holds nothing back. Just as God – because he loves you – was prepared to sacrifice his precious Son to save you from sin, you must be prepared to sacrifice everything to him – because you love him. He does not expect you to sacrifice more than your love and your life; but he expects nothing less!

Lord, I dedicate my whole life to you – as well as my love. Sanctify my gift through the love there is in Jesus Christ.

God forces nobody, because there is no tyranny in love. Those who serve God are therefore completely free – HANS DENK.

Have faith today for the future

D on't ever lose faith in the future. Never measure the future against the present. What you are today is largely the result of yesterday's thoughts and deeds. Today you can already determine what you will be tomorrow.

Don't waste your time complaining about what could have been. Go to meet the future in true faith and in complete trust because you have given your utmost for "today".

> *Put your faith in God, for I will yet praise him, my Saviour and my God.*
> PS 43:5

Don't entertain negative thoughts. The worst stumbling blocks in the way of a future full of promises are bitterness, hatred and jealousy. These emotions paralyse your actions, obscure your outlook, interfere with your thoughts and prevent spiritual growth. You are the one who have to decide what powers will dictate your thoughts and actions. Are you prepared to accept the challenges with a positive, trusting attitude or will you isolate yourself by indulging in negative thoughts?

On the road of faith tomorrow and the next day hold no dangers, because God is with you. In his hands you will be safe. The precipices will still be there; however, instead of stumbling blocks, they will present themselves as challenges.

F ather, transform my thoughts so that I shall be able to face the challenges of each day with faith in my heart and in the name of Christ.

Man cannot live without faith: the primary requirement for the adventure of life is courage, and the lifeblood of courage is faith
— HARRY EMERSON FOSDICK.

Your life is your testimonial

People who experience the impact of the sacrificial love of the Holy Spirit can find charity the most exciting and satisfying experience of their entire lines.

People who need help are often not aware of their need. They might have closed their minds to influences of any kind. They can be cynical about everything you hold holy and can regard your help with contempt. If you are dedicated to your charitable cause, such an attitude can easily discourage you. Remember, however, that this unapproachable exterior hides a spirit which is yearning to be liberated.

Spiritual and intellectual liberation cannot be achieved by preaching or by laying down rules. You should live in such a manner that your conduct is beyond criticism. In

> When they saw the courage of Peter and John and realised that they were unschooled, ordinary men, they were astonished . . .
> ACTS 4:13

fact, your conduct should awaken the desire in others to share the same spiritual experiences you have gained through the Holy Spirit.

The best way to "help" a person is to reflect a quality of life which will inspire them to become in Christ what he had intended them to be. Then you will be testifying to the glory of your Lord.

Holy Spirit, thank you for teaching me that the spiritual quality of my life is far more important than the words that pass over my lips.

Witnessing means removing the stumbling blocks so that Christ, who lives in us, may reveal himself to others – PAUL FROST.

We shall be comforted

G rief is a reality in our lives. It is therefore a comforting thought to hear our Redeemer, who himself has suffered, saying, "Blessed are those who mourn, for they will be comforted" (Mt 5:4).

Do you experience need and poverty in your home? Christ had nowhere to lay his head (Lk 9:58). Has your friend disappointed you? His friends betrayed him and renounced him (Lk 22:48, 58). Are you trying to come to terms with grief? He battled in Gethsemane to accept the cup of sorrows which was awaiting him (Mt 26:36-46). Are you grieving about the death of a loved one?

> *He has sent me*
> *to bind up the*
> *broken-hearted . . .*
> *to comfort all who mourn.*
> IS 61:1-2

He wept at the grave of his friend Lazarus (Jn 11:35). Do you feel deserted, even by God? He cried out in a loud voice on the cross : "My God, my God, why have you forsaken me?" (Mt 27:46).

This life is characterised by setbacks, poverty and cares. But Christ came to comfort us: "As a mother comforts her child, so will I comfort you" (Is 66:13). Not far from Marah, meaning "bitter water", you will find Elim with twelve fountains with sweet water and many palm trees. There you will be able to camp again in peace. Simply trust God who is sure to comfort you.

T hank you Lord, that you have sent us the Comforter to remain with us for ever. Thank you that my grief is teaching me that what I have lost is not important; much more important is what I have left through your grace.

Nothing is more beneficial for those who grieve than to comfort others — MAURICE HULST.

Read JOB 2:1-10

How shall I ever cope with my grief?

I f we rebel against our "unkind fate" – as we often incorrectly term it – we rebel against God. Death forms part of his plan for our lives. Accepting it in faith is a sign of spiritual maturity.

To turn your back on God when faced by grief means trying to cope with your grief on your own. This drives us to despair. It puts up a barrier between us and God because God cannot comfort a rebellious heart.

God never subjects his children to suffering without being there with them himself. If you don't learn something in times of trials and tribulations your suffering will never serve any purpose. Thousands of God's children have proved that such times are often times of optimal spiritual growth – provided you have the correct approach to your suffering. The only way in which the Christian can recognise his grief and work through it, is if he follows Christ's example: Accept life calmly and with courage and submit to the cross with a fearless heart filled with courage. The liberation lies in the knowledge that life's real significance can be found beyond Calvary and the grave.

> *Shall we accept good from God, and not trouble?*
> JOB 2:10

L ord, my Redeemer, I know that I don't have all the answers, but I know that I can hold onto you and that your love for me will never fail.

We can accept whatever God has brought about in our lives without really knowing how it works; in fact, you will certainly not know how it works until you have accepted it – C S LEWIS.

Read JEREMIAH 18:1-17

Hearing God's voice

S ometimes it is a real problem for us to know what God's will is for our lives. God, however, makes his will known to us in his own time and in his special way. It sometimes happens in the most unexpected places and in the most unusual ways, as in the case of Jeremiah.

We can seek God's will for our lives by withdrawing from the world around us and by concentrating on him with all our strength. We might seek out the quiet and solitude of a church or a lovely spot in nature. We can even have our own special place where God has often become a reality in the past.

> *"Go down to the potter's house,*
> *and there I will give you my message."*
> JER 18:2

Principally God reveals himself to all who seek him with all their hearts. Where this happens is not the decisive factor. God is able to meet you in any place and under all circumstances. Jeremiah went to the potter's house to listen to the voice of God. Despite the unusual circumstances the Lord spoke to him in an extremely powerful way.

If only we listen sensitively and obediently we shall hear his voice distinctly.

T hank you, Lord, that hearing your voice is neither dependent on time, nor on place or circumstances. Make me sensitive to your voice and willing to obey you.

If you want God to listen to you when you pray, you must be prepared to listen whenever he tries to speak to you
— *THOMAS BENTON BROOKS.*

Cast your anxiety on him

C onstant worry is self-destructive. All of us suffer from this ail-
ment because we still do not understand the essence of Christ's
words when he told us, "Therefore I tell you, do not worry about your
life, what you will eat or drink; or about your body, what you will
wear . . . Who of you by worrying can add a single hour to his life?"
(Mt 6:25, 27).

How often have we experienced how useless and damaging it is to
worry all the time. Disasters which we feared, never happened to us,
while others which we had never
even thought of, caught up with us.
Only afterwards could we witness
that at the time we received sufficient strength to bear our cross.

All our worrying and sighing cannot add even one second to our lives.
Worry and unfounded fears only rob
us of our joy and peace in life. Let us

> *Therefore do not worry*
> *about tomorrow,*
> *for tomorrow will worry*
> *about itself.*
> *Each day has enough*
> *trouble of its own.*
> MT 6:34

rather treasure the words of 1 Peter 5:7 in our hearts and use it to
hold God to his promise when we feel overcome by worry, "Cast all
your anxiety on him because he cares for you."

L ord, please strengthen my faith. Thank you that I need not
fear anything, because you are with me. Help me to
keep my eyes fixed on you.

---

*There is no doubt that death and danger only bring us nearer to
God* — *DIETRICH BONHOEFFER.*

16 MARCH

Read LUKE 2:8-20

Peace – God's loving gift

M any people approach life with the attitude of, *Life owes me something.* Christians, on the other hand, ask, *What do I owe life?*

If being a Christian is only a matter of what we can gain and not what we can contribute, we have no understanding of God's peace. Giving is a godly principle. God gives all the time: He gives life and strength; forgiveness; his Son and also his peace. In answer to his love we should dedicate our lives to him and become messengers of his peace.

> *Glory to God in the highest, and on earth peace to men on whom his favour rests.*
>
> LK 2:14

When we accept God's gift of love we become committed to glorifying his Name. In addition we are called upon to become peacemakers who constantly try to convince the world that its only hope for peace is rooted in God. When we love God and glorify him in everything we do it gives us the power to serve him and to be true peacemakers.

The Holy Spirit will equip us for this task; he will teach us and guide us; he will illuminate our minds, warm our hearts and lift our souls in adoration. God's gift of love will become a reality in our lives through the working of his Spirit.

D ear Lord, I desire to be your messenger of peace in this world and I wish to share your love and peace with others. Please equip me for this task through your Spirit.

Words of love serve little purpose. Only when love is demonstrated in deeds does it become meaningful – ENA MURRAY.

You have an identity

"Identity crisis" has become a buzzword in our time. "Who am I?" is the question on our lips from our youth until we are old and grey. Let us therefore immediately put one thing right: You are God's unique creation; in his own image he has created you. You are the child of a King, even though sin has marred this image. God, your Father, calls you to fulfil your task as his child with dignity.

> *And who knows but that you have come to royal position for such a time as this?*
> ESTHER 4:14

Every child of God has been created with his or her own identity, nature and personality. No other person on earth can take your place. You must therefore ensure that you are not swallowed up by the faceless masses which have no identity of their own. Never consider yourself better than others because you are a child of God. For it is only through God's grace that you have been saved and therefore you are called to live your life with dignity and confidence.

Faith in Jesus Christ helps you to discover who you really are. False pride; inferiority which handicaps your spiritual growth; impure values which mar your perspective on life – all these things can be conquered and purified through the power which Christ has granted you.

To be yourself guarantees the highest fulfilment in life and there is no greater joy on earth than to know that you are living your life according to God's will.

Lord, I want to humble myself before you so that you can teach me through your Holy Spirit what you wish me to become.

Self-knowledge prevents us from becoming self-satisfied
– MIGUEL DE CERVANTES.

Wait in good faith

S ome or other time in life all of us need help, sometimes rather urgently. If we then ask God to help us, we must give him time to answer us. For the manner in which God deals with our crises and distress often differs considerably from the way in which we would have done.

We often turn to God with panic in our hearts. We rattle off a quick prayer and expect God to answer straightaway. But God expects us to wait upon him in good faith – that way we shall never be disappointed.

> *"For my thoughts are not your thoughts, neither are your ways my ways," declares the LORD.*
>
> IS 55:8

Moreover, we should not just wait for his guidance in silent prayer but should try listening to him with a sensitive ear to find out his will for us. However, we must be prepared to listen and obey whatever he dictates.

This kind of obedience time and time again opens up new perspectives for us. Things we would never have deemed possible start happening in our lives. We see God at work in our lives in such a marvellous and exciting way that we are often left speechless. Life is no longer dull or mere routine and his presence becomes a wonderful reality in our lives. What more could we desire?

F ather, keep me from trying to bend your will according to my needs. Help me to submit to your ways and thoughts, because you know all my needs and will provide in them.

Faith mounts the steep stairs which Love has built and views life through the window which Hope has opened
– CHARLES HADDON SPURGEON.

Fear unmasked

Throughout the Bible God tells his children, "Do not be afraid!" At the Red Sea he said to Israel, "Do not be afraid. Stand firm and you will see the deliverance the LORD will bring you today . . ." (Ex 14:13). He encouraged Joshua with the words, "Be strong and courageous. Do not be terrified; do not be discouraged, for the LORD your God will be with you wherever you go" (Josh 1:9).

When Christ was born the angels said to the shepherds, "Do not be afraid . . ." (Lk 2:10). When Jesus walked on the water and his disciples were afraid, he said, "Take courage! It is I. Don't be afraid" (Mt 14:27). When he spoke to them for the last time, Jesus comforted them by saying, "Do not let your hearts be troubled and do not be afraid" (Jn 14:27).

> *Surely God is my salvation; I will trust and not be afraid. The LORD, the LORD, is my strength and my song; he has become my salvation.*
> IS 12:2

When you are trying to cope with stress, grief or pain, God's loving voice says to you, "Do not be afraid." Know that you are safe with him, because you are his child. Hold onto him, for he loves you. Live life to the fullest in the knowledge that his love will never fail. The way to victory over fear is rooted in faith and love.

Glorious Lord Jesus, deliver me from the darkness of my fears. In your omnicience, know that I love you.

When a storm rages, the wise man prays to God, not for protection against danger, but for deliverance from fear. It is not the storm outside that is dangerous, but the storm that rages inside ourselves – EMERSON.

Do not be amazed

The church of the early days was experiencing a crisis. Their leader was in jail, the authorities were persecuting Christians and the believers were scattered across Asia Minor. Then they did the best thing possible: They prayed! (12:12).

When Peter knocked on the door and a servant girl named Rhoda heard his voice, she ran back to tell the praying church members that God had answered their prayers. They were astonished beyond description. How hesitant we are to take answered prayers at face value! Instead of glorifying and praising God for his goodness and omnipotence we seek explanations.

> *When she recognised Peter's voice, she was so overjoyed she ran back . . . and exclaimed, "Peter is at the door!"*
> *"You're out of your mind," they told her.*
> ACTS 12:14-15

When we pray, we should implore God to give us the ability to recognise his answers. Sometimes we continue to pray for things God has already given us. Because God has not granted us our prayers precisely as we had expected or had wanted, we fail to recognise that God has heard our prayers. God always knows what is best for us. We must, however, develop a sensitivity to recognise God's answered prayers without doubt and with joyful and believing hearts.

Lord, help me to await your answer to my prayers with excitement. Thank you that I may be sure that you will always hear and answer my prayers.

God does nothing except in answer to prayers — JOHN WESLEY.

A feared friend

There are times when we realise that the death of a loved one is imminent. But when we are faced with the finality and inevitability of death, it invariably comes as a shock and we experience grief and profound sorrow.

Death accompanies us through life like a feared friend. We recognise its signs within our own bodies or in the body of a loved one. These signs are all proof of God's grace and should remind us that we have no eternal house on this earth and that we are citizens of heaven.

This world, however unsatisfactory and transient it may be, holds an unavoidable attraction for us. We cringe at the thought of having to leave it behind. We regard death as an enemy, firmly believing that we are unable to triumph over it. Instead we should realise that it is a messanger who opens the door of immortality for us.

> *But Christ has indeed been raised from the dead, the firstfruits of those who have fallen asleep.*
> 1 COR 15:20

Our hearts are sorely lacking in faith. Death is after all the illuminated entrance leading into the brightly shining glory of our Father's house. How insignificant our fear will prove when we step inside!

Lord Jesus, you have conquered death and have paved the way to eternal joy. Allow your love to free us from all fear when we walk through the valley of death.

God's road begins where my road comes to a dead end.

22 MARCH

Read JAMES 1:2-8

Triumph over your circumstances

We can react in different ways to the circumstances in which we find ourselves. We can surrender completely and refuse to do anything to try and change things, in which case we shall tell ourselves that success is out of the question. We can convince ourselves that our circumstances are too difficult to cope with, in which case we shall accept them with bitterness in our hearts. We may even rebel against our fate and blame God and others for it.

> *Consider it pure joy, my brothers, whenever you face trials of many kinds, because you know that the testing of your faith develops perseverance.*
> JAS 1:2

However, the best response would be to accept our circumstances and all it entails, supported by the will and determination to overcome them. No matter how intimidating our circumstances, we can be assured that God's power is at our disposal. He will help us to solve our problems and triumph over them.

This power to be stronger than our problems, is a gift from God to all who allow the Holy Spirit into their lives. We are called to surrender to its influence and to realise that Christ is at work, trying to perfect his will in our lives. With Christ in our lives we are blessed with faith and confidence. And this enables us to cope under all circumstances and conquer all.

*C*hrist, I trust you to grant me wisdom and guidance to conquer all circumstances and not allow myself to become despondent.

God gives us the nuts, but we have to crack them open ourselves — ANDERSON.

Faith which opens the eyes of the blind

There is a vast difference between true faith and wishful thinking. Many people never learn to distinguish between the two. This eventually leads to spiritual blindness and poverty. Some people desire certain things fervently, yet they are convinced that they will never fulfil these desires. Their minds become wrought with conflict, their spiritual strength fails them and their vision becomes blurred.

True faith means to be convinced that all desires can be realised in the Name of Jesus Christ. For true believers Christ is the power at work in their lives. They put their trust in the Omnipotent to reveal himself in their everyday existence.

> *Then Jesus touched their eyes and said,*
> *"According to your faith will it be done to you."*
> MT 9:29

The kind of faith that yields results must have its inspiration and its origin in God himself. If we expect great things from God, we shall receive great things and we shall be able to perform mighty deeds in his Name. If your faith is rooted in him you shall become a channel through which his mighty deeds will be performed. A new world of spiritual energy will be revealed to you. If you dedicate yourself to God, your faith will become a glorious reality.

Father, make me your faithful instrument. Uphold me through the power of Christ, my Redeemer, to keep serving you with dedication.

It is through faith among people that the moral elements of the community are upheld, and it is faith in God which binds the world to his throne — WILLIAM MAXWELL EVARTS.

Read ROMANS 8:31-39

Don't run yourself down

T here are people who underestimate their God-given talents to such an extent that their talents eventually fall into disuse. Others complain that they are not gifted at all. These attitudes do not honour God.

God gave every human being at least one talent. Perhaps you cannot recognise what it is, but you definitely have one or more talents. It is your responsibility to discover what your particular talent is and to develop it to its full potential.

Initially you will undoubtedly experience problems and you will even find all kinds of excuses to leave this talent undeveloped. Perhaps you are afraid to start working on the particular talent God has given you because you doubt whether you will be able to use it to the full. You might even consider the task of making the most of your talents too overwhelming and simply leave it lying undeveloped.

> *No, in all these things we are more than conquerors through him who loved us.*
> ROM 8:37

God will never entrust you with a talent if he thinks you are unable to develop it fully. Granted, it may require effort on your part and initially the task may seem completely beyond your capabilities. But the Holy Spirit will grant you the grace and strength to grow both intellectually and spiritually and to develop and use the talent he has entrusted to you to the full.

I thank you, Lord, that you make it possible for me to fully develop the talents you have given me. In honour of you I accept the challenge.

Never think that we need to be stars if we wish to shine for the Lord. It was through the muted light of a candle that the woman found her lost penny – HENRI AMIEL.

Be still and know that he is God

Prayer is like a precious diamond with many facets. Adoration, praise, supplication, dedication, confession and intercession are all facets of prayer. However, there is one facet which few people are willing to practise and with which they are consequently not well acquainted. That facet is to be still in the Lord's presence.

In general people do not find it difficult to talk to God because most people are naturally talkative. But in order to listen to what God wants to tell you, you need to be still in the presence of the Lord. This means that you must invite Christ to enter your thoughts and your life through the Holy Spirit and that you must allow him to make his will known to you. Then you will receive his guidance.

> *The Lord came and stood there, calling as at other times, "Samuel! Samuel!" Then Samuel said, "Speak, for your servant is listening."*
> 1 SAM 3:10

Initially it might not be clear where God is leading you and you will hesitate to obey. You may even make mistakes. But if you persevere, a special relationship will develop between you and the Lord and you will be sure that whatever you are doing is his will for your life. Without becoming still in the presence of the Lord, this is not possible.

Father, grant me a sensitive spirit so that I shall always know your will for my life. Teach me to be still in your presence, my God.

Prayer is not a magic formula which you can use to make God fulfil your desires, but the only way of being transformed into the person God wants you to be – STUDDERT KENNEDY.

Let them go

All of us who have lost loved ones must allow them to go to a new and glorified life with Christ. This is one of the most difficult things to do, not only because our memories are still so vivid, but also because we can hardly imagine what eternity is like. However, Isaiah brings us this message from God, "Forget the former things; do not dwell on the past. See, I am doing a new thing!" (Is 43:18).

> *"Take off the grave clothes and let him go."*
> JN 11:44

God wants us to part with the past and our loved ones who have passed on, and surrender them into the hands of the Lord. Having done that, we must proceed with courage and in faith. Even the good can handicap our spiritual growth if we cling to it too desperately. We can even defeat God's purpose for our lives. For only if we submit to his will can we find peace.

If we commit our loved ones to God, his perfect will for our future can unfold. This does not mean that we have to forget our loved ones, but we must, however, face the future and not dwell on the past. God will then lead us to the feast in his house where we will all meet again and our hearts will be filled with everlasting joy.

Lord, help me to cope with my present sorrow to the best of my ability and to look forward to all the blessings you will one day share with me.

Worry does not release tomorrow from its sorrow; it robs today of its power – CORRIE TEN BOOM.

Forgive and forget

I f only we could estimate the enormous damage wrought by an un-forgiving heart, we would hurry to put things right with those against whom we have transgressed.

Time cures sorrow, but if we are loathe to forgive, it cuts deep into our spiritual life and cripples us spiritually. Our unforgiving attitude is like an infected wound that causes unpleasantness and even bitterness.

We are called to be forgiving. This is one of the central themes of Christ's message to this world, "But I tell you, Love your enemies and pray for those who persecute you" (Mt 5:44).

Christ did not only preach this, he also demonstrated it on the cross, "Father, forgive them, for they do not know what they are doing" (Lk 23:34).

> *For if you forgive men when they sin against you, your heavenly Father will also forgive you.*
> *But if you do not forgive men their sins, your Father will not forgive your sins.*
> MT 6:14-15

Is there someone in your life whom you have not yet forgiven? Does this make you deeply unhappy? Don't hesitate – do something about it right now!

L ord Jesus, you can heal the sick – therefore you can heal my sick, unforgiving heart which causes much suffering. Grant me your mercy and heal me today so that joy and peace can fill my heart again.

We all agree that forgiveness is a wonderful idea – until we have to forgive someone who has hurt us deeply – C S LEWIS.

28 MARCH

Read MATTHEW 6:5-8

Your Father knows

In Matthew 6 Christ speaks about the troubles and worries of life and how we should overcome them. The key to his whole argument lies in verse 8 where he says, ". . . your Father knows what you need . . ." In many cases people who have suffered from a serious illness or who have been sorely afflicted, confessed, My Father knows! They hold on to this truth with all their hearts.

It is very easy to make this confession when life is good and there is reason for joy, but we struggle to confess this when our earthly

> . . . your Father knows what you need before you ask him.
>
> MT 6:8

supports start failing us one by one. We expect joy, but sorrow comes our way. We bargain on getting better, but instead we get worse. We believe that the light will shine through, but instead it gets darker

and darker. Bitterness enters our hearts and we feel like sighing, "Where is God now?"

When you feel like asking this question, remember that God will never leave you. Jesus Christ is the guarantee of the promise which God has made. If you hold onto this, you shall remain steadfast in your faith and your courage will not fail you, in spite of your trying circumstances.

Father, I marvel at the thought that I am your child and that I have the guarantee that you will never fail me, particularly in hard times. Thank you for knowing what I need.

We have a God who rejoices in making the impossible possible
— ANDREW MURRAY.

Peace requires communication

Communication is extremely important in our search for peace. It is only possible to communicate with God if we have a relationship with him. This line of communication must remain open if we wish to experience peace. If there is a breakdown in communication – whether it involves man and God or man and man, all peace will disappear.

When God spoke to Moses as a man speaks with a true friend, peace entered the heart of Moses. The Lord's loving assurance, "My Presence will go with you, and I will give you rest," was followed by Moses' reply, "If your presence does not go with us, do not send us up from here" (Ex 33:14-15). Moses thus maintained a close relationship with God.

> *The LORD would speak to Moses face to face, as a man speaks with his friend.*
> EX 33:11

If we continue to talk to the Lord, we shall have hope, peace of mind and inward peace, however dark our circumstances in life might be. Through Jesus Christ, God came to speak to us in a perfect way about all the things that contribute to our peace.

God speaks to us in every situation, if only we would listen to him. He tells us about redemption from sin; about grief turned into joy; hatred turned into love and he promises peace to all who would speak to him, listen to him and then go forth to convey his message to a world longing for peace.

Open my heart, dear Lord, so that I can make your promises my own. Teach me to depend on you completely and to rely on you in unconditional faith.

There must be a consensus between two parties to accomplish peace, but only one of them is needed to take the first step
— JOHN KENNEDY.

Become aware of God's love

W hen we are devastated by suffering, we tend to want to isolate ourselves. In this desolate loneliness we lose our grip on life. We cannot experience the reality of God's presence and we begin to believe that he has rejected us; that he is to be blamed for our pain.

We may feel like that about God, but that is definitely not the way he feels about us! God's love for us is unchangeable. Our emotions and perceptions may change when our circumstances change, but God never stops loving us, even though we might reject him, "For I am convinced that neither death nor life . . . nor anything else in all creation, will be able to separate us from the love of God" (Rom 8:38-39).

> *If God is for us, who can be against us?*
> ROM 8:31

Being aware of God's love implies more than a mere emotional experience – it is a way of life, of full surrender to God. God's love has a wonderful and healing power. You might have turned your back on him, but the moment you turn back to him, he will meet you halfway. He is yearning for your love. That very moment you will know: God's love has always surrounded you and he loved you even when you strayed from him, not deserving his love.

M erciful Lord, your unfathomable love for me is the source of my greatest joy and strength. Thank you that I can depend on it, even when I go through depths of darkness.

Love can still hope where the mind would despair – LYTTELTON.

Seek the kingdom of God

S ome people make themselves profoundly unhappy because they are so anxious to correct all the wrongs in life. They believe that they have the solutions to all problems, but in their enthusiasm they tend to forget that imperfection is part of human nature.

To create a new world without new people is impossible. Also, it is no use trying to change others first. The best place to begin to change and heal a sick world, is to start with ourselves. We don't find it easy to accept this truth, but unless our own lives are in harmony with God it will be impossible to change others. After all, Jesus said that the kingdom of God is within us.

> But seek first his kingdom and his righteousness, and all these things will be given you as well.
>
> MT 6:33

Only if we become aware of this kingdom and allow it to come into its own, will it be revealed in our lives and influence the lives of others. We must keep striving for spiritual maturity, in spite of all our short-comings. Jesus has promised to be with us always – in victory and in defeat. He will enable us to be a positive asset in the particular area of his kingdom where he places us.

H oly Lord Jesus, I put you in the centre of my life. Thank you that I know that you will help me to live a victorious life.

Perfection defeats men in their thousands, but imperfection defeats ten thousands – ANDREW MURRAY.

Notes

APRIL

PRAYER

O Lord, our Lord
how majestic is your name in all the earth!
In this month we praise you as Christ Triumphant!
On Golgotha you overcame death
    and destroyed Satan's power.
The grave is empty! You have truly risen!
The heavens rejoice and proclaim your glory!
Thank you that even in your death you were obedient;
    that God has accorded you the highest honour;
    that you sit at the right-hand side of God and intercede for me.
Thank you that I may accompany you on your triumpant journey
    through time and eternity.
Because you have risen from the dead
    I can also triumph over death
    to arise to a new life.
You are the Resurrection and Everlasting Life
    and therefore I shall live in the eternal home which you have
    gone to prepare for me.
Never let me forget your living presence;
    and strengthen my conviction that nothing and no one
    can ever separate me from your love.
Dear Lord Jesus, forgive me when at times my life
    does not proclaim your triumph over death.
Every day of this month and for the rest of my life
    I am comforted by your promise,
    "Behold, I am with you . . ."
In the Name of Jesus Christ, the Victor!

*A*men

A refuge in danger

A n experienced police officer always wore a bullet-proof vest even though a shot had never been fired at him in his thirty years of service. One day he was shot in the back and the bullet-proof vest saved his life. He realised that as long as he wore his uniform he would always be a target and therefore he had taken precautions.

God is our bullet-proof protection. We must arm ourselves with this wonderful truth because we belong to Christ and are therefore always Satan's target. He tries to destroy us with the "bullets" of doubt, despair and temptation. We make good targets, particularly when troubles threaten to overwhelm us or in times of illness and grief when we are very vulnerable.

> *Every word of God is flawless;*
> *he is a shield to those who take refuge in him.*
> PROV 30:5

That is why an intimate relationship with the living Christ is essential. He is our shield and protector.

Let us then, whilst we are at our most vulnerable, take refuge under the Rock of Ages because with him we are safe and comforted.

*A*lmighty Protector, I pray that you may be my shield in times of grief, weakness and doubt, when my strength is depleted.

The only safe haven for us is to focus on God's will. If he leads us along thorny paths he will provide us with strong boots
— CORRIE TEN BOOM.

APRIL

Read JEREMIAH 23:33-40

Be ready to have your prayers answered

M any people do not expect their prayers to be answered and therefore they do not receive any answers. This results in spiritual impoverishment which prevents them from seeing their prayers answered.

When you have prayed in the belief that your heavenly Father will answer you, you await his answer with excitement and in expectation of how that answer will come. This type of attitude makes it easier for God to work in your life. There is also no danger of dismissing answered prayer as mere coincidence.

> *"What is the LORD's answer to you"*
> *or "What has the Lord spoken?"*
>
> JER 23:37

However, you must realise that when you have prayed you cannot prescribe to God how he should answer your prayer. You will only be disappointed and become blind to the miracles which he performs in your life.

When God answers, he does it in his perfect way. When you come into his presence with a prayerful heart you will be able to see the design underlying his answer. You will become a willing and joyful worker in God's kingdom and you will be ready to accept the answering of your prayers as part of your spiritual experience.

D ear Lord, help me to follow your example and to say, "Not my will but your will be done." Open my eyes to see your answers to my prayers.

Daily prayer exercises the soul – *C E COWMAN.*

"Teacher, don't you care?"

Sometimes death is unleashed on our lives like a sudden storm. Then we lash about in fear and trepidation of the mighty elements and our fear drives us to the depths of despair and loss of faith.

This once happened to the disciples, "A furious squall came up, and the waves broke over the boat . . ." (37). They were panic-stricken and it seemed as if there was no hope for them. Even Jesus seemed indifferent to their plight.

We are totally unprepared when a storm suddenly breaks in our lives. We experience it as cruel and senseless. We demand answers to our many questions. Our faith and trust in God are tested to the utmost. In despair we also cry out: "Teacher, don't you care if we drown?" (38).

> *He got up, rebuked the wind and said to the waves, "Quiet, be still!"*
> MK 4:39

Is there anyone who cares or sees and understands our grief? Does someone have the answers to the troubled questions of our fearful hearts? *God* hears your anguished cry and cares about you. In Jesus Christ he is with you in the storm to enfold you in his loving arms and protect you. He is God, the Almighty – he can answer your questions and calm the storm in your troubled heart.

Thank you, Lord, that you are always by my side. You are my best friend and through my vale of tears you will lead me to joy.

Your name also is written in the palm of God's hand.

Enthusiasm

M any people base their lives on negative attitudes. They dwell on all that is wrong, the things which they dislike and which make them angry and despondent. This type of attitude destroys your ideals, your motivation, your zest for life and your relationship with God and others.

God has a message of hope for everyone who falls into this category, "But those who hope in the LORD will renew their strength" (Is 40:31).

> *For our light and momentary troubles are achieving for us an eternal glory that far outweighs them all.*
> 2 COR 4:17

Accept this encouraging promise with a positive and joyful heart and watch how circumstances undergo a radical change. Be enthusiastic about life – let your life become a song of praise for everything which God bestows on you – particularly his gifts of life and health.

Life does have a dark side. But it is not necessary for us to dwell in darkness. God intended life to be good. Forget the wrongs of the past and remember the positive – that is what God wants to teach us.

God created us to live life to the fullest and with a positive attitude. Let us therefore seize every day with gratitude as coming from your hand.

F ill us, o Lord, with your goodness so that we can rejoice in you. Help us to seize every day that you give us with gratitude.

No one is as old as the person who has lost his enthusiasm
– HENRY DAVID THOREAU.

Victory through faith

We can overcome the world because of our steadfast belief that Jesus Christ is the Son of God who was sent to this world to demonstrate God's love for us. Through him God entered this world in a physical form. He cared enough about us to come in the form of a servant. This is love. This fact assures us of God's love and that he understands and cares. He is not oblivious to our trials, temptations, grief and suffering.

Because we obey his commands in love they are not onerous and when we execute them we have the opportunity to demonstrate our love and to live according to his will. Through this faith and love we have the strength to withstand the blows of misfortune. Many things can be a threat to our faith but Christ, who as a human being also experienced these threats, can and will help us when storm clouds darken our horizon.

> . . . *for everyone born of God overcomes the world. This is the victory that has overcome the world, even our faith.*
> 1 JN 5:4

In the same way as Christ overcame the world, we shall also be able to be victorious through our faith and love for him. After the cross a crown; after defeat a glorious victory!

Loving God, in faith and love I want to follow where you lead, because I know that I have been assured of victory.

Prayer is the most important act in my life. If I should neglect to pray for one day, I would loose much of the fervour of my faith
— MARTIN LUTHER.

6 APRIL

Read LUKE 18:9-14

Followers of Christ

S ome people constantly compare themselves with other Christians and conclude that their faith is better. They are like the Pharisee who compared himself with the tax collector.

When we consider ourselves superior to other children in God's kingdom, we become conceited. Our spiritual power can decline and we become ineffective disciples of the Master. The Christian has only one role-model – Jesus Christ! His is the only standard against which we can gauge ourselves. If you have him as your role-model, you cannot but experience a deepfelt unworthiness, for who can ever hope to lead as perfect a life as he?

> "God, I thank you that I am not like other men – robbers, evildoers, adulterers – or even like this tax collector."
>
> LK 18:11

Having Christ as your role-model could result in a feeling of frustration were it not for his grace, love and encouragement. He calls us to follow him and when we do so he bestows on us the indescribable gift of his presence. When you offer yourself completely to Christ you will become what Christ has envisaged for you all along.

T hank you Lord Jesus, that you are my perfect example and guide through life. Help me to faithfully follow in your footsteps.

How can we be the salt of the earth whilst we pepper others when they fail? – G K CHESTERTON.

God is always there for us

Many Christians often wonder if God knows about them and whether he cares about them. Then, like David, they ask, "How long, O LORD? Will you forget me for ever? How long will you hide your face from me? (Ps 13:1)

However, a dark period in your life can be followed by a revelation from God in which he shows you what he expects of you. When you feel alienated from God and allow the searchlight of the Holy Spirit to probe your life, remain sensitive to his guidance and consider how you can serve him better. "He does not ignore the cry of the afflicted" (Ps 9:12). It's easy to be a disciple in good times when you experience God's presence and you are full of confidence, but things are different when you feel that God has withdrawn from you. In times like these you must walk in faith and not according to what you feel. To continue to grow spiritually you must persevere in prayer, even if you think that God is not listening or does not care. When the world around you becomes dark and lonely always remember: God is always there for you. He knows about you and he does care. If you are steadfast in your faith, you will be richly blessed, even in the darkest moments.

> *You hear, O LORD, the desire of the afflicted; you encourage them, and you listen to their cry...*
>
> PS 10:17

Lord Jesus, once you also cried out that you had been forsaken. But then you committed your spirit into the hands of your Father. Help me to follow your example and cling to God, even in my darkest moments.

For the person who remembers that his help comes from the almighty God, it is impossible to be discouraged
— *JEREMY TAYLOR.*

To remember and to forget

It is not hypocritical to remember only the good qualities of our deceased loved ones. However, we are often extremely forgiving of the dead, but very unforgiving of ourselves. We regret not doing or saying certain things to the deceased. This feeling of guilt intensifies our grief.

> *This is love: not that we loved God, but that He loved us and sent His Son as an atoning sacrifice for our sins.*
>
> 1 JN 4:10

If we find it so easy to forgive the departed, why can we not forgive ourselves? Let us claim God's forgiveness for ourselves. In his grace he sent his Son to wipe out our sins. If we accept this loving gift from God our grief will be tempered and we shall find peace of mind.

It is laudable to cover the weaknesses of others with our love, to overlook their faults and to lovingly remember their virtues. But be just as generous towards yourself as you are towards others.

*H*eavenly Father, teach me about the values which are important to remember. Enfold me with your love in my grief.

It is noble to cover the shortcomings of a friend and to pardon his failures; to draw a curtain over his shame and to display his good points; quietly to bury his weaknesses but to shout his virtues from the rooftops – ROBERT SOUTH.

He invites you to rest

I nvitations can be so exciting – especially when issued by someone we respect and love.

Have you heard about this invitation? The Lord invites everyone! The only qualification is that you must bring your troubles and burdens to him.

When something upsets or worries us, we becomes burdened and stressed. However, 1 Peter 5:7 tells us, "Cast all your anxiety on him because he cares for you."

When we experience deep sorrow we become exhausted and burdened. We feel lonely and despondent. It is then that the Lord says to us, "As a mother comforts her child, so will I comfort you" (Is 66:13).

> Come to me all you who are weary and burdened, and I will give you rest.
>
> MT 11:28

Do you feel forgotten, forsaken and pushed aside by those with whom you have shared so much in life? "The Lord himself goes before you and will be with you; He will never leave you or forsake you" (Deut 31:8).

If you believe God's promises you will truly find rest for your troubled soul, because, "We know that in all things God works for the good of those who love him" (Rom 8:28).

G od of love, I hold you to your word and now come to you with all my troubles and burdens. Thank you for your assurance that I shall find rest with you.

I find the name of Jesus Christ written at the top of every page of modern history – GEORGE BANCROFT.

10 APRIL

Read REVELATIONS 1:4-8

The enchantment of the Lord's peace

T he humble acknowledgement that all true peace comes from God is the highest level of human wisdom. We must become enchanted by God's peace before we can truly find peace. This has been the case since the beginning of time and will be so until the end of time.

> *Grace and peace to you from him who is,*
> *and who was and who is to come,*
> *and from the seven spirits before his throne,*
> *and from Jesus Christ, who is the faithful witness,*
> *the firstborn from the dead, and the ruler of the kings of the earth.*
>
> REV 1:4-5

Every generation has produced poets, philosophers, prophets and teachers who have joined their voices to the innumerable masses who together with St Augustine acknowledged that, "In all the wide world there is no peace until we have found your peace."

Happy is the person who has found his peace within God's sanctuary; within the sphere of his boundless love. The knowledge that we are his children and that his peace supports us, is more precious than possessing the most fabulous jewels. Those people who have made their home with God tread lightly on the road of life with an inner calm and peace. We constantly marvel at this boundless grace and can only gratefully whisper, "Lord, your peace has enchanted me!"

T hank you, Lord, that I can succumb to the enchantment of your peace and that I can take safe refuge in your sanctuary.

Our peace lies in doing your will! – DANTE.

Read 1 CORINTHIANS 10:1-17

Through his power we can withstand temptation

How uncomplicated and carefree life would be if Christians could be free of all temptation. We, however, all need grace in order to expose the malignancy of temptations which hide behind the mask of friendliness and not to underestimate and trifle with the power of temptation.

Satan calls up all types of wonderful images for us. We start living in a dream world where we constantly assure ourselves that we are in full control of our deeds and emotions. In a moment of weakness the fantasy of the temptation becomes a cruel reality. We are trapped in a prison of our own making.

What a wonderful assurance to know that God will not allow us to be tempted beyond our endurance.

> *And God is faithful,*
> *He will not let*
> *you be tempted beyond*
> *what you can bear.*
> *But when you are tempted*
> *He will also provide*
> *a way out so that you can*
> *stand up under it.*
> 1 COR 10:13

All we need to do is to remain dedicated to God and reject the temptation before it becomes a powerful passion in our lives. We must ask him for the wisdom to recognise these temptations and to overcome them with his grace and power, before they get hold of us. He will sustain us.

Invincible Saviour, give me the strength, in your power, to withstand and overcome temptation when I am tested.

How is it possible for man to walk without stumbling over his own ruins? – MUSSET.

Put God first

Every day so many important tasks demand our attention and energies: our studies, our careers, the education of our children, care of the aged. In spite of all these important tasks we must place God first in our lives.

God is the Alpha and the Omega, the First and the Last, the Beginning and the End. That is why his position in our lives is the thing that matters the most. He claims the highest priority in our lives, not only because he has the right to do so, but especially because it improves the quality of our lives. If he is first in your life he can also influence other aspects in your life which are under his control, to his glory and to your immeasurable benefit.

> And this is my prayer: that your love
> may abound more and more in knowledge
> and depth of insight, so that you may be able
> to discern what is best . . .
>
> PHIL 1:9-10

Honour God with your time, your talents, your possessions, your plans. Allow his spirit to control all areas of your life. You will be amazed when you discover that when God is first in your life all other things fall into perspective. That is what we call being at peace with yourself.

Heavenly Father, help me always to put you first in my life through the power of Jesus Christ, who lived and died to glorify you.

A self-sufficient person always looks down upon objects and people; and, naturally as long as you look down you cannot see what comes from Above – C S LEWIS.

Living love

There is no substitute for love. It is the most powerful and noble emotion. There is no way that we can banish it from our lives and think that we can be fulfilled.

Owing to its unique quality we cannot describe love in terms which are easily understood. We are inclined to confuse love with sentimentality and then this dynamic force becomes ineffectual and weak. Love in action is far more than the mere execution of good deeds, although these deeds may be an expression of love. True love is lasting, even through the greatest trials. It is deep and unselfish and epitomises the qualities of loyalty, faithfulness and high principles. These values enrich the spirit and the thoughts of those who love.

> *Dear children, let us not love with words or tongue but with actions and in truth.*
>
> 1 JN 3:18

Love can never be bought; that is why it is so precious. True love is shown in your actions. If you want this type of love in your life you must find the Source of true love: God. Your love can feed from this Source and then it will produce abundant fruit in your life and the lives of others.

God of Love, thank you that through the example of Jesus Christ I can experience true love. Guide me through your Holy Spirit so that my love can live and flourish.

Only love is eternal. Only love has the quality of eternity in man's brief stay on earth – *POPE JOHN PAUL II.*

14 APRIL

Read PSALM 94:1-9

We worship a God who hears

How comforting it is to know that we worship a God who hears, listens and cares! Our prayers are never untimely, God is always available and longingly waits for us to spend time with him. In his eyes no one is too insignificant or unimportant. Everyone has access to the throne of grace because through his sacrifice on the cross Jesus Christ opened up the way into the holy sanctuary for us.

Age is also not important with God. He does not believe in, "children should be seen and not heard". On the contrary, he invites the children to come to him.

> *Does he who implanted the ear not hear?*
>
> PS 94:9

People grow old and lonely and long for someone to talk to. Not one of them is forgotten by God. They can talk to him at any time. The fears of a child, the stormy years of youth, the weary years of middle age, the loneliness of old age – all these phases of life are known to God and all of us can go to God in prayer with the assurance that he will listen.

For this reason prayer should not simply be a desperate cry in a crisis, but must form part of our relationship with God. Most marvellous of all is that God listens to each person as though he or she is the only person on earth.

Lord, I confess that I sometimes doubt whether my prayers reach you. Thank you for the assurance that you hear and answer my prayers.

Prayer is the unconditional requirement for everything God wants to achieve in this world – ANDREW MURRAY.

Read 1 CORINTHIANS 2:6-10

Death is a natural progression

We fear death because we think that death is life's enemy. We love life so much that we cling to it, but we forget that death enables us to become immortal.

If life on earth were the only life available to us, then the death of a loved one would be the pitiful end of it all. However, everything that Christ has told us bears witness that the opposite is true. Death is merely a bend in the road and once we have rounded the corner, a better and wonderful life awaits us.

> *No eye has seen,
> no ear has heard,
> no mind has conceived
> what God has prepared
> for those who
> love him.*
> 1 COR 2:9

It is God's perfect will that we can only attain the blessings which he wants to bestow on us in eternity, through death and the grave. Because this is God's will we accept it with a childlike faith.

Death is not merely God's planned end for our earthly life; but the beginning of a glorious eternal life which awaits us and our loved ones.

Spirit of God, help us to understand that death is merely one incident on the path of life. Bear us up out of the shadows of this world and give us the strength to put all our trust in you.

Every person who has heaven in his heart will have an eternal share of heaven – HENRY WARD BEECHER.

16 APRIL

Read JOHN 10:1-10

Life in abundance

Many people have lost the ability to lead a full and rich life and consequently lead a humdrum existence. The future no longer holds any exciting surprises for them and their hope and enjoyment of striving towards an ideal have faded.

If your life is like this, remember that we were created by God to live a full and rich life, to radiate love and to make the world a better place because God allows us to live in it.

> *I have come that they may have life and have it to the full.*
>
> JN 10:10

When we have a relationship with God and because we love him, our life can never degenerate into a humdrum existence. The fact that we live in Jesus Christ frees us from the danger of leading a useless existence. By working for God in his world, witnessing, loving others and praying for them, our own inner tensions and frustrations will disappear and every day will be a new adventure.

It is Christ who makes this fundamental difference in your life. He makes everything new and the strength of those who wait upon him is restored. May he keep you from a colourless existence and grant you a full and rich life through the grace of Jesus Christ, our Lord.

Lord, grant me your wisdom so that I may glorify you through living a full and meaningful life.

A quality life is one which is lived for others — ADRIO KÖNIG.

A living faith

Your faith can die if it is not fed with the nutriment of grace which God makes available to you. A living faith needs the essential nourishment of prayer, Bible study, worship and praise. Without it your faith can be pushed aside by other matters and become totally powerless.

Someone whose faith has died normally becomes embittered. However, God is still there for that person. He never changes, whatever our condition, he is still the source of all life. Because God is the very centre of all true faith we should put our spiritual barrenness in his loving hands. Through Jesus Christ he gives himself to us as the way, the truth and the life.

> . . . and to put on the new self, created to be like God in true righteousness and holiness.
>
> EPH 4:24

Don't allow anything to take God's place in your life. Whilst your life is still filled with the things of the world, God cannot fill you with his Spirit. In order for you to have a living and powerful life filled with faith, he must be at the centre of your life and his mighty power must encompass every area of your life. When this happens, love will take the place of hate, strength will supplant weakness and you will again experience a sparkling, living faith.

God of grace, strengthen me through your Spirit so that my faith can withstand all attacks.

Faith is the beginning and Love the end, and in God both are united – IGNATIUS.

Read ROMANS 8:1-16

Who is in control?

A re you a well-balanced person, in control of yourself or are you a slave of your circumstances or moods? Do you sometimes say and do things which are contrary to your true nature? This is a common phenomenon with people. That is why we need a power greater and stronger than ourselves to control us when we are unable to do so ourselves.

> *You, however, are controlled not by the sinful nature but by the Spirit, if the Spirit of God lives in you.*
>
> ROM 8:9

We are often enslaved by bad habits. Consequently our whole being and spirit are in bonds. Even though we long to be free it is impossible to experience the freedom which we instinctively know is our right. Do you feel like this? Listen to the wonderful truth of the Christian teaching, ". . . where the Spirit of the Lord is, there is freedom" (2 Cor 3:17).

If you allow the Spirit of Christ to take up residence in your life and to lead you in truth, your life will gain a new meaning and you will be filled with power which enables you to bear fruit worthy of your conversion. This means the subjection of self, but also the triumphant victory through the Spirit of Jesus Christ. Then he is in full control of your life.

S pirit of God, saturate my life so that I can be focussed and directed to live and work to God's glory.

One is tempted to expect things from God without longing for God himself – as if the gift is preferable to the Giver
— ST AUGUSTINE.

In the school of suffering

O ne of the greatest mysteries of our human existence is that of suffering. For centuries mankind has been searching for an answer to this problem. Some have even tried to explain away the existence of suffering, but it remains a most painful and confusing reality. However, suffering must be borne in quiet acquiescence because God wants to tell us something through that experience.

The Son of God suffered mentally, physically and emotionally in the Garden of Gethsemane and on the cross at Calvary. Our suffering is but a poor imitation of the pain which he had to suffer. He accepted his suffering and did not try to escape it. He suffered

> *Although he was the Son he learned obedience from what he suffered . . .*
> HEB 5:8

because he was truly human in every sense and identified with suffering humanity. Through his suffering he brought redemption to the world because he was obedient to God unto death.

To be a pupil in the school of suffering, is to participate in God's plan for your life. To pass the test you must follow the road of obedience.

T hank you Lord, that you took our weaknesses and sorrow upon yourself. If I have to suffer, may it bring me closer to you.

Our suffering is not worthy of the name. When I consider my cross, my afflictions and temptations, I am ashamed because I tried to compare them with the suffering of our blessed Lord
— MARTIN LUTHER.

20 APRIL

Read 2 CHRONICLES 4:1-22

You are the Potter, I am the clay

The church father John Chrysostom relates that if you have a statue which rust and age has spoilt, you can break it into pieces and place it in a furnace. After it has been melted down and cast, you have the original statue back again. The furnace did not destroy it, but renewed it. In the same way our physical death does not destroy life, but renews it in Christ.

God used a clay mould to create man. From this mould emerged a beautiful living creature. But man was marred by sin. To repair this damage God used the redemption at Calvary and brought about our renewal through his Holy Spirit. This was God's way of refining us to become committed people who to an ever increasing extent display the image of Jesus Christ.

> *All the objects that Huram-Abi made for King Solomon for the temple of the LORD were of polished bronze. The king had them cast in clay moulds . . .*
> 2 CHRON 4:16-17

Life is therefore a process by which something beautiful can be created in a simple clay mould. Death destroys the imperfect clay mould and exposes the wonder of a new life. The final product is fit to take its place before the throne of God.

*H*eavenly Potter, take my insignificant life and cast me into an object worthy of a place in your kingdom.

Obedience to God is the most reliable proof of a pure and genuine love for him – NATHANAEL EMMONS.

Read JOSHUA 1:1-9

The Lord your God is with you

At times we all look into the unknown future, either with joyous expectation or in abject fear. The uncertainty of the future fills us with trepidation. Often we not only fear for ourselves, but also for those whom we love: possibly a loved one sick at home or in hospital; a child far away from home; a grieving friend.

In these circumstances God's words to Joshua stand steadfast and firm. As a child of the almighty Creator you need not fear anything. There is nothing in the present, past or future which is beyond his control. With this knowledge you will be able to take courage even though the fear may not have disappeared – because courage does not mean that fear is absent, but that you have triumphed over it.

> *Be strong and courageous. Do not be terrified; do not be discouraged, for the Lord your God will be with you wherever you go.*
> JOSH 1:9

The only thing that God asks from you is that you put your complete trust in his guidance. You will be able to deal with any situation if you know that God is with you. Sometimes you will doubt the direction in which he leads you, but if you always trust in him he will lead you into the eternal light.

*H*eavenly Father, thank you that I can pray: Take my hand every day and lead me, for I am weak and helpless.
I cannot take one step further on my own, but in faith
I can walk by your side wherever you lead me.

Without God's presence we would live in eternal fear
— LEO TOLSTOI.

Peace through faith

G od's peace is beyond man's understanding (Phil 4:7) and quite different to that of the world (Jn 14:27). Paul tells us that Christ is our peace (Eph 2:11-22). He creates and proclaims peace. He, alone, has removed the enmity between us and God by his death of atonement on the cross.

> *You will keep in perfect peace*
> *him whose mind is steadfast*
> *because he trusts in you.*
>
> IS 26:3

The richness of God's peace is overwhelming (Eph 1:15-19). It encompasses far more than we are able to imagine. However, to make this peace our own, we must trust God, we must rely on him only for our strength. We must control our thoughts and lift them up to God (Phil 2:5; 4:8). That means that we must consider God's almighty and wonderful deeds. No disappointment, grief or trial must prevent us from trusting in him.

Proverbs exhort us to, "Trust in the Lord with all your heart, and lean not on your own understanding" (3:5). Because you have sought your peace outside yourself, in Jesus Christ, God's peace will not evade you.

*F*ather, we know that our strength lies in quietness and trust. Help us not to rely on our own understanding of things.

Why must we learn to trust God anew every day? Did he not prove his faithfulness yesterday? And the day before? And the day before that? – C S LEWIS.

Christ is with you all the time

To lead a meaningful life you must constantly guard against your faith deteriorating into a lifeless and powerless tradition. This can easily happen if you do not have a continuous relationship with Christ.

Christ reveals himself in your life because you believe in him and have invited him to take control of your life. Many people find it very difficult to give themselves completely to Someone whom they cannot see or hear. However, if you accept the Word of God that says that you can always know the Lord through the power of his resurrection, there will always be new horisons of spiritual experiences for you.

> *And surely I am with you always,*
> *to the very end of the age.*
> MT 28:20

Christ is with you every moment of each day. This you can believe with conviction. Become aware of God's loving company and dwell in it. Then you will receive the strength to meet the challenges of each day. Whether in prosperity or adversity, in joy or sorrow, his liberating presence will guide you to a life filled with inward peace and strength.

Thank you, Lord, for your presence which fills me with confidence and joy. Grant that the world will never rob me of this glorious privilege.

The future is not determined by fate or by a specific horoscope.
Christ is the pilot of my life – J CILLIERS.

24 APRIL

Read 2 CORINTHIANS 4:7-18

God is with us even in old age

G od's wonderful orchestration which we know as "life" consists of many facets; the cute baby stage, the effervescent expectations of youth, the confidence of maturity, the tranquility, wisdom and peace of old age.

One can easily fold under the burden of memories of the past, particularly when we think about our sins. The sin of worldliness, when you sought pleasure at all costs; of lust, when you were caught in the coils of passion; of unfaithfulness, when, like Peter, you denied knowing the Lord.

> *Therefore we do not lose heart. Though outwardly we are wasting away, yet inwardly we are being renewed day by day.*
> 2 COR 4:16

When we get older, however, God releases us from the bonds which bind us so firmly to the world. Then the world becomes less important and God more important. Your obedience and faithfulness to him increase and together with Peter you can say, "Lord, you know everything. You know that I love you." You see things so much more clearly because you can share in the sentiments expressed in 2 Corinthians 5:1, "Now we know that if the earthly tent we live in is destroyed, we have a building from God, an eternal house in heaven, not built by human hands."

T hank you Lord, that you are also with me when I grow old. I accept my old age as a gift from you and praise you for every new day.

My head is crowned with the snow of winter, but spring is in my heart – VICTOR HUGO.

Caught between hope and despair

Paul, the foremost example of a faithful servant of God, knew what it was like to sink into the depths of despair. Nevertheless he rose to great heights where he could praise God for his victory and liberation.

At some time or other you will also experience these two extremes. You will have to decide for yourself in which of these areas of emotion you want to exist. God wants only the best for you. He wants you constantly to experience the joy and power which is the result of his presence in your life. By abiding

> *No, in all these things we are more than conquerors through him who loved us.*
>
> ROM 8:37

in him, submitting yourself to him completely and living in strict obedience to his will, you will be able to rejoice, whether you are on an emotional high or stranded in the valleys of depression.

See yourself as a victorious child of God. Look past your failures and discover the wonderful life which can be yours through the power of Christ. Become aware of your human dignity. This will add a new quality and excitement to your existence. Then you will start to glorify God through your life and you will become a channel for God's love and power. And then you will know beyond any doubt that in his Name, you can be victorious.

Lord, my God, thank you that through Jesus Christ I may be your child! I put myself at your disposal so that your Spirit can make a new creation out of me.

Do not lose courage during the great sorrows of life . . . If you toiled during the day, you will be able to sleep peacefully. God is awake! – VICTOR HUGO.

26 APRIL

Read PSALM 62:1-13

How much time can you spare God?

A re you longing for a deeper, more meaningful prayer life. Perhaps you have already pleaded with God to do something about it. The fact is that God has already done everything necessary – He loved you before you even knew him. Christ died to prove God's love for you and promised to be with you always, through his Holy Spirit. How much time are you prepared to devote to him?

> *Trust in him at all times, O people; pour out your hearts to him, for God is our refuge.*
>
> PS 62:8

If your prayer life lacks power, the problem lies with you. After all, you determine how much time you devote to praying. The responsibility of developing a meaningful prayer life rests on your shoulders.

Time spent with God forms the basis of your spiritual existence and growth. Remember that it is possible to experience God at any time and in any place by simply focusing your thoughts on him and making your mind receptive to his Holy Spirit.

G od of grace, you who hear your children's supplications, help me to consciously make time to spend with you in prayer, so that I can experience true spiritual growth.

The most important cause of spiritual barrenness is a tardiness to pray. If I can get my heart in a state of boldness in prayer, everything else becomes relatively easy

— RICHARD NEWTON.

Read JOB 2:1-10

Accepting death

For many years Job enjoyed the love of his children. Yet there was no rebellion against God when they were taken away from him. He did not reproach God.

It is difficult to be as patient as Job was. However, to rebel against our "unfortunate fate" as we often incorrectly term it, is to rebel against God. To rebel against it, or to try to escape our sorrows, results in our having to bear the burden of our grief alone and without help. This rebellion opens up a deep chasm between us and God, because he cannot penetrate a rebellious heart.

The only way in which a Christian can come to terms with his or her grief is to follow the example of the

> *Shall we accept good from God and not trouble?*
> JOB 2:10

Master: to accept life calmly and courageously, knowing that the meaning of life is not found on this side of the grave but on the other side, because Christ triumphed over death.

Most wonderful of all is that each one of us can find this courage if we keep the path open to him who wants to give us that strength.

Lord, be with me and let me experience your grace. Help me to deal with life and death calmly and courageously.

The deeper sorrow cuts into your soul, the more joy you can contain — KAHLIL GIBRAN.

28 APRIL

Read PHILIPPIANS 3:7-14

Leave the past behind

N ever allow the past to dominate your life. If you exhaust yourself trying to bear the heavy burden of self-reproach over things which happened in the past, you will never develop the ability to place it in God's hands. If you are not constantly on your guard, past experiences or failures can cast a shadow over your life and have a paralysing effect on your peace of mind and spiritual growth.

One of the direct results of faith in God is a positive attitude towards life – a life free of self-reproach and feelings of guilt about the past. Then the quality of your life is determined by your faith in Christ and not by the past.

> But one thing I do: Forgetting what is behind and straining toward what is ahead . . .
> PHIL 3:13

The living Christ wants to take control of your thoughts and your spirit and he wants to change your whole attitude towards life. Allow him to do this and you will have confidence that everything will go well. Your fear will be replaced by a living, liberating faith. Damaging habits or thoughts will be replaced by a disciplined way of life. This is how the miraculous power of our Saviour renews everything in our life.

G od of my life, help me to meet the future with confidence knowing that you renew everything in my life.

The fleeting moment has passed; the future may never dawn.
You are only master of the present – JEAN JACQUES ROUSSEAU.

Faith and character

E ven in live's worst trials, a child of God can reveal a radiant faith. Stephen is a speaking example of this faith.

The early church of Christ was growing, but so was the opposition. As Stephen was above reproach in his teaching and lifestyle, false witnesses had to be produced to testify against him and he was summoned before the Jewish court. But Stephen had the inner assurance that he belonged to God. No persecution or suffering could rob him of this conviction. It was the determining force in his life. He firmly believed that whatever happened to him was part of God's perfect plan for his life. Stephen did not know any fear because he knew that he lived and worked within God's will. The by-products of his faith were peace, joy, wisdom and power.

> But Stephen, full of the Holy Spirit, looked up
> to heaven and saw the glory of God and
> Jesus standing at the right hand of God.
>
> ACTS 7:55

Everyone who loves and serves the Lord can share in Stephen's experience. Irrespective of your circumstances, first seek the will of the Lord for your life. Even if you encounter great opposition, through your faith you will always be conscious of God's presence and grace.

L ord, thank you that I can tackle life in the conviction that I am in your loving care. I want to abide in you, because that is where I find my strength.

Even though you know the whole Bible by heart and have the words of the prophets at your fingertips, of what use would that be without God's love and grace? — THOMAS À KEMPIS.

Be careful not to judge others

Hannah was not drunk, on the contrary, she was praying. Eli was too hasty in his judgement and thought the worst of her. We often fall into the same trap. However, Eli immediately gave Hannah the benefit of the doubt – and we must do likewise. Jesus told us not to judge others so that we do not bring judgement upon ourselves. We must not dwell on the weaknesses of others but attend to our own shortcomings (Mt 7:1, 3).

> Eli thought she was drunk and said to her, "How long will you keep on getting drunk? Get rid of your wine."
>
> 1 SAM 1:14

Sometimes we condemn someone for being proud, whilst he of she is simply shy or find it difficult to communicate. When we suspect people of pride we avoid them and make things worse, because in turn they then think that we are proud.

Think before you judge someone. There could be underlying reasons for someone's apparent irrationality, anger or stubbornness. Perhaps they are battling through a traumatic experience. Perhaps they are suffering from a terminal illness which only they and God know about. These circumstances take their toll on human behaviour. Therefore, be careful not to judge others. Like Eli, rather give them the benefit of the doubt and treat them in a Christ-like manner.

Father, you forgive me and have so much insight into my weaknesses. Help me to be slow to judge, but quick to forgive.

The one act which the Lord asked us to leave in his hands is that which we are most eager to take out of his hands – that of passing judgement – C J LANGENHOVEN.

MAY

PRAYER

❖ ❖ ❖ ❖ ❖ ❖ ❖ ❖ ❖ ❖ ❖ ❖ ❖ ❖ ❖ ❖ ❖ ❖ ❖ ❖

*E*ternal God and Father through our Lord Jesus Christ
During this month we remember the
Holy Spirit coming at Pentecost.
As always you have kept your promises:
You sent us the Spirit, our Counsellor
    to support us in our deepest sorrow;
    to guide us when we are at a loss as to
    which road to follow;
    to show us what your will is for our lives;
    to reveal it to us and teach us how to love you
    and serve others in love.
Lord, send the flame of your Spirit to purify me
    from all selfish motives, all envy,
    all unforgivingness, hate and all pride.
Send your Spirit to bring me renewed strength and growth.
Send your Spirit as the dove of God's peace to be with me.
Send your Spirit to cleanse me from sin,
    to make me whiter than snow
    and to help me grow spiritually and bear fruit
    worthy of you, my Redeemer.
Send your Spirit to restore and nourish me
    with power from heaven.
Recreate me, Holy Spirit, bring life anew,
    let your kingdom come with power.
This we pray in the name of the Father,
and the Son and the Holy Ghost.

A men

Read ACTS 2:1-13

Filled with the Holy Spirit

On the day of Pentecost God's time was fulfilled. The house was filled with all those who were together and they were filled with the Holy Spirit in a glorious way.

Each year we celebrate Pentecost. In accordance with God's will, the desire is awakened in the hearts of God's children to be abundantly blessed by the Spirit. God wants each of us to be filled with the Holy Spirit. Moreover, we may expect it with boldness and in great faith.

> Suddenly a sound . . . came from heaven and filled the whole house . . . All of them were filled with the Holy Spirit.
>
> ACTS 2:2-4

Many people got to know God through Christ, but chose not to walk with him. Many walked with him for a short way only, but turned away after a while. Many lack the fire of a living faith . . . the fire of the Holy Spirit.

In the book of Acts we note that prayer was always necessary before a person could be filled by the Spirit and experience his mighty power. When we pray we must fervently desire the blessing we are praying for and we must be prepared for a full surrender before God can give us what he is waiting to give us – to be filled with the Spirit of Pentecost.

Spirit of truth, fill us; unite us in our zeal for your kingdom. Touch us with your fire and prepare us to be true messengers, rejoicing and proclaiming your Name wherever we go.

Each time we confess "I believe in the Holy Spirit" we confess that we believe in a living God who is willing to make man's heart his home and change his personality – J B PHILLIPS.

Our Counsellor

T he disciples realised that they would lose Jesus and they were sad about it. That is why Jesus comforted them by giving them the promise that he would be leaving them for their own good, because when he left, he would send the Holy Spirit, the Counsellor, to them.

To be present in a physical form held limitations for Christ. However, nothing can restrict the Holy Spirit. Wherever we are, he will be with us. Throughout the world the Spirit works in people's hearts.

> *It is for your good that I am going away. Unless I go away, the Counsellor will not come to you.*
>
> JN 16:7

Through the Holy Spirit we can maintain an unbroken relationship with our Redeemer. Through the Holy Spirit the Word of God will speak to peoples' hearts and bring them to repentance (Acts 2:37). The Holy Spirit makes us aware of the saving grace of our Redeemer and convicts us of the wonder and truth that Christ is the Son of God.

The Holy Spirit also brings the conviction that a just God will judge us, but also that through his death on the cross we are no longer under the law but can share in his grace. Through the Spirit we get to know Christ as Immanuel – God with us!

F ather, thank you that your Spirit brings the conviction that we shall live *with* you. Grant that we may also live *for* you – Immanuel, God with us.

God is always with us; why shall we not be with God always?
– S KIERKEGAARD.

The Paraclete

"Paraclete" means "someone who is called upon to witness in our favour". How comforting to know that the Holy Spirit will always be our advocate and plead for us whenever Satan, our conscience or our fellow man accuse us before God.

He fills the hearts and minds of the despondent with courage and inspires them to face life's struggles with enthusiasm. When we descend into the valleys of despondency, we are in great need of these heartening and encouraging words.

The paraclete can be called upon in times of distress and grief, when we doubt the Word of God or are confused. Whenever you feel overcome by the mystery of suffering, remember that there is a Counsellor who pleads for you before the Throne of mercy. We can find renewed strength and courage in this knowledge and can live a victorious life.

> *Unless I go away, the Counsellor will not come to you.*
>
> JN 16:7

In times of danger the paraclete will intervene for us. He will be the railing that protects us from falling into the abyss. He keeps us from stumbling, and this encourages us to proceed fearlessly, even when the light grows dim. He always intercedes when we fall short and enables us to face life's problems.

Spirit of God, you are the Paraclete who guides us. You are the source of Life, a gift from God who stays with us and kindles in our hearts the fire of your glowing love.

The Holy Spirit is the living presence of God in our existence
— ROMANO GUARDINI.

Receive the Holy Spirit

How do we receive the Holy Spirit? God cannot fill us if we don't belong to him. Therefore dedicate your life to him. Commit yourself to his service. This is a simple action – and yet it is difficult because you must surrender yourself to him with a genuine heart and you must fervently desire to be filled with the Spirit. Do this if you desire to receive the Spirit.

Ask God to grant you his Spirit. He wants us to ask him, although he is of course capable of giving it without us asking. Why are we so unwilling to make use of this wonderful privilege? Man has become so independent that he feels ashamed to ask. Still, we should not hesitate, because an unwillingness to ask often leads to spiritual poverty.

> *Did you receive the Holy Spirit when you believed?*
> ACTS 19:2

God gives his Spirit to those who obey him. Are you prepared to do what God asks of you? All he asks of you is that you should live according to his Word.

We must have faith. We receive the Holy Spirit through faith, in the same way in which we are redeemed – through faith in Jesus Christ. The Spirit comes to us as a wonderful gift from God. He works in us so that we can be born again; he leads us on the road to holiness so that God finds a dwelling place within our hearts.

Heavenly Father, we dedicate our lives to you. Fill our lives with your Spirit and grant that we may forever be your obedient servants.

We must not be satisfied only to be cleansed from sin; we must be filled with the Holy Spirit *– JOHN FLETCHER.*

Teacher of the Truth

O ne of the tasks of the Holy Spirit is to bring God's truth to people. This revelation is a continuous process. At a given time the Spirit leads us to all those truths which we are able to understand at that stage. He will expose our sins to us, he will lead us to repentance, redemption and sanctification. He guides us in our understanding of the Word of God and teaches us how to be obedient. He teaches us the truth about the indescribable power of prayer.

The Holy Spirit reveals to us the liberating truth about Christ's life on earth, his death and resurrection. When our understanding of these truths fails us, the Holy Spirit will guide us into all truth. He helps us to cope with every situation in

> But when he, the Spirit of truth,
> comes, he will guide you into all truth.
>
> JN 16:13

life: with our sorrow and pain; with our spiritual distress and poverty. He provides in every need. He breaks open the truth of God's loving Father-heart and consequently his soothing comfort flows through our aching hearts.

God reveals this truth to us through his Spirit. Without the workings of the Spirit we shall never have a full understanding of Christ's true value in our lives.

S pirit of God, we praise you. Comfort our hearts, be our Guide in this life and guide us in the Truth.

Heaven is waiting to help those who have discovered and obey God's will for their lives – J ROBERT ASHCROFT.

Read ACTS 1:1-8

Witnesses of Pentecost

hen we encounter and get to know Christ through his Word the Holy Spirit convinces us that Christ is the Son of God. If our hearts and minds turn to God in answer to his call, it is the work of the Holy Spirit. He works within us so that we are able to answer Christ's invitation to be cleansed from our sins. Moreover, the Spirit himself convinces us that we have been saved.

Led by the Spirit we also become witnesses. A witness is a person who can talk from first-hand knowledge. Without this, we cannot be reliable witnesses. Only when we have met Christ personally and have committed ourselves to him, can we be reliable witnesses. The Holy Spirit brings about this relationship. The world will judge our every word and attitude to see how reliable we are as witnesses. However, if we are not truly convicted, the world will not find Christ in our lives. This intimate relationship with Christ is only possible if the Holy Spirit makes it possible for us.

> *But you will receive power when the Holy Spirit comes on you; and you will be my witnesses . . .*
> ACTS 1:8

As Christians we have the firm conviction that Christ lives and saves and this makes us willing to testify and to proclaim it. The Holy Spirit knows how strong Christ's love is, and he wants others to share in this love too.

*D*ear Lord, anoint me with your Spirit, sanctify me and use me in your service. I want to pray to you, testify for you, serve and love you with a fearless heart.

The Lord anoints us with his Spirit and sanctifies us for his service; He calls us to be kings, priests and prophets – to be true Christians.

A promise of comfort

Are you acquainted with the Counsellor, the Comforter? Not merely through an intellectual knowledge of him; but because you have experienced that Christ sent this Spirit into your life as a living presence?

Jesus Christ knows how badly we need consolation, particularly in our hour of separation and grief. That is why he gives us this wonderful promise of a Counsellor. He comforts the broken heart, he strengthens the desolate soul; he leads us to victory in every situation in life; he strengthens us in the hour of temptation.

> *I will ask the Father, and he will give*
> *you another Counsellor to be with*
> *you for ever – the Spirit of truth.*
>
> JN 14:16

Each one of us suffers pain which gnaws away at us : We are left with the remains of our ideals. We try fighting against a weakness which we seem unable to conquer. We live with remorse. We fear the future because our health has suffered. In such circumstances the Lord's promise comes to us like a shining star in a pitch-black sky: There is comfort ! I am sending a Comforter!

Surrender yourself into his gentle and comforting hands: He will never break a bruised reed; he will restore a wounded spirit: a new day will dawn and the shadows will disappear.

Holy Spirit, you are the comforter who leads us; you are the gift of God who lives in us. You are the source of life who fills us with your love.

God does not comfort us to make us comfortable, but to use us to comfort others – *JOHN HENRY JOWETT.*

8 MAY

Read ROMANS 5:1-5

The Holy Spirit – the one who kindles love in our hearts

The Holy Spirit assures you that you have been united with the Source of true love – God. However, this love must be firmly rooted in faith.

If you claim that you love Jesus Christ but refuse to lighten the burden of the less priviledged, you will be denying that love. If you truly love him through the Holy Spirit, you will become aware of the needs of others and feel compelled to do something about it.

If you claim the love of God in your heart, the Holy Spirit will give you the power to make this love visible through your words, your attitude and your willingness to serve others. Through the working of the Spirit God's love is expressed and becomes a reality in your life. You will be willing to accept the full responsibility of your faith. Moreover, through the Holy Spirit, this love will enable you to seek only the best for others.

> *Because God has poured out his love into our hearts by the Holy Spirit, whom he has given us . . .*
> ROM 5:5

Spirit of God, enlighten our minds and kindle a fervent love in our hearts. We are so weak. Please strengthen us with your power.

Whoever sees someone in need and waits to be asked to help, is so lacking in love that he might as well have refused to help
— DANTE ALIGHIERI.

The Spirit glorifies Christ

T he disciples' deepest desire was to have Christ with them permanently. Because Jesus was aware of this desire he promised them the Holy Spirit who would come to comfort them and reveal Christ to them.

It was a wonderful gift. And what makes it even more wonderful, is that this merciful gift is still available to every disciple of Jesus Christ. All the gifts which the Spirit receives from Christ, will be made known to and shared with us: love, joy and peace. In fact, through his grace the Lord will share every possible blessing with us.

The Holy Spirit will endow every believer with the enriching presence of Christ each day. With his dynamic power the Spirit will help us to remain in close communion with Jesus, get to know him better, to love

> *He will bring glory to me by taking from what is mine and make it known to you.*
> JN 16:14

him more and to serve him daily. Gradually the fruit of the Spirit will grow in us and be revealed in our lives. Christ Jesus will be glorified in our lives through the work of the Holy Spirit. All our deeds and prayers should be to this end.

S pirit of God, I pray that people will start worshipping you, convicted by your persuasive power. Grant that Christ may be glorified in us. Assure us of God's love and let us be ever watchful in prayer and in service.

The future of the human race depends on whether we can bring the individual more completely under the rule of Christ and the Holy Spirit — ISAAC THECKER.

10 MAY

Read ROMANS 8:12-16

I am God's child

T he essential truths of the gospel are that we have a *Father* in heaven and are *children* of God; we have been *redeemed* and we have the *assurance of faith*; we are *heirs*.

God so loved man that he sent Christ to the world to reconcile us with him and to remake us into what God meant us to be. You are so precious to God that he invites you to call him "Father". You may therefore never run yourself down or consider yourself worthless. The Spirit will always lead you to rejoice gratefully about the wonderful truth that Christ has saved you from sin and has made you his child. He calls you to put your sinful past behind you and to accept that you are his child.

> *Those who are led by the Spirit are sons of God.*
> ROM 8:14

If you call yourself a child of God, but keep on dredging up sins which have been forgiven, you will be denying God's love and his grace. Through his Holy Spirit God leads you to accept his forgiveness through Christ's sacrifice of atonement, and helps you to live a triumphant life.

You are God's child and heir! How indescribable is the miracle of God's grace!

*D*ear Father, we are your children. Your Holy Spirit testifies that we are your heirs. We thank you for the indescribable grace which allows us to call you "Father".

Be content to be his child and allow the Father daily to give you light, power, toil, problems, fears, joy, peace and trials to the extent that he deems fit – I PENINGTON.

Leading you to a life of holiness

"H oly" means to be set aside. To be able to live a holy life, you must live in an intimate union with Christ. Many people avoid this relationship – to their spiritual detriment. Others reject it because they find it too demanding.

It is possible to live a holy life if you have dedicated yourself to God. A truly holy person is fully obedient to the Lord. A holy life demands of you to be constantly aware of your attitude, your deeds and motives. As a disciple of the Lord there is no excuse for continuing to be ruled by a particular sinful practice. You cannot hold onto the world with one hand and hold out the other wavering hand to the Lord, thinking that you will be able to live a holy life in that way.

> *Be holy, because I am holy.*
> 1 PET 1:16

All the guidelines for a holy way of life can be found in God's Word and in Christ, our perfect model. Furthermore, God gave us his Spirit to lead us on our road to holiness. The more attuned we are to his quiet voice, the more holy we shall become. He will help us to travel along this difficult road joyfully.

S pirit of God, grant that I may grow in holiness and purify my heart with a spark of your holiness. I want to put my trust in my Saviour and be more faithful to him. Grant me joy in labour and more power in prayer.

You must be holy in the sense in which God asks you to be holy. He never asked you to be a Trappist monk or a hermit. His desire for you is to make the world a more holy place in your daily walk – VINCENT PALOTTI.

The Spirit sets us free

"Freedom" is a popular word. Many people interpret it as being free to do whatever appeals to them. All those who restrict them and try to wake them from this illusion are regarded as oppressors.

True freedom comprises far more than a political or social aspiration. It is a profound spiritual experience which expresses itself in a moral obligation, which amounts to doing what you *must* do and not to do what you *want* to do. It implies becoming what God has ordained you to be. You can be truly free only if you joyfully accept and fulfil the responsibilities which God expects a child of his to fulfil.

> *Then you will know the truth, and the truth will set you free.*
>
> JN 8:32

Freedom is an attitude to life. When you allow Christ to become Lord of your life, you experience the joy of being set free from the bondage of sin. Faith replaces fear; love replaces hate; freedom inspired by Christ replaces negative attitudes and thoughts. If your life is controlled by the Spirit, sin has no power over you and you are free to serve him gratefully and joyfully through his Spirit. Christ promises you this freedom which will lead to eternal peace.

Holy Spirit, deliver me from my own will and selfishness so that I may live a pure and holy life. Help me to accept my responsibilities and to experience your freedom and peace.

We must be firmly rooted in self-discipline if we wish to risk stepping out into freedom — HEROLD E KOHN.

Read 2 CORINTHIANS 5:1-10

On losing courage

T he ability to remain courageous cannot be separated from obedience to God. You gain the greatest confidence and the wisest insight when you realise that obedience is synonymous with a joyful acceptance of God's will for your life.

All of us experience moments of depression and despair and it takes
courage to do what God wants us to do. However, it is then that God
allows the Holy Spirit to kindle new hope in our hearts. In obedience
to him you feel drawn towards fulfilling the will of God in every situation in which he leads you. The Holy Spirit will work the power in your
heart and enable you to live a good life in the sight of the Lord.

A surprising bonus of obedience
to the will of God is that your self-
confidence and faith are boosted.
You start living withour fear and develop spiritual courage. The key to
this approach to life is the fruit of
love which the Holy Spirit makes
possible for you. Love drives out all

> *God . . . has given us the
> Spirit as a
> deposit, guaranteeing what
> is to come.
> Therefore we are always
> confident . . .*
> 2 COR 5:5-6

fear. If you live your life inspired by the love of God and you obey him,
you will never lose confidence. May the Spirit of the Lord grant that
you never forget this wonderful lesson.

H oly Spirit, please help us never to let go of you. Show us the
right way. Make us faithful and help us never to lose faith.

Confidence is not the absence of fear, it is conquering it
— *ROBERT LOUIS STEVENSON.*

Inspiration

The Holy Spirit is eternal and omnipresent. That is why our lives are under his control. Wherever we can be enriched and inspired in life, the ministry of the Holy Spirit inspires us with bounteous blessings. Wherever our thoughts and hearts can be uplifted, the Holy Spirit is at work.

In the field of art, the Spirit reveals and inspires the love of beauty.

> . . . *it is the Spirit in a man, the breath of the Almighty, that gives him understanding.*
>
> JOB 32:8

Music reflects the harmony of God's almighty power of creation. Science and technology reveal mysteries and give a foretaste of further mysteries still to be revealed. The science of medicine brings us nearer to the sympathetic heart of the great Healer. All the good things in life are brought into perspective when viewed in the light of God himself and of his Spirit. Whatever your calling in life, God can approve of it and you should be able to benefit from the inspiring ministry of the Holy Spirit.

The Holy Spirit can inspire you to achieve complete fulfilment in life and can inspire you with ideas which will enrich your life. He gives you vitality and calls forth the noblest fruit you are capable of bearing. Allow him to inspire you and follow the road on which he wishes to lead you.

Communion with you, o Holy Spirit, feeds our soul. You clarify our own understanding of the Scriptures. Please help us to walk the road you wish us to follow.

First of all the Holy Spirit shares love. Then he inspires us with hope and sets us free – and, sad to say, in many of our churches that is the last characteristic of the Spirit we ever see
– DWIGHT L MOODY.

Read 1 CORINTHIANS 3:9-17

God's temple

Man must glorify God by allowing God to dwell in him and by glorifying his majesty. Sin interfered with this aim of God; however, God did not abandon the works of his hands.

Through the Holy Spirit God came to live in every heart which had been renewed and purified and he made these hearts his dwelling-place. Therefore we must listen to the following question responsibly and with an introspective heart, "Don't you know that you yourselves are God's temple?" The Holy Spirit came to live in us and made our hearts suitable for God to live in. Thus Christ's promise is fulfilled that he and the Father would come and make their home within us. This is such an amazing gift of his grace that it makes us bow down in awe before God. The Holy Spirit makes us temples of God by cleansing us, provided we obey him and surrender to him completely. There is no doubt as to whether or not he will enter our hearts, because the Word says, "And this is how we know that he lives in us: We know it by the Spirit he gave us" (1 Jn 3:24).

> Don't you know that you yourselves
> are God's temple and that God's Spirit lives in you?
> 1 COR 3:16

Holy Spirit, we pray that you will make our hearts your dwelling-place. Illuminate our hearts and let the darkness disappear from our lives. Fill us, your temple, adorn us with your virtues and grant us your joy.

If it is a characteristic of a sinner to desecrate all that is holy, it should be a characteristic of a Christian to introduce the holiness of God into secular life — THOMAS CHALMERS.

16 MAY

Read 2 PETER 3:14-18

Grow in the knowledge of Christ

A Christian's life must never be characterised by stagnation, because that leads to deterioration. We must constantly strive towards a growing knowledge of God.

Peter called upon the first Christians to "grow" in the grace and knowledge of Christ. We cannot do this through our own strength. That is why Christ sent the Holy Spirit to lead us into all truth, including the truth about Christ. While your growth and your experience of God deepen and you dedicate and surrender yourself to the guidance of the Holy Spirit, his image is revealed in your life to an increasing extent.

> But grow in the grace and knowledge of our Lord and Saviour Jesus Christ.
>
> 2 PET 3:18

The true disciple is constantly aware of his or her shortcomings and sinfulness, but it is exactly this awareness which is a sign of growth in the grace and knowledge of Christ through the powerful work of the Holy Spirit. God conveys this knowledge to his believing children through his Word. Through the work of the Spirit he brings the Word to life for each of us. He leads us to accept what is required for our spiritual growth and development. Each one of us must fervently pray for this growth.

Father, lead us through your Spirit to a better knowledge of your Word and of yourself, as our almighty God. Bless us on the road of spiritual growth so that your image will be seen in us.

True growth only begins when we start confessing our own weaknesses – JEAN VANIER.

Grant me insight through your Spirit

J ohn 14:17 says that the world cannot accept Jesus Christ because they do not know him. "The world" refers to those who live as if there is no God, those who leave the Spirit of God no room in their planning. The result is that they become spiritually dead.

One can only see those things for which one has developed an ability to see. What we see, hear and experience, therefore, depends to a large extent, on our personal contribution to the experience. If a person makes no room for God in his life, he cannot experience the work of the Holy Spirit. Something will be lacking in respect

> *The world cannot accept him, because it neither sees him nor knows him. But you know him, for he lives with you and will be in you.*
>
> JN 14:17

of his knowledge of God, and something will be lacking in his dealings with people. We therefore need to pray for and look forward to receiving the Holy Spirit into our lives. We shall be deprived of his comforting influence in our lives if we are so preoccupied with worldly things that we grant him no space in our lives.

The Holy Spirit waits patiently to enter into our lives. Make time to wait quietly for his coming into your life. Only then will you receive the Spirit in all its fullness and will you be able to fight the battle of truth in this sinful world.

S pirit of God, teach us always to strive towards holiness. Strengthen us through your grace. Always make us aware of our vanity, sinfulness and weakness.

Spirituality really means: the Holy Spirit at work. It is the surprising activity of the Holy Spirit in the church which renews and activates the members of a congregation – LEON J SUENENS.

18 MAY

Read ACTS 2:1-13

Spirit of grace

The people of Jerusalem did not deserve what they experienced and received on the day of Pentecost! The "fire" which they saw coming from heaven, ought to have been a fire of judgment. Instead they saw the purifying flame of the grace of the Holy Spirit.

The "tongues" in which they spoke, ought to have been cutting condemnations from a just God. Instead they heard about the loving deeds of God. The "violent" wind should have been a destructive hurricane of God's wrath let loose over unloving people who had nailed his Son to a cross. Instead it was the promise of his Spirit proclaiming forgiveness and redemption. The crowd who were together had reason to panic, yet they observed in surprise how God sent his Spirit to all believers.

> When the day of Pentecost came, they were all together in one place . . . All of them were filled with the Holy Spirit . . .
> ACTS 2:1, 4

Thus the coming of the Holy Spirit became a mighty demonstration of the grace and love of God. Death was turned into life; despair was turned into hope; hate into love; judgment into grace. All of this was the result of Christ giving his blood at Calvary. He earned the life-giving Spirit for us all.

Spirit of God, your glowing light allows us to find our Father again. Let our praises resound around the earth in all languages: Halleluja, praise the Lord!

Grace is God himself; his loving energy at work in his church and in the hearts of the redeemed — EVELYN UNDERHILL.

Read JOHN 14:25-31

God-given teacher

No Christian can claim that he or she has the full truth. We must therefore always allow ourselves to be instructed by the Holy Spirit who will lead us in the truth of God. We should yearn for this truth in the same way as we yearn for God himself. Any child of God who would claim that he or she has nothing more to learn, has not even begun to understand the rich blessings God is constantly waiting to bestow upon his children.

The Holy Spirit stands behind us like a sympathetic teacher behind the dependent pupil. He places his hand on the pupil's shoulder and forms the letters with him, until the pupil has acquired the ability to write beautifully. The Holy Spirit teaches us to come to terms with sorrow, to deal with life in such a way that we shall eventually recognise God's work of art in the kaleidoscope of life's colours. He teaches us the truth about ourselves and the grace of God, and the meeting of these two poles. During this journey

> But the Counsellor, the Holy Spirit,
> whom the Father will send in my name,
> will teach you all things and will remind
> you of everything I have said to you.
>
> JN 14:26

of self-discovery we realise how greatly we have sinned, yet at the same time we realise God's endless love for us. The Spirit brings us to the knowledge that our Redeemer lives, that through him we are reconciled with God and he instructs us how to walk on the road to holiness.

Spirit of God, we pray that your love may burn within our hearts. Strengthen us with your power. Allow our spiritual insight to be clear and equip us to serve you in truth.

God the Father is the giver of the holy Word; God the Son is the theme of the Word; God the Holy Spirit is the author of the Word; he makes the Word true and interprets it for us. —J I PACKER.

20 MAY

Read GALATIANS 5:22-26

The Holy Spirit and my example

M any people claim that they are fully dedicated to God. Serving others is their motto in life. But often they see only those needs which they prefer to see. Moreover, they become so involved with people that they eventually have very little time to spend with God; they become more and more self-sufficient and less dependent on God.

When charity begins to take the place of the worship to which God

> *Since we live by the Spirit, let us keep in step with the Spirit.*
>
> GAL 5:25

is entitled and upsets our communion with him, we run the risk of losing our contact with the real Source of inspiration and power. The busier we become in the service of God and in serving others, the more essential it is to spend more time with him. It is from God that we get the inspiration which he can only give to those who wait upon him in prayer.

The Lord gives us his Holy Spirit to guide us each day, particularly in our service of him. Our most urgent need is to spend time with the Father every day and to plead with him to fill us with his Spirit. We must lift up our hearts in faith over and over again so that God can remind us that his Spirit should always be our companion and co-worker. Let us thank God continually for this faithful Counsellor who works within us and enables us to walk and work in Christ.

A noint us with your Spirit, dear Lord, so that we can serve you, be sanctified, become kings, priests and prophets, and be true Christians in your service.

With all our efforts to be faithful in the service of our Lord, we are often unfaithful to the Lord of our service – A W TOZER.

Freed from the shadows of the past

M emories from our past has an influence on the present as well as on our future life. Unpleasant memories has the persistent habit of sticking to your mind and to become more painful as the years go by. We don't always realise that these memories influence our thoughts to such an extent that we become embittered and unforgiving. They even tend to rob us of our spontaneity and friendliness.

This vicious circle can only be broken if you allow the Holy Spirit to work in your life and if you yourself are prepared to grant forgiveness. This is indeed a difficult and challenging aspect of our Christianity. But hatred is not God's will for us and does not contribute to our spiritual growth. When you refuse to forgive, you destroy the bridge which you must also cross on the road to spiritual freedom.

> *But one thing I do: Forgetting what is behind and straining towards what is ahead . . .*
> PHIL 3:13

Only if you have experienced God's forgiveness can you truly forgive. If you are guided by the Holy Spirit to accept God's forgiveness in Jesus Christ, you are also expected to grant forgiveness and purify your memory from all negative influences. Forget all that lies behind you and strain towards the rich blessings which Christ make available to you.

B e merciful unto us, Lord, and forgive us our trespasses. Help us to forgive those wo have trespassed against us as you forgave us.

The best way to assure the future is to deal with the present constructively and courageously – ROLLO MAY.

The Holy Spirit, our source of power

Every human being needs a source of power and inspiration in life. Through Jesus Christ God gave us the Holy Spirit to be such a source of power – a source of power which cannot be surpassed by anything or anybody.

When we get to know Jesus, we are introduced to the source of true inspiration. When you know him, love him and believe in him, you start to worship him and your life becomes a song of praise to his glory. This faith is nourished through the Holy Spirit. He kindles the fire of love in your heart, because it is the foundation of your prayer life and the start of your inner power.

> *I pray that out of his glorious riches he may strengthen you with power through his Spirit in your inner being, so that Christ may dwell in your hearts through faith. And I pray that you, being rooted and established in love . . . may be filled.*
> EPH 3:16-18

Your innermost life is therefore sanctified through the work of the Holy Spirit and Christ becomes King of your heart and thoughts. He is always ready to let his power and love flow to every part of your life. Whenever you experience problems, the Holy Spirit will guide you day by day and fill you with renewed hope and courage. Open your heart to the Spirit and you will become even more rooted in the Lord of your life.

Holy Spirit, fill our hearts. Teach us, guide us, comfort us in our grief. Thank you for continuously confirming that we are your children. We praise you.

Dear Lord, give me mountains to climb and your strength to do it – *ARTHUR GUITERMAN.*

Being filled with the Holy Spirit

I f you desire to be filled with the Holy Spirit you must be convinced that it is God's will for you and that it forms part of our redemption through Jesus Christ. You must fervently desire to be filled with the Spirit. You must long for him to have full control of your life.

Don't ask him half-heartedly to take control of your life because you consider your life to be spiritually reasonably sound. You pray regularly, read your Bible, go to church, neither drink nor gamble, and enjoy praising the Lord. But is it sufficient? Do you wish to follow God to the utmost? Do you desire a deep

> *Whoever believes in me, as the Scripture has said, streams of living water will flow from within him. By this he meant the Spirit . . .*
>
> JN 7:38-39

spiritual experience with him? Then you must pray fervently that God should fill you with his Spirit. You will enjoy abundance and it will also ripple outwards to others around you. This is the difference between "being filled" and "overflowing". To be filled with God's love completely, and still have love left to give to others, an overflowing abundance is required. The Lord blesses his faithful children with this abundance when his Spirit fills us.

S pirit of God, who lives for ever, come in the abundance of your power and fill our praying hearts.

Life only becomes worth living when Jesus Christ enters into your heart – STEPHAN NEILL.

24 MAY

Read JOHN 14:27-31

The Holy Spirit leads us to peace

I n today's rushed life everyone is subjected to stress. Every day we are expected to meet higher and higher demands. And all over the world people are trying to be relieved of this unbearable pressure; all of us try to find peace and peace of mind.

There is only one way in which man can be assured of the rest which both body and soul are yearning for, "My soul finds rest in God alone; my salvation comes from him" (Ps 62:1). To know him and spend time in his presence, brings us true peace, because he is our power station where we can find renewed strength.

> *Peace I leave with you; my peace I give you . . . Do not let your hearts be troubled and do not be afraid.*
>
> JN 14:27

Our relationship with God must be a lasting union, like that of the branch and the vine. We can achieve this through the discipline of prayer, medidation, Bible study, and in being attuned to the work of the Holy Spirit in our lives. That was how Christ managed to remain steadfast in the trials of live without succumbing to pressure and stress. And now he invites all those who are weary and he waits for them to accept his loving invitation. If we take his yoke which is light upon us and learn from him through the Holy Spirit, we shall find rest and we shall experience the peace of God which transcends all understanding.

*H*oly Spirit, guide us in the truth. Take complete control of our lives and grant us your peace.

No form of peace can ever be bought over a counter
— CAREY WILLIAMS.

Guiding us to Jesus Christ

Jesus is King! The moment you say this, you commit yourself to the Lord and you declare that you will be faithful to him. You state that you have fully surrendered you life to him and that you trust him with unyielding faith; that you will obey him and will live through your faith in him.

When your life is ruled by Christ, it is no guarantee that you will not be faced by temptations or failure. You may still find yourself floundering between your own sinful nature and the wonder of God's healing power. However, God promises you his presence through the Holy Spirit. He promises to be with you, to renew you and to live and work through you so that his kingdom can be established on earth.

> *No one can say,*
> *"Jesus is Lord,"*
> *except by the Holy Spirit.*
> 1 COR 12:3

When you dedicate yourself to Christ, you will experience a feeling of being completely accepted by him, and an indescribable certainty of God's love and presence will fill your life. Every moment you will be aware of this certainty: Christ is the Lord of my life! The Holy Spirit will further lead you to a stronger awareness of Christ's majesty and your life will be filled with this glorious reality.

Confirm your relationship with your King this very moment and confess your loyalty and trust in him.

Spirit of Father and Son, lead me towards a renewed confirmation of my relationship with my King. I confess my loyalty and faithfulness to you.

The human race will be lost without religion, but without Christ man will be lost – DAVID F STRAUSS.

The Spirit which reveals

M any people know exactly what they want in life and spare no effort to achieve their goal. This characteristic could be commendable, but is could also degenerate into a foolish independence which leaves the Spirit no room for convincing you of wrong and selfish views. To stick to your point of view just because you are to proud to admit that you are wrong, is self-destructive. It is not a disgrace to admit that you have made a mistake.

> *But when he, the Spirit of truth, comes,*
> *he will guide you into all truth.*
>
> JN 16:13

Some time or other we all have to ask ourselves: Am I doing the right thing? Or: Is my faith the real truth? Examining oneself in this way shows that you are serious in your search for the real truth and that the truth is more important to you than your own opinions or meaningless traditions.

When you explore new ideas and new schools of thought you must be willing to listen to the Holy Spirit. Free yourself of ideas which no longer satisfy your needs or no longer serve a purpose. When the Holy Spirit is your guide you need an open and sensitive mind to understand the message the Spirit is trying to convey to you. Make sure that this truth has been inspired by God by comparing it with Christ's example and teachings as revealed in his Word.

H oly Spirit, grant that we may believe in the real truth. Strengthen us with power from above and perfect our weak prayers.

We must merely be obedient. Each one of us will be guided; if only we would humbly listen, we shall hear the correct word
— RALPH WALDO EMERSON.

Recreator of our thoughts

M any people simply follow the masses. Now and again they raise their voices in protest, but soon enough they conform to the masses again, preferring to keep quiet, safe and popular. They refrain from giving their own opinions and show no respect for the individuality with which their Creator has endowed them.

When you dedicate your life to Christ you receive new values in life. At the same time, however, you are faced with new responsibilities. Selfishness is replaced by sympathy; dishonesty by honesty; your love grows to include even those you have never been able to love. You become willing to ask God what his will is and you find joy in obeying him. The Holy Spirit works in your life and you no longer resist him.

> *Do not conform any longer to the pattern of this world, but be transformed by the renewing of your mind. Then you will be able to test and approve what God's will is.*
> ROM 12:2

Such a change in your thinking and conduct is often marred by setbacks. However, when you fail, always seek the road which will lead you to God again. If you repent and confess, the Holy Spirit will over and over again purify and renew your thoughts. Then you will experience joy, deliverance and peace and complete willingness to live within the will of God and to do whatever is acceptable in his eyes.

*D*ear Lord, recreate my life to your glory. Sanctify me and guide me to dedicate my life fully to you.

Fill your mind with positive thoughts, otherwise the enemy will fill it with negative ones – your mind can never be vacant
– THOMAS MOORE.

Am I wallowing in a spiritual quagmire?

We must realise that God gives us his Spirit so that we can be sanctified. He calls us to venture bravely out into spiritual depths and not to wallow in shallow sludge.

If you try to remain steadfast in a faith which lacks life and sparkle, hoping that it might get you somewhere, it is equivalent to rowing around in circles in shallow waters of

> *"Put out into deep water..."*
>
> LK 5:4

spiritual ineffectiveness. If this is true of you, you will never reach the fullness of life in which Christ has meant you to share through the Spirit.

The tragedy of Christians who lack spiritual depth is that they hamper the testimony of Christ's church and remain unfulfilled themselves. If that is the situation with your spiritual life, it is imperative that you do something about it. Approach your spiritual growth with the seriousness it deserves. Don't be satisfied with second best. Find your security in Christ and then pray to the Spirit to help you find rest and peace. With the Spirit as your guide you will be enriched and strengthened to sail triumphantly towards the spiritual depth to which he wants to lead you.

Holy Spirit, it is a great comfort to know that you desire to live in me forever. Sanctify me and grant that I may reflect the image of Christ more and more. Make me your own.

Faith is the courage of the soul to go further than it can see
— WILLIAM NEWTON CLARK.

Spirit of God – source of strength

M any Christians, when they compare themselves with others who have a sparkling faith, believe that they have no spiritual strength whatsoever. This is not true. When a new Christian's faith starts to grow, it draws from the source of power – God's Holy Spirit – to let it grow into maturity. This power reveals itself in different ways. All of us who have become new creatures through Christ's redemption, will experience its impact in a different way.

Therefore, never measure the power of the Holy Spirit in your own life against the lives of others. Allow him to reveal his power through

> . . . *having a form of godliness but denying its power.*
> 2 TIM 3:5

your life in a way which is true to your own personality and spiritual development. God does not make all his children the same. He creates each with an own identity and strength in a particular area as it pleases him. The Holy Spirit guides us to the discovery of that area and allows that power to be released in its own unique way.

S pirit of God, you are the power in our lives, therefore our faith can bear fruit. Use us in your kingdom through your power which works in us.

There is a source of power that is stronger than any disappointment, bitterness or inherent mistrust. That source is Jesus Christ who bought forgiveness and reconciliation for this world – and paid for it with his blood – POPE PAUL II.

30 MAY

Read COLOSSIANS 2:6-11

Spiritual maturity

Many people surrender themselves to Christ, but their love grows dim and they stop growing spiritually. When this happens, an honest evaluation of your spiritual life becomes essential.

The point of departure is a personal encounter with God through the sacrifice of his Son. God guides us to Christ through his Word and his Spirit. However, this encounter should not mark the beginning and the end. We must allow the Spirit to guide us into a deeper knowledge of our Saviour.

On the road to spiritual maturity we become more and more aware of Christ's presence and power in our lives. We experience the desire to know him better, to nourish our minds with enriching thoughts from his Word. This in turn leads us to be obedient to God's will as the Holy Spirit makes it known to us.

> So then, just as you received Christ Jesus
> as Lord, continue to
> live in him,
> rooted and built up in him,
> strengthened in the
> faith . . .
>
> COL 2:6-7

As you grow spiritually more mature, Christ's image is reflected in your life more and more and your faith begins to enrich the environment in which God has placed you.

Father, teach us to grow in our understanding of you, through the work of the Holy Spirit in us. Guide and teach us through your Word and Spirit in such a way that we shall always glorify your name through our lives and work.

Spiritual maturity is not attained through learning, but by being obedient to the revealed will of God – D W LAMBERT.

Read GALATIANS 5:13-26

Live by the Spirit

Living by the Spirit implies that you should follow his guidance faithfully in all you do and think, in all your struggles and strivings. This is the essential characteristic of each Spirit-filled person who serves God with dedication.

The guidance of the Holy Spirit is not an isolated compartment of our lives, which is only unlocked on Sundays or on particular occasions. The Lord blesses us with his Spirit in its fullness to lead us each day. The force of the world is so strong that we desperately require the guidance of the Spirit. We must daily plead with God to fill us with his Spirit. And throughout the day we must assure ourselves that the Holy Spirit lives within us and controls our lives.

> *So I say, live by the Spirit . . . Since we live by the Spirit, let us keep in step with the Spirit.*
> GAL 5:16, 25

If we step outside the sphere of influence of the Holy Spirit our sinful nature gets the better of us. Then we become the prey of Satan who prowls around like a roaring lion, looking for someone to devour. However, if we are guided by the Spirit, we shall bear his abundant fruit: love, joy, peace, patience, kindness, goodness, faithfulness, gentleness and self-control.

Spirit of life, teach me to honour only God. Sanctify my every deed so that I shall remain pure and untouched by evil. You are the ruler of my life – I praise you for that.

The duty of man is summarised in his obedience to the will of God – *GEORGE WASHINGTON.*

Notes

JUNE

PRAYER

❖ ❖

Holy Father,
Creator of heaven and earth
    winter brings its own pleasures
    but also its own anxieties.
Thank you for the winter blossoms
    even though they are untimely.
They remind us how almost impossible your love
    for us, who are hopeless sinners, appears to be.
Thank you for the rain and cold, a time to read,
    for slumbering nature waiting on new growth.
Through this winter teach me to make time for you,
    to acquire peace in your presence.
Allow me sometimes to slow down
    so that I may think about the essential things in life
    and store energy for a new period of growth.
Father, the winter cold also has its share of anxieties;
    the aged and poor die in poverty
    whilst I sit in front of my cosy fire;
    the unemployed who do not know
    where they will find food for tomorrow;
    the hungry who pass me with pleading eyes;
    the destitute who must suffer in the cold outside
    as well as suffer the unfeeling coldness of unsympathetic people.
Help me to be a caring, loving person
    who reaches out a helping hand.
Warm this winter season
    with the spirit of Christmas in June.
In the name of the Merciful One.

Amen

Count your blessings

Some people always expect the worst from life. If you are experiencing difficulties, don't assume that an even more difficult time lies ahead. With such pessimism you will never know the joy of a living faith.

Faith does not make us blind to our problems, but takes away the fear. If we trust in God, we can embark on life with a calm assurance. When faith in Christ is the focal point of our life, we are able to look past the trials and heartache to a future filled with promise, because we receive that future from him.

> *I will bless them and the places surrounding my hill. I will send down showers in season; there will be showers of blessing.*
> EZEK 34:26

God envisages only the best for us. You might be battling your way through a taxing time in your life and doubt God's goodness, but he loves you and wants to bless you and lead you along his perfect way. Be aware of all the blessings which could come your way. Spend more time in prayer. Become aware of God's presence; thank him for his love which enhances life. Always be joyful in the Lord and streams of blessings will descend on your life.

God of grace, forgive me when I doubt you and become depressed. I accept your rich blessings and thank you for them. Help me to use them to your honour.

The world is charged with the grandeur of God
— GERALD MANLEY HOPKINS

2 JUNE

Read PHILIPPIANS 1:12-26

From caterpillar to butterfly

I n God's plan death to the caterpillar means life to a butterfly. In the same way death is also not our final destination. If God wants us all to die, he intends something good to come out of it, because he is good. For believers death only means that we enter a higher dimension of life. That is why we need not fear death. Through our Saviour, who has risen, we have been victorious over death and we have the assurance that our life, like trees in spring, will again burst forth in full bloom.

> *For to me, to live is Christ and to die is gain.*
>
> PHIL 1:21

Death is the final chapter in the redemption of mankind. Through his death on the cross Christ freed us from the *power* of sin and God's *judgement* of sin. But only after our death and resurrection in Christ will we be totally free from our *natural inclination* to sin.

If we want to experience God's comfort as a positive force, we must understand something of his holy purpose. In his omnipotence God tames even death for the sake of those who love him.

*T*hank you, Lord our Creator, that you have made death a thoroughfare to victory. Comfort us with the assurance that death's sting has been removed through Jesus Christ.

Our Lord etched the resurrection not only in print, but in every leaf of spring – MARTIN LUTHER.

He helps us to get up again

We often hear people who have been beaten by life say, "I cannot go on any longer." When we have been knocked down by circumstances, the most sensible thing to do is to get up again. Unfortunately there are people who, when life has dealt them a telling blow, are convinced that they will never be strong enough to carry on.

Amidst the supposed ruins of their lives, they are filled with self-pity and cry out against the terrible injustice of life. They become embittered and unfriendly and want to

> *When men fall down, do they not get up?*
> JER 8:4

revenge themselves on their fellow man. Soon these people become very lonely, because their friends eventually tire of listening to their complaints.

However hard life might have hit you, remember that God does not want you to be constantly depressed. He wants you to live victoriously. Therefore, don't waste your time on useless self-recrimination and self-pity. Look up towards him who renews all things. He will lead you on the road to recovery and happiness.

In moments of defeat I need you so badly, Lord. Please help me to get up every time I have been knocked down by life's cruel blows and to press on in faith, in your strength.

To be healed we can concentrate on two characteristics of God: his omnipotence and his love. Every healing has a measure of both – FRANCIS MCNUTT.

4 JUNE

Read JOHN 14:27-31

Peace – God's gift to us

In a world seemingly on the edge of a precipice it seems naive and idealistic to talk about peace. Do we still have the right to expect it? Is peace not just an idle dream?

No! Even though the rumble of weapons of war might announce devastating times, the peace which Christ gives, is an indestructible reality for each person who loves God. His peace is the stabilising factor in this disrupted world. Those who have accepted God's peace through Jesus Christ, do not try to escape trials, dangers and problems. They deal with them, because they know that they have a precious treasure, infinitely more important than the spirit of the times in which they live. When others become panic-stricken, they press on with peace in their hearts. They have peace of mind in every circumstance and situation.

> *Peace I leave with you;*
> *my peace I give you.*
> JN 14:27

Peace does not imply that you close your eyes to the realities of life, but it gives you a positive attitude founded in a living faith in Jesus Christ. Peace is a gift from the Spirit of God and it enables you to face life's challenges with faith and strength. In any situation you can depend on the promise of your living Saviour: "My peace I give you!"

Lord, source of peace, thank you that, in the midst of the raging storms, I can find a place of peace and quiet with you.

We do not know what is coming, but we do know Who is coming. He who knows to whom the last hour belongs, does not have to fear the next minute – HELMUT THIELICKE.

Overcome your inferiority complex

An inferiority complex stunts our spiritual growth. We know that this feeling is at odds with God's desire for our lives, but we don't know what to do about it.

The only antidote for a feeling of inferiority is to put all your trust in God. To arrive at this type of faith you must invite Christ into your life and devote yourself to him completely. Then his power will be manifested through you. Prayer and meditation strengthen your self-confidence and your faith in God. If God in Christ works in your life you can live a trusting, victorious life, because the more you become aware of Christ's omnipotence, the stronger your faith and trust in him will become. In this way you will overcome your inferiority and lead a fruitful, satisfying life.

> *I am the vine; you are the branches.*
> *If a man remains in me and I in him,*
> *he will bear much fruit;*
> *apart from me you can do nothing.*
> JN 15:5

Remember, nothing is impossible if we are anchored in Christ's power. The doors to God's house are wide open for those who wish to enter through Christ to a fruitful and victorious life.

Eternal God, abide in me through your Holy Spirit, so that I may never feel inferior. With you in my life I am able to do everything through Christ who gives me my strength.

We cannot change people, or ourselves, but the gospel can . . . that is my consolation — *J CILLIERS.*

A living faith

To have a living faith is absolutely essential in this world in which we live. When everything around you falls apart it is necessary to have a firmly established faith; to believe without any doubt that this world still belongs to God.

In the chaos in which we live we often wonder what the future holds for us. Lawlessness is rampant and the powers of justice seem to be limited and worthless. However, don't allow appearances to mislead you. God still cares about us; he is still in control of the world. Without this belief in an omniscient God who holds the fate of nations and individuals in his hand, we are lost.

> *The earth is the Lord's and everything in it; the world and all who live in it.*
>
> PS 24:1

Jesus Christ came to this world not to establish a new theology, but to bring life in all its abundance. To all who accept him he gives the strength to believe, so that they can live a purposeful and victorious life – even when circumstances are uncertain. If you believe in him you can approach the future with confidence in the knowledge that he is the Guide and the Anchor in times of trouble.

*A*lmighty God, thank you that through Jesus Christ I can be certain that I share in your peace, even in the midst of the storms of this world.

It is as impossible for an unbelievier to detract from God's majesty by refusing to bow before him as it would be for a madman to extinguish the light of the sun by scribbeling "darkness" on his cell wall – C S LEWIS.

Approaching the future with faith

When Columbus sailed away to discover the new world, he and his crew lived through difficult times. They were faced with famine and sickness. The crew were considering mutiny. However, the determined Columbus insisted that they "hoist the sails and push on". What a demonstration of faith in the unseen and unknown this was, even in the most perilous of circumstances! His joy must have been indescribable when he first cast his eyes on the New World.

> *And without faith it is impossible to please God, because anyone who comes to him must believe that he exists, and that he rewards those who earnestly seek him.*
> HEB 11:6

In difficult times we need a steadfast faith which will say, "hoist the sails and push on". Such a faith helps us to deal with our problems and to trust in God for the future. God knows about us, cares about us and supports us in every situation. His only condition is that in faith we must place our complete trust in him.

Faith is when the heart dares to step out beyond what the eye can see. With this type of faith we can approach life with courage. We shall be able to navigate through unknown waters to God's "new world" – a world of beauty and joy which will far surpass our dreams.

Compassionate God, thank you that you reward those who place their trust in you. Help me to trust in you, through your Spirit, even when everything is dark around me.

I don't merely want to possess a faith; I want a faith which possesses me – CHARLES KINGSLEY.

Read JOB 23:1-17

God is only a prayer away

Millions of people all over the world are searching for certainty about God. Some try to suppress this longing by claiming that they are not interested in religion. However, deep in the heart of everyone of God's creatures there is a longing for a Truth which can give significance and meaning to their lives.

> *If only I knew where to find him; if only I could go to his dwelling! I would state my case before him and fill my mouth with arguments. I would find out what he would answer me and consider what he would say.*
>
> JOB 23:3-5

When one realises that one needs God, the immediate question is, "Where can I find God?" Thereafter one experiences either a joyful discovery or frustration – depending on whether you find him or continue to search.

You may look for God in many places and later reach the point where you are ready to quit. Then you must remember that the One you are looking for, is with you. The Lord is only a prayer away. Stop your feverish search to find him. In faith accept his comforting presence in your life and say with gratitude: Now I have truly found him! Praise the Lord!

Lord God, I receive you into my life with joy and thankfulness. Thank you that I am aware of your presence when I pray to you.

Prayer is often compared with breathing. With every breath we exhale the unhealthy air . . . and inhale the fresh air of God's promises and love and his life in Christ. This we do through the Holy Spirit which is the very breath of life to us
— ANDREW MURRAY.

The problem of suffering

Why do bad things happen to good people? Why do some people suffer more than others? Why did this have to happen to me?

The answer to these questions is probably found only by those who have suffered and survived victoriously. Through suffering we discover the true meaning of life. After all, it is only through death that we begin to understand the significance of the resurrection.

Suffering and love are so intertwined that it is difficult for us to distinguish between them. We can plummet from the heights of blissful joy to the depths of utter sorrow

> *My God, my God, why have you forsaken me?*
> MT 27:46

and suffering. What is more, the greater our love, the greater our suffering.

The great tragedy is not our suffering, but that we see only our own problems and turn a blind eye to the Man of Sorrows – He who never changes and is closest to us when we are suffering. In our darkest, most helpless moments he teaches us the true meaning of the word "love" – that love which gave us the cross *and* our salvation.

O Lord, I place my sorrow and suffering at the foot of the cross and I trust that you will know what to do and that everything will work out for the best in my life.

Let circumstances be what they will, always keep your eyes on Jesus – OSWALD CHAMBERS.

10 JUNE

Read PSALM 118:22-29

The day of the Lord

Sunday is a day of rest, it is God's day . . . our day. He gave this day of rest to us for a specific purpose: so that, for a short while, we can withdraw from the exhausting, rushed life we lead to find our Lord and ourselves again; to break away from the wearisome tempo of our lives so that we can come to rest in the company of our Creator and see the significance of our existence in perpective.

> *This is the day the LORD has made;*
> *let us rejoice and be glad in it.*
> PS 118:24

The day of the Lord was instituted for our benefit, but also to God's honour. On this day we must be reinvigorated so that we can meet the challenges which we shall encounter during the week. We must find the time to take our battered lives to God so that, through his Holy Spirit, he can heal and strengthen us. The day of rest also gives us the opportunity of seeing our loved ones so that we can enjoy one another's friendship and love. Close to one another, close to God – in his house and in our home.

May you find this special significance in every Sunday. May you have many meaningful encounters with God and be richly blessed.

Father, thank you for instituting your day. Help us on this day to draw on all the many blessings you so lovingly made available to us.

If we are willing to learn the true meaning of discipleship and become true disciples, the church will undergo a revival and its effect on society will be astounding – DAVID WATSON.

Love is . . . faith in God

L ove is a renewing power in the life of every Christian. Christian love cannot be experienced or given superficially. When you confess your love for God, you are compelled to open your life to him and his Spirit and to give Christ a free hand.

Love leads you to submitting your life to God's will. It evokes the desire in you to get to know him better and to obey him. Love gives you access to God and you receive the blessings which he has intended for you. Love elevates your spirit and fills your life with thankfulness towards the God who pours blessings on you. It assures you that you are in God's hands and that his hands are loving and caring.

> *God is love. Whoever lives in love*
> *lives in God, and God in him.*
> 1 JN 4:16

This love is not false or a fleeting emotion. Therefore, open your heart to the Spirit of God. It is an act of faith, even though emotion plays a role. You must believe, irrespective of how or what you feel. You must believe that your life is God's loved possession. Then your faith will become alive and real, because the love of God is in you and works through you.

*G*od of love, thank you that your love in my life is steadfast.

All we need is a believing heart. God will lead us by the hand – that is why we must concentrate more on our love for him than on our fear of failure – FRANCOIS FÉNELON.

12 JUNE

Read ACTS 17:16-33

Someone cares

When your world collapses like a house of cards and you have no one to turn to, your loneliness becomes unbearable and you may easily become desperate.

When you are on the verge of losing hope, remember that Jesus Christ experienced similar trials. Think about the dark shadows which descended upon him in Gethsemane; the darkest of moments when as a lonely outcast he cried out on the cross with these dying words: "My God, my God, why have you forsaken me?" (Mt 27:46).

> *He is not far from each one of us.*
> *For in him we live and move and have our being.*
> ACTS 17:27-28

The scriptures confirm that God did not forsake his Son at all. On the contrary, he was with Jesus in that moment to give him strength to overcome the forces of evil. God gave Jesus the power to be victorious over death and to rise again triumphantly and to have his will done.

Instead of despairing in your lonely plight, turn to Christ. He understands your crisis better than anyone else. He will never forsake you. He is there now, willing to take your burden upon his shoulders. Place yourself unconditionally in his care. He will give you his peace because he cares about you.

*C*rucified Saviour, thank you that in my worst trials I am never alone, that you are always by my side. That is why I am never afraid.

People are lonely because they build walls instead of bridges
— *JOSEPH NEWTON.*

Don't be afraid

Change is part of life. For a while everything may seem to be going well and then suddenly things may be disrupted. Everything appears to be going wrong and you feel disorientated and overwhelmed. Life requires tremendous courage from us. It is then that you need the encouragement that Isaiah 43:5 offers, because fear paralyses your thoughts and it is difficult to think clearly. It destroys everything beautiful and worthwhile in life.

How can one fight fear? By remembering that God your Father is greater than anything which threatens your life. Trust in him – always expect the best and not the worst.

> *Do not be afraid,*
> *for I am with you . . .*
> IS 43:5

Share your fears with him before they start to take over your life. If you allow fear to dominate your life, the knowledge of Christ's presence in your life will grow so dim that you will not have the strength to fight against your fear.

A living faith in God is a sure antidote against fear. It enables us to live a full, rich and powerful life in the knowledge that God holds our lives in his hands.

Heavenly Father, I place my full trust in you and shall face the future without fear. Hold my hand and lead me in your truth, in the name of Jesus Christ.

You can fight with conviction when you are sure of victory.
With Christ and for Christ, the victory is assured
— BERNARD VAN CLAIRVAUX.

14 JUNE

Read PSALM 56

Comforting tears

Tears alleviate our grief and prevent sorrow from turning into despair. Tears are not shed by weaklings only, but also by the strong, because tears have their source in love, tenderness and sympathy.

God views our sorrow sympathetically and provides comfort through our tears. Through the tears shed by Jesus God also sanctified our tears. He was God enough to take away tears, but also human enough to share the sorrow of those in tears.

> *Record my lament; list my tears on your scroll – are they not on your record?*
>
> PS 56:8

Thank God for the healing power of tears. They alleviate grief, bring acceptance and eventually lead to joy. The soul would not have known a rainbow if our eyes had not filled with tears. Furthermore, we also have God's promise that there will be an end to our tears. God, himself, promises to wipe away the tears (Rev 21:4).

If there have to be tears in your life, may they be like dewdrops, heralding days of happiness and joy.

My Comforter, thank you that through my tears I can find comfort; that it makes my sorrow more bearable and draws me closer to you.

Tears can be holy. They are not a sign of weakness, but of strength. They say more than ten thousand words. Tears may herald overwhelming grief or complete repentance but also demonstrate inexpressible love – WASHINGTON IRVING.

God's purpose for your life

Perhaps at this point in time your life has become very difficult and pressurised and you would rather have been anywhere else. Because you are experiencing problems you may be praying earnestly that God should change your situation or solve your problem. What if nothing happens? Have you considered that God might have placed you in your present situation with a specific purpose, that you may be his representative, so that through his Spirit and wisdom you can be his instrument of change?

> *And who knows but that you have come to royal position for such a time as this?*
> ESTHER 4:14

When everything is mixed-up don't harbour thoughts of defeat and surrender, but earnestly ask God what he expects of you. If you are sincere about asking God what you must do, he has his ways of showing you what his will is.

Does he want you to bring peace to a situation fraught with discord? Or does he want you to demonstrate his power to those who are weak? Are you required to show understanding where there is misunderstanding? Must you show loyalty to him where others have spurned him? Before asking God to change your situation, first make sure that the place in which you are at the moment, is perhaps not where God needs you most.

Heavenly Father, keep me from blundering blindly on paths where I think I should be. In your grace let me live as close to you as possible, to enable me to understand your will for my life.

If you recognise the authority of Jesus Christ in your life, also accept the authority of his Word – COLIN URQUHART.

16 JUNE

Read JOHN 14:1-14

Peace which banishes our troubles

Faith in God gives us peace of mind. Obedience to his will leads us to peace. His Holy Spirit, our Advocate and Comforter, is the gift from God which drives out our fears and fills us with peace, courage and calmness.

The door to God is always open through our prayers (Mt 6:6). He invites us to speak to him when we are in trouble. He is the giver of all good gifts, the most important of which is his presence. God also gives us communion with other fellow believers. Through going to church and praising God together with other believers, we receive the power which emanates from them to us and which we, in turn, pass on to others.

> Do not let your hearts be troubled
> Trust in God; trust also in me.
>
> JN 14:1

The knowledge that the Lord will come again to claim what belongs to him also gives us peace. Then the struggle against sin will be over and death will be finally defeated. Together with others who have been redeemed we shall rejoice in our everlasting joy and peace.

God wants us to be courageous and calm in spite of our circumstances. We must trust in him and believe in his Son Jesus Christ and then we shall experience peace in our hearts.

Banish my troubles, O Lord, and let me experience your peace from day to day, because I trust in you.

I believe in the sun, even though it is not shining today. I believe in love, even though I see so little of it. I believe in God, even now, when I no longer hear his voice
— POLISH JEW IN THE WARSAW GHETTO, SECOND WORLD WAR.

Read 1 JOHN 4:7-21

Let love be the victor

L ove conquers everything. It is the most amazing power on earth. Its most outstanding quality is to give – always the best and the most precious. No one can take love away from you and the more you give, the stronger its influence on your life will be.

The martyrs of old refused to be controlled by bitterness and hatred. They chose to endure physical suffering. Their love for those who persecuted them could not be extinguished. And when, with broken bodies, they could lose nothing more, their love carried them through victoriously.

> *We love because He first loved us.*
> 1 JN 4:19

This love they learnt from the source of all true love; the One who lovingly gave himself for the redemption of the world. The purest demonstration of Christian love is Christ on the cross. His love's shining light shone down triumphantly, even though he suffered indescribable agonies.

Let God's love work through you and move in ever widening circles to the world around you. That is how you, a dedicated person, can demonstrate Christ's love in this world.

G od of grace and love, thank you for sending Jesus Christ to demonstrate your love for us. Let his perfect love saturate, purify and strengthen my life.

The lost opportunities that people will regret most, are the opportunities they had of loving someone – F B MYERS.

Read PSALM 28

God shall answer you

God is still capable of peforming miracles. Every time that someone is healed in answer to a prayer, God has performed a miracle. Every time that peace returns to our hearts after a time of tension and trial; when our suffering becomes more bearable or is transformed to exultant joy, a miracle has taken place.

The proof that God answers our prayers is overwhelming. Many Christians can give testimony of a miracle in answer to their faithful prayers. Lives have been reshaped; the sick have been healed; degrading habits have been beaten; distorted relationships have been restored. Many people have first-hand experience of the fact that God gives us his guidance when we ask him for it.

> *Praise be to the Lord, for He has heard my cry for mercy.*
> PS 28:6

Therefore, hand today's problems over to God in prayer and wait on him in faith. If there is something which you must personally do, then do it, without delay. Do not be overcome by despair in your distress. God shall answer your prayer at the right time and in the right way and you will be amazed at his deliverance.

My God and heavenly Father, I know that you are able to do far more than I can pray for or even imagine, because you are almighty. May this truth be my guiding light through this day.

Prayer is not to hear yourself talking, prayer is to be quiet and wait until you hear God's voice — S KIERKEGAARD.

The comforted become comforters

Suffering and afflictions weave a special type of beauty into the lives of the faithful, because in the darkest valleys of life we sometimes discover the most precious of life's treasures.

Paul taught us through his trials that God can comfort anyone at any time. He abounds in grace and is a God "who comforts us in all our troubles" (2 Cor 1:3) and gives us courage. This courage is a direct consequence of our communion with God. It emanates from us to others who are suffering and brings a special comfort to them. It often happens that our own grief is alleviated whilst we comfort others. Happiness, tenderness and love is not necessarily to be found in a

> *. . . the God of all comfort, who comforts us in all our troubles, so that we can comfort those in any trouble with the comfort we ourselves have received from God.*
> 2 COR 1:3-4

carefree home, but is often present where the shadow of sorrow has fallen and where Christ's comfort has come from the hands of his children.

That is why every burden and trial which God brings upon us, hides a blessing. Just ask for grace to be able to identify it and share this blessing with others. Soon our own grief will be tempered and we will be able to reach out to others with open hands and hearts.

God, our Comforter, let your healing love fill our hearts. Teach us to be as tender in our dealings with others as you are with us.

Earth has no sorrow which heaven cannot heal
— THOMAS MOORE.

Read MATTHEW 26:36-46

Too tired to pray?

We often start our quiet time with God with such good intentions, but physically we are so exhausted that we are unable to concentrate. All we can think of is sleeping. Then our prayers are fruitless and ineffective. In the same way unhappiness, distorted relationships or frustration can disrupt our prayer life.

> *Then he returned to his disciples and found them sleeping. "Could you men not keep watch with me for one hour?" he asked Peter. "Watch and pray so that you will not fall into temptation. The spirit is willing but the body is weak."*
>
> MT 26:40

When Jesus was tired he prayed and it refreshed and strengthened him. When he was downcast in spirit he prayed even more earnestly. Through this example he teaches us that prayer is as essential as the air we breathe. When you share your whole life with your Heavenly Father you will find that your quiet time is a time to be reinvigorated and to experience spiritual renewal.

If you are tired and sleepy, speak your words to God out loud. Read a prayer from the Bible aloud; make time to pray early in the morning when you are still fresh. Let prayer be the key to every day and the lock to close every night of your earthly existence.

Lord Jesus, so often when I pray the only thing I really want to do is sleep. Help me to overcome this weakness through discipline and love for you.

I have so much to do that if I do not spend several hours in prayer, I would never get through all my work – JOHN WESLEY.

The mystery will be solved

Questions are asked either in a spirit of rebellion or with the desire to obtain knowledge and understanding. God does not mind that we ask questions. He wants us to understand and he will reveal himself to the extent that he judges best.

This brings us to the question often asked, but not properly considered: I know that God is good and God is love, but then why does he allow sorrow in the lives of those who love him?

Our love for God is not a guarantee of a carefree existence. Suffering and death is also not a sign of God's displeasure with us. The purpose of this life is to prepare us for eternity. Life offers boundless opportunities but also surrounds us with countless dangers, such as death. Through dealing with life and death we learn the best lessons. If we achieve success God is pleased. When we fail he is sad, but it does not alter his love for us at all.

> *For the Lamb at the centre of the throne will be their shepherd, he will lead them to springs of living water.*
> REV 7:17

*H*eavenly Father, thank you that you have all the answers to the questions in our hearts. May we wait patiently until you provide us with the solution in Jesus Christ.

If life knocks your feet out from underneath you, it is time to fall on your knees — FREDERICK BECK.

Acknowledge God in every facet of your life

Many people have witnessed something of God's unmistakable guidance in their lives. However, there are days which dawn grey and without any prospects, days when we only too readily query God's guidance .

However, God never stops offering us his guidance. To experience his guidance you must have an intimate relationship with God and live in close communion with him. You must make time to be quiet in his presence so that you can hear his voice and become aware of the directions for the road he wants you to follow. You must lay your confusion, your desires, your problems before him in prayer.

> *In all your ways acknowledge him and he will make your paths straight.*
>
> PROV 3:6

When you place God's will above your own desires, your faith will become stronger. You will start every day in faith and become sensitive and obedient to every step which God wants you to take. Initially it could be difficult to submit your will to God's will and progress along God's way will be slow. However, the conviction that you are on the right road will gradually grow stronger. Then you will joyfully do the will of your Father and follow his guidance.

Lord, I rejoice in doing your will. Make me ever more obedient and willing to follow where you lead me.

Do not pray for an easy life – pray to become a stronger person. Don't pray for tasks according to your strengths – pray for strength according to the task – PHILIP BROOKS.

Faith in the unseen

When you try to understand who Christ really is and what he does, you find that it is impossible to explain. Who can explain the mystery of God Incarnate?

Life is infinitely more than just our allotted seventy odd years. We experience eternal qualities such as love, purity, unselfish service and sacrifice, but do not quite understand them. Through them we are given just an inkling of what eternity means. It is enriching when in faith we can look beyond this temporary world. Whilst you lose your life in the living Christ, you become increasingly aware of your union with the eternal.

> *But he said to them,*
> *"Unless I see*
> *the nail marks . . . I will not*
> *believe it."*
> JN 20:25

This experience has a practical implication for your life. You perceive the abundance and magnanimity of God's deeds around you with a new perception. Your develop a broader view of the temporary and all pettiness disappears from your existence. Then you realise that the most precious treasure on earth is not God's gifts, but God himself and you grow in knowledge of him and his grace.

Eternal God, make me aware of your goodness, so that I shall understand something of eternity. Help me to get to know you better and to serve and love you more.

Faith sees the unseen, believes the unbelievable and receives the impossible – *C S LEWIS.*

24 JUNE

Read MATTHEW 18:1-5

Humble yourself before God

Children place a simple faith in those people whom they respect and love. Their faith and acceptance is a lesson in humility for us adults. And that is one of the biggest lessons which we must learn, because often the fact that we are not humble becomes a stumbling-block in life. Soon we start to query and analyse our faith and trust in God and his eternal Word.

> Therefore, whoever humbles himself like this child, is the greatest in the kingdom of heaven.
>
> MT 18:4

The leaders of the early church were simple people, yet the church grew under the guidance of God's almighty hand and in the power of his Spirit. In spite of the advantages which we enjoy, the modern day church is often the scene of disagreement and division. This seriously affects and sometimes even wrecks Christ's work, and the working of the Holy Spirit and the church fathers.

It is so extremely important that all Christians remember that one of the most endearing characteristics of our Lord was his humility. Only when we forget our pride and social status and become washers of feet, like him, can we expect to make a contribution to the expansion of his kingdom.

Show me, o Lord, how to humble myself before you. Make me modest and help me to live according to your will.

The reason why God loves a humble person, is because he loves the truth. Humility is after all nothing other than the truth, whilst pride is a lie – VINCENT DE PAUL.

Christ stays the same

Life seldom runs smoothly and without problems. Sometimes everything is going well and we are filled with a feeling of satisfaction. Then, suddenly, without any reason, problems arise and dark shadows move across life's horizon. One moment we are in a state of joy, only the next moment to plummet into the depths of despair.

Our life constantly moves between a state of hope and hopelessness; joy and sorrow. It is because of these extremes that we desperately need a stabilising force in our lives – the power of Jesus, the living Christ.

> *Jesus Christ is the same yesterday, today and forever.*
>
> HEB 13:8

Christ is eternal. He never changes. Even though we are temperamental and our feelings vacillate according to our circumstances, if Christ is the Lord of our life and his Holy Spirit lives in us, we experience a stability which we have not known before. Our lives become centred in Christ and this gives us, at all times, a balanced and stable outlook on life. Then we experience a joy so great that we cannot find the words to express it.

*H*oly Father, I accept in faith that your Spirit lives in me. I want to live in accordance with your direction, so that my life can be balanced.

Time leaves nothing unchanged. O Lord-who-never-changes, stay with me! – HENRY FRANCIS WHYTE.

26 JUNE

Read ROMANS 8:18-30

Do things always work for our good?

When we are grief-stricken it is difficult to believe that every-thing God does and will do, works for our good. How ever much we may lose in life, enough always remains for God to execute his eternal plan for us.

God's almighty power is unlimited, his love is boundless. He not only wants us to accept his intervention in faith, but he also requires our acquiescence. In our sorrow it might sound out of place to say that God will work for the good in that situation, but this is where our comfort and healing lies.

> *And we know that in all things God works for the good of those who love him, who have been called according to his purpose.*
>
> ROM 8:28

If we have no hope for the future, we do not have enough strength for today, because our hope for tomorrow must be engendered in today's inspiration. If it were not for hope we would all be broken people. Those who truly love God know – God wants only the best for us and proves this through Jesus Christ. Good always comes out of our love for him and particularly his love for us. The more we love Christ, the more our trust in him grows. Then we shall see that even the trials and tribulations of life can be converted into something good and wholesome.

*T*hank you, Lord, that everything will work for our good. I shall love and trust you every day of my life.

We place our trust in the one we love and the degree to which we love determines how much we trust. If we love Christ dearly, surely we shall also trust him to the utmost – PHILIP BROOKE.

Only your best is good enough

The prophet Malachi here emphasizes an important rule – second best is not good enough for God.

If you are one of those people who place God at the bottom of your list of priorities, if you give him only the remnants of your life, you must not be surprised if you do not experience any of God's miracles or blessings or if your life is ineffective and drab.

To give anything less than your best to God is an insult to him. It implies that there are matters and circumstances in your life which enjoy a higher priority than your heavenly Father. In your eyes the temporal is more important than the eternal. If this is your attitude you will very soon find out that nothing in your life seems to be going right. Your sense of values becomes warped, because they are based on shaky foundations.

> *"When you bring injured, crippled or diseased animals and offer them as sacrifices, should I accept them from your hands?" says the LORD."*
>
> MAL 1:13

Only when you are prepared to give God your very best and put him first in your life, your values will become solid and effective.

*O*nly the best for you, my Lord, because nothing less will suffice. After all, you gave your best for me in the person of Jesus Christ.

People notice your deeds, but God notices your motives
– THOMAS À KEMPIS.

28 JUNE

Read LUKE 19:28-44

Recipe for peace

Some people live in enmity. They go through life with rage and hatred in their hearts. Employers and employees, neighbours, friends and families live in discord. In so doing people are also in conflict with God, because they do not want to understand which qualities are necessary to achieve peace. The more sensitive we become to the voice of Christ and the workings of the Holy Spirit in our lives, the clearer those qualities required to achieve peace will become.

> *If you, even you, had only known on this*
> *day what would bring you peace –*
> *but now it is hidden from your eyes.*
> LK 19:42

We must acknowledge God's sovereignty. Other things, people or self-interest have priority in our lives. We refuse to worship God and as a result other less important things take God's place. Eventually we become as shallow as the things we love and serve.

We must acknowledge the worthiness and dignity of the individual before God. Christ always showed people that he sincerely cared for them. We love possessions and use people. This leads to envy and strife.

We must accept that we are bound to and dependent on one another. If we cannot live together in harmony, hate will destroy us. To achieve harmony we must submit our thoughts, words, deeds and ideals to Christ and strive for his peace.

God of peace, allow your Holy Spirit to open my eyes so that I can clearly see what I need to do to achieve peace in my life.

Peace cannot be maintained by force; peace is achieved only through understanding one another – ALBERT EINSTEIN.

Your relationship with God

Some Christians are always happy and cheerful. They never seem to get depressed and have the ability to deal with setbacks that will make others grind to a halt and become discouraged. However, for the latter there is hope and comfort.

Many of God's children wallow in the depths of despair and wish, like Elijah did, that God would end their lives. Spiritual depression, however, is not necessarily synonomous with spiritual failure. Even Jesus was very distressed at times. Only when you stop trying to grope your way from the darkness to the light, have you failed.

> You . . . clothed me with joy, that my heart may sing to you and not be silent. O Lord my God, I will give you thanks forever.
> PS 30:12

Restore your relationship with God. Eliminate everything from your life which separates you from him. Don't place your own desires above your obligation to be obedient to his will. And if there are sins which hinder your communication with God, confess them to him and experience the liberation of God's forgiveness. Then you will spontaneously burst into songs of praise; for then the dark times are only a prelude to a brighter light and a deeper love for God.

Loving Lord, lead me, especially in the dark times of my life, to a sure knowledge of your unfathomable love.

Our unique joy lies not so much in the fact that we hold firmly unto God, but rather that we are held firmly by him
— ROBERT M HEROLD.

30 JUNE

Read ISAIAH 41:8-20

God is our comfort

rief and suffering can radically change our lives, particularly the grief surrounding death. Where shared love, understanding and experiences used to be, there is now only a painful, gaping void. Only those who have experienced this separation can truly understand the pain. For years you may have shared your love with someone, but now that person has died and you are devastated. However, there is comfort for you in the sure knowledge that your loved one is safe with the Lord and that you will meet again in a different life.

> *So do not fear for I am with you; do not be dismayed for I am your God. I will strengthen you and help you; I will uphold you with my righteous right hand.*
>
> IS 41:10

There are also other forms of grief which are equally bad – maybe even worse. When someone brings shame and degradation upon a family you often hear the words, "Death would have been better than this!" A beloved child with a physical disability or a terminal illness can also bring the deepest sorrow and suffering into our lives. In these circumstances we raise our tearful eyes to the heavens and hear the God of love say, "I will uphold you with my righteous right hand." Believe in this God and trust him. He is your Comforter.

oving Lord, your comfort uplifts me. In faith I place my sorrow at the foot of the cross and with quiet conviction I know that you will comfort me here and now.

God did not come to take away our suffering. God did not come to justify our suffering. God simply fills our suffering with his presence – PAUL CLANDEL.

JULY

PRAYER

*L*oving Father
It is the holiday season!
Everybody is en route: up country to go hunting;
    visiting relatives; to a game reserve or to the seaside.
And on our roads many motorists pay with their lives
    – unnecessary loss and grief which might have been avoided.
You gave us life – our most precious possession.
Help us to drive carefully.
Thank you for time available to relax with our family.
Bind us together as a family and to you, our Saviour.
Thank you for friends with whom we can share our holidays,
    and for sweet memories which we can treasure in our hearts.
We pray for those who have to work while we are relaxing.
Thank you for the beauty of winter landscapes.
Renew our spirits while we are at rest.
Help us not to neglect our Bible study,
our prayers or our quiet times in your presence during the holidays.
Make us the salt of the earth and the light of the world.
In the powerful name of Jesus Christ.

*A*men

Inner healing

We cannot possibly move towards a promising future if we are inhibited by the scars of old wounds. Gentle and loving hands are needed to heal these inner wounds. These hands belong only to Christ. All of us are tortured by things we would much rather forget. Certain memories keep haunting and upsetting us. Don't try to suppress or expel these memories. Bring them before God in prayer so that his forgiveness can erase them.

> *Forget the former things; do not dwell on the past. See, I am doing a new thing!*
> IS 43:18-19

Try as far as possible to redress all the wrong you have done, then you can boldly claim the forgiveness in which you can share through Christ's grace. It is one of the most enriching experiences in life when you experience his forgiveness.

Are you tormented by memories of disappointments, failures and mistakes in the past? Only if you allow them to oppress you will they have dominion over you. If you trust Christ fully, penitent prayer will have a healing power and will ban these memories from both mind and life. Christ makes you victorious.

*F*ather, I thank you and praise you for healing the painful memories and for granting me peace
through Jesus Christ.

For why, the Lord our God is good: his mercy is for ever sure; his truth at all times firmly stood, and shall from age to age endure
– WILLIAM KETHE.

2 JULY

Read HEWBREWS 7:11-28

Christ our Intercessor

J esus is our High Priest for ever, "because he always lives to intercede for us" (24). What a blessed comfort that in our ever changing
world something is permanent!

When Christ came in the flesh he also came as the mighty Inter-
cessor. He prayed for his disciples and for all those who would come to believe in him (Jn 17). He assured Peter that he would pray for him so that his faith might not fail him. On the cross he prayed that God would forgive those who had nailed him to the cross.

> *Therefore he is able to save completely*
> *those who come to God through him, because*
> *he always lives to intercede for them.*
>
> HEB 7:25

Now he has been exalted into the highest glory and sits at the right
hand of the Father. There he, the High Priest, performs his tasks eternally and continually for his children. In his name we can bring all our
prayers and needs to the throne of God.

Christ also gave us his Holy Spirit who teaches us to pray and who
sanctifies and purifies our prayers. He intercedes for us with groans
that words cannot express and also lays the duty upon us to be intercessors according to his example.

T hank you, Lord Jesus, that you lay our weak prayers before
the Father. Thank you for the privilege to be able to intercede for others. Make us faithful in this calling.

---

*A person who prays must necessarily elevate himself above
time and link himself to eternity* – ALEXANDER WHITE.

We are not of this world

We can hardly picture eternity for ourselves. We see only a poor reflection as in a mirror, and when we are caught up in sorrow of some kind we cannot see anything beyond our pain.

When a loved one dies, for instance, we can comfort ourselves with the thought that he or she has come to the crossing where they step over from this limited, physical existence into a wonderful, full life without any limitations. We must therefore not view death as the end, but rather as a new beginning. Our deceased loved ones have a far richer and more wonderful life beyond the grave. Their only sorrow could be the fact that we who are left behind, are unable to understand the truth about life and death.

> *For the perishable must clothe itself with the imperishable, and the mortal with immortality.*
> 1 COR 15:53

On many occasions Christ assured us of a life after death. That is why we believe in continued, sanctified love; in mutual prayer; in a wonderful reunion in a better world.

If we look at life in its entirety from the perspective of eternity, would it matter at all if death came sooner or later? It is not the length of our life on earth that counts, but the quality of the life we live. For the believer death has no sting, only victory.

*T*hank you, Lord Jesus, that you have conquered death and that we can therefore be victorious.

Don't cling to the world; there is more than enough room in heaven.

4 JULY

Quality of life and faith

If your faith has become powerless and you cling to it only because you are afraid of letting it go, it is time for spiritual stock-taking. God is not responsible for this recession in your faith – you alone are to blame. It is by no means the will of the Father that your faith should be a burden to you; on the contrary, you should continually reach new spiritual heights on wings of faith.

> *I will make breath enter you, and you will come to life . . . Then you will know that I am the LORD.*
> EZEK 37:5-6

You might be so industrious in your efforts to serve God through good deeds that you have no time left to find out what God's will is for your life. You could be so busy with God's work that you forget about God. You lose your awareness of his inspiring presence and power in your life and your work.

There is only one way of living a spiritually qualitative and jubilant life: Allow your life to be a temple of the Holy Spirit who will help you to know and to do God's will. Through the Spirit who lives within you a new life and a victorious faith is kindled. Consequently you will again experience a dynamic spiritual life and Christ will become a reality to you.

God did not call us to his service because of our strength and goodness, but because he desires to realise his plan for our lives. He wants us to be victorious in our faith.

When your Spirit lives in me, dear Father, I can see my faith gaining in spiritual power. For that great gift I thank you.

Without faith we can achieve very little; for those who believe, all things are possible – WILLIAM OSTER.

Soul-searching

Do you sometimes stop and prayerfully think about the direction your life is taking? If you do, you will find that all the choices you have had to make have led to the situation in which you find yourself at that moment, whether it be favourable or unfavourable.

Make time to compare your present circumstances with your aim in life. By regularly checking your ideals in life, you will avoid monotony. You will also gain new inspiration if you allow the Source of all truth to search your soul. Keep your prospects for the future strong and cheerful; don't let them become uninspired and vague, for then your daily existence will seem equally drab.

> *What is man that you are mindful of him, the son of man that you care for him?*
> PS 8:4

If you feel discouraged and depressed about your current situation and start querying the purpose of life, allow your heavenly Father through his Holy Spirit to take control of your mind and to guide you. He will inspire you to achieve what you have never thought possible. You will become a completely new person through God's grace, power and love.

Thank you, dear Creator and God, that your Spirit can re-create me to live a satisfactory, creative life because Jesus Christ has saved me.

What people think and say of you is indeed important, but what you know in your own heart is far more important
— ENA MURRAY.

Read 1 Timothy 6:3-21

Pursue your ideals

All of us have a desire to be successful in life. Yet more people fail than those who succeed. Why?

It is most surprising how many people don't have any goals in life. They accept every day from God's hand without considering how they can improve their quality of life. They lack a spirit of hope and expectancy, and because they expect nothing from life, they also don't get anything out of life.

Others have remarkable ideals, but believe that they will never reach these ideals. In the end they cry over lost opportunities or complain that they were never given a chance in life. Meanwhile they simply lacked a spirit of perseverance. There are also those who realise all their ideals in life, but are still unhappy because they are yearning for something which worldly treasures cannot give them.

> *Fight the good fight of the faith.*
> *Take hold of the eternal life to which you were called . . .*
> 1 TIM 6:12

Success is not the realisation of a burning ambition. It is the profound satisfaction that you are striving towards a worthy goal. Always set your goal to strive forwards and upwards so that you can reach a spiritual level where you have surrendered to God wholeheartedly. He will achieve his purpose for your life.

I thank you, Lord Jesus, that my success is not dependent on
this world, but that it depends on the work of
the Holy Spirit in my life.

Ideals are like stars: we never reach them, but like the mariners we use them to determine our direction in life – CARL SCHRUZ.

Read PSALM 31:20-25

Take heart!

There is no time when our courage is tested more than when we have lost a loved one. During these sad times we desperately need courage: to face the future alone; to be strong; to reach out to others; to make decisions. Death has already robbed you of so much that was dear to you – don't let it rob you of your courage as well!

Courage is built on two pillars: faith in the integrity of your goals, and confidence in your own capabilities. God provides both the sense of purpose as well as the power for these two components. We must therefore remain steadfast and not lose heart.

> *Be strong and take heart, all you who hope in the LORD.*
>
> PS 31:25

Faith and perseverance guarantees victory. In faith we can look past the earthly life and focus on eternity. Then we realise that death is only a milestone on the way to God's promised land. If we hold onto his promises, our courage will grow and flourish.

The most profound emotions are experienced when we are faced by grief. Grief can therefore serve a holy purpose for God grants us the grace to take heart and be courageous.

*A*lmighty God, renew my courage every day and help me to cling to your unfailing promises. Make me a courageous disciple of Jesus Christ.

Worry is the natural result when we put our hope in anything less than God and his will for our lives – BILLY GRAHAM.

Read MATTHEW 1:18-25

God with us

My prayer for you is that you will experience the presence of God today and that your heart will rejoice in it. May, for this day, these powerful words be engraved upon your armour: Immanuel – God with me. May it not be only a powerful saying in your life, but also a wonderful experience.

> *And they will call him Immanuel –*
> *which means, "God with us".*
> MT 1:23

God above you – to protect you against the heat of the sun in your everyday struggle.

God behind you – to keep you upright and support you whenever you are depressed and in danger of slipping.

God before you – to guide you in the way of righteousness and to teach you the way you should go.

God around you – to enfold you with his love and protect you against visible and invisible dangers.

God within you – to be the way, the truth and the life and to provide in every need according to the richness and glory of his grace.

May God be the All-sufficient with regard to all matters in your life, at all times, under all circumstances – from now unto all eternity.

My Saviour and Lord, words fail to describe the truth of your Immanual presence. I experience only gratefulness that I may be your child. I praise your holy name.

Man's source of happiness is neither centred within himself nor outside himself; happiness is man being reconciled with God
— BLAISE PASCAL.

Patriotism and peace

True patriotism is a love for your country which strives for peace for all.

The peacemaker yearns for the day when we shall be released from the sword, when money will be spent on food, housing and health services for the less privileged, instead of on weapons. This is the hope of the patriotic peacemaker.

Many dedicated patriotists don't march with flags or revel in war cries, but they work ceaselessly and in silence to establish peace among people by ensuring that righteousness prevails and by displaying goodwill. They pray that the nation will be strong enough to prefer peace to war. These are the people the Lord was referring to when he said, "Blessed are the peacemakers, for they will be called sons of God" (Mt 5:9).

> *Extol the LORD,*
> *O Jerusalem;*
> *praise your God,*
> *O Zion, for he strengthens*
> *the bars of your gates*
> *and blesses your people*
> *within you.*
> *He grants peace to your*
> *borders . . .*
>
> PS 147:12-14

If our ideal is to bring peace by establishing reconciliation and righteousness, we have begun to understand what is meant by true patriotism.

Father of peace, thank you that I can contribute to peace, that I may love my country, but above all, that I can love you!

I hope that my generation will be remembered for being the first generation to have firmly believed that there can be peace on earth – ARNOLD TOYNBEE.

Discover your happiness in God

All of us seek happiness, yet it seems to elude most of us. Perhaps it is because we tend to forget that the true source of happiness is the knowledge that our spirit is in harmony with God. If God is in the centre of our lives, it is possible to experience permanent happiness, even in the most distressing circumstances.

> *For whoever wants to save his life will lose it, but whoever loses his life for me will find it .*
>
> MT 16:25

Many people seek happiness in material things and treasure that which can be destroyed by moth and rust. These people do not possess their possessions, their possessions possess them. Others who believe that freedom from all restrictions will bring them happiness, lead a life of debauchery and too late they discover that they have strayed. You could try to find happiness in life by living for yourself only, without being aware of the needs of others, but then you will be isolated and unfulfilled.

Love is a precondition for happiness; love finds its highest fulfilment in serving others. Allow God in his love to control your life. Then you will experience happiness and inner peace. In Christ Jesus this ideal can be realised by one and all.

I search for you, Lord, with all my heart, because I know that I will only find true happiness in you. Find me in your great love, even when I have strayed from you in sin and vanity .

Outside himself God cannot give us happiness and peace, simply because there is no such thing as joy without God
— C S LEWIS.

Read PHILIPPIANS 4:10-20

Turn to God again

Sometimes we find it difficult to keep up with the rat race. It feels as if we are losing control of our circumstances. We feel overcome by the demands of life. These are the times when we fear that our faith will not carry us through. When circumstances seem to become more hopeless every day, when all our relationships seem to go wrong, we feel as if we are losing our grip on life.

When you feel that way, the balance between your spiritual attitude and the challenges of life has been disturbed. The demands of life seem greater than your faith.

> *I can do everything through him who gives me strength.*
> PHIL 4:13

When you have reached breaking point, go back to the basics of life which can activate and strengthen your faith and you will be assured of God's presence. Your equilibrium will be restored and you will see people and events in the correct perspective again. A living faith in God will have a stabilising effect when you find yourself in distressing circumstances. Turn to God with your needs, trust him unconditionally. He will bear your burdens every day.

Loving Father, I confess that I can do nothing without you. Thank you that through your grace and power I find it possible to tackle the demands of life and to triumph over them.

For those who share in the grace of God, no confession will ever come too late. God's grace is available at all times and those who seek the truth will enter into his grace
— ST CYPRIAN.

---

12 JULY

Read JAMES 1:2-8

Joy born out of suffering

Jesus asked us to obey his commands as he obeyed the commands of his Father so that joy can be in us and our joy may be complete (Jn 15:11). Christ's obedience included a cross and the sacrifice of a life, but this resulted in indescribable, eternal joy. That is why he can transform our grief into a joy of which nobody can rob us.

> Consider it pure joy, my brothers, whenever you face trials of many kinds . . .
> JAS 1:2

Joy is the flag waving at the top of the palace to show that the King is home. Our Lord knows that we are weak and sinful, therefore he fills us with an inner fountain of joy. This joy is manifested when we remember his birth, his death and resurrection, his ascension and the day of judgment; when we keep his commandments; when we witness for him and rejoice in those who accept the testimony.

If we are joyful children of God, particularly in times of trial, it will be a powerful testimony to the world. If the peace of God works within our hearts, the world will see something of his love. They will also desire to share this love and in that way we shall honour him.

Redeemer, help me to be joyful and to witness for you in this world. Help me to reflect your love to others.

Whenever I think of God, my heart is filled with such joy that the notes dance and leap from my pen; and since God has given me a joyful heart, I shall be pardoned for serving the Lord with a joyful spirit – FRANZ JOSEPH HAYDN.

A prayer in distress

Sometimes we find ourselves in a situation where we need an answer immediately. In such a situation, do what Nehemiah did: find immediate refuge in God.

It is astounding how God answers the prayers of those who fully trust him when they go through a crisis. Extreme emergencies require a "hotline" directly to God. If we fully submit to God's will, he will listen and answer even before we have formulated our prayer.

However, prayers in times of emergency should never take the place of regular and peaceful seclusion and quiet times with God. Only when a crisis requires immediate action can we call upon God using a "hotline" prayer, and then only because we can rely on a close relationship between God and us.

> *O LORD, God of heaven, the great and awesome God, who keeps his covenant of love with those who love him and obey his commands, let your ear be attentive and your eyes open to hear the prayer your servant is praying before you day and night . . .*
>
> NEH 1:5

God is always available when his children call to him with heart-rending cries of distress. He is already waiting to answer.

Lord, my God, I thank you for the assurance that my prayers in times of emergency will also reach you and that you wil do with them what you think best. Thank you, Lord Jesus, that you have made it possible for me to go to God unhindered.

If you are too busy to pray, you are indeed too busy – F B MYER.

14 JULY

Read ROMANS 8:31-39

Are you afraid to die?

Many Christians are afraid to die. However, we should try to unmask this enemy and struggle against him until the triumphant end.

Most people find the thought of physical death extremely intimidating. However, Christ freed us from the slavery of the fear of death. "Since the children have flesh and blood, he too shared in their humanity so that by his death he might destroy him who holds the power of death – that is, the devil – and free those who all their lives were held in slavery by their fear of death" (Heb 2:14-15).

> For I am convinced that neither death nor life . . . will be able to separate us from the love of God . . .
>
> ROM 8:38-39

Fear of the unknown could be the overpowering emotion when we think about death. However, Christ – who returned triumphantly from the grave – was the One to tell us about the place of glory we shall be going to after death. Why should we be afraid?

We fear death only if we regard it as the "end". When a person dies, people say, "He has gone". But in heaven it will resound, "He is here!" We therefore need not fear physical death. All we really need to fear, is to be separated from God.

Almighty Father, when I am faced with death and I tremble with fear, may I hear your Son saying: Do not let your hearts be troubled. Trust in God; trust also in me.

I shall not be going into darkness, because God is Light; I shall not be lonely, because Christ will be with me; it will not be unfamiliar country, for my risen Lord will be there!
— *CHARLES KINGSLEY.*

Triumph through faith

So many people have the wrong idea about faith. They think that they are incapable of living a dedicated life and are blinded by this fear; they don't believe that they can succeed and live a victorious life. They keep asking God for more faith; and yet their faith seems to remain ineffective.

It is not a matter of requiring more faith; it is merely a matter of using correctly what we already have. When Jesus called upon his disciples to have more faith, he appealed to them to lead a positive and constructive life. All of us can believe in something or someone, but without faith in Christ nobody can please God.

> *Now faith is being sure of what we hope for and certain of what we do not see.*
>
> HEB 11:1

Faith is the essence of our spiritual life. Without faith we cannot have communion with God; we can neither face life, nor can we deal with grief or problems. Faith is trusting God and accepting his guidance. The rewarding fruit of this faith is the assurance that he is with you and that he loves you. Faith makes everything that comes your way fall into place and become meaningful. In this way you will live a victorious life.

I thank you, God, for the faith that your Holy Spirit engenders in my heart, and that I can be triumphant through Jesus Christ who assures me of your love for me.

Faith is believing what you cannot see. The result is that you see what you can hardly believe – ST AUGUSTINE.

God is love!

As a result of broken relationships, misunderstandings, disillusion-ment, criticism or indifference many people feel rejected or are convinced that nobody loves them. If this emptiness in their lives is not dealt with in time, it could have tragic effects.

> *Who shall separate us from the love of Christ?*
> ROM 8:35

During his imprisonment and trial Jesus's friends deserted him. His enemies hated him. There was no vestige of love when he was humiliated, tortured and crucified. However, he was upheld by God's love and God exalted him through his triumphant resurrection.

If you feel deserted or unloved; if you feel convinced that life cannot offer you anything; if everything around you seems to fall apart – take heart! Your living Saviour has not deserted you. He, the One who knows what you think and understands how you feel, will fill your life with his love and grace.

Turn to Christ right now. Open your heart to him. Your life will be brightened by his grace and love and you will be uplifted from the depths of darkness. The Lord will fill you with hope and confidence to face life. Don't hesitate: just do it!

Eternal Rock, thank you that I have found a safe haven in you. Thank you that your love also guides me through the depths of darkness.

I am convinced that nine out of every ten patients in a psychiatrist's consulting room don't need psychiatric treatment; all they want is love, the kind of love God has taught us: unconditional love – PAUL TOURNIER.

Forget the past

N ever allow regret over the past to dominate your thoughts. If you dwell on your failures and defeats of the past you will hamper your spiritual growth. Forget about the times when a tardiness and a lack of enthusiasm robbed you of your ideals. Memories of that kind can cast a dark shadow over your life.

A living faith in Christ will always bring a fresh approach to life. The mistakes of the past will no longer have a paralysing effect on your life. Your whole attitude to life will change. Instead of always expecting the worst to happen, you will live in faith that God has prepared great things for you. Fear of the future will be replaced by faith and courage. An unforgiving attitude will be replaced by a will to forgive and forget. Even

> *. . . put off your old self, which is being corrupted by its deceitful desires . . . be made new in the attitude of your minds; and . . . put on the new self, created to be like God in true righteousness and holiness.*
>
> EPH 4:22-24

your health will improve. You will develop self-discipline and healthy habits. Your spirit will no longer be dominated by the failures of the past, but will be inspired by the Spirit of God, who will make you aware of all the wonderful prospects around and within you.

I praise you, holy Lord, for the past. I rejoice in the challenges that my present life is offering me and I put my trust in you for the unknown future through Jesus Christ who will give me strength.

Success can be achieved in anything for which you have unlimited enthusiasm – *CHARLES SCHWAB.*

18 JULY

The comfort of the Resurrection

Blessed are those who have a complete understanding of communion with the living Christ, since that is the true meaning of Christ's resurrection. This is our hope amidst our most profound sorrow. God gave us eternal life through Jesus Christ. That is the seed which makes it possible for us to reap the rich harvest of a future life – in spite of our tears and toil. The night of our deepest sorrow can never be so dark that is will blur the glorious image of our resurrected Lord.

> *I am the resurrection and the life. He who believes in me will live, even though he dies; and whoever lives and believes in me will never die.*
> JN 11:25-26

When loved ones die, or when our death is imminent, we are comforted by the joyful assurance of our Lord who promised that those who believe in him would never die. We are therefore not on our way to death, but to life eternal.

After having spent years in our earthly tent we shall move to a new eternal house in heaven. Our mortal bodies will be clothed with immortality. Death has been conquered and life will forever be triumphant. We shall be with the Lord eternally. This truth will help us to face and cope with any situation in life.

Jesus, I rejoice in your promise of resurrection. Help me to hold on to this hope through my faith in you, my Saviour.

Do not weep, because I shall not die; I am merely leaving the land of the dying to step over into the land of the living
— THE FINAL WORDS OF EDWARD THE CONFESSOR.

Read COLOSSIANS 3:1-4

Peace when tension mounts

Day after day the rat race seems to get worse. Efficiency and productivity have become all-important. As a result tension has become part of our lives. Our minds are overloaded with trivialities and we don't nourish ourselves with strong and positive thoughts. The result is that we are spiritually undernourished; we could even suffer from spiritual starvation. As a result of this our relationship with our heavenly Father becomes shallow and our attitude to life becomes gloomy.

To prevent this, we need to spend time with God. Christ was our perfect model: in stressful situations he isolated himself to find his strength and peace with his Father. If you have

> *Set your minds on things above, not on earthly things.*
> COL 3:2

strayed from God, try to find your way back to him immediately. Two minutes of fruitful communion with him, is worth more than twenty minutes during which your thoughts go astray. God does not judge you by the length of your prayers, but by the quality and sincerity of your love.

Ask God to take control of your life and ideals. Keep your conversation with him simple and honest. Look upon your time of prayer as a place of rest in your rushed life. Then you will feel his peace enfolding your entire being.

*H*oly Lord, you know how easily I become caught up in the rat race. Thank you that I can be quiet in your presence and rest by still waters where I can find peace.

You can easily build a throne for yourself with bayonets, but you will not sit on it for long — BORIS JELTSIN.

God's timing is perfect

God's timing is always perfect. You must therefore never become impatient if God allows delays in your life. The more you surrender to him, the clearer you will observe his perfect timing in your life. Never try, in your impatience, to force God to match his timing with your time schedule. You see your problems bound by an earthly time, whereas he sees them from an eternal perspective. God is perfect wisdom and he knows what is best for you.

> *I am the LORD; in its time I will do this swiftly.*
> IS 60:22

We don't always find it easy to accept God's timing. Sometimes we rush into his holy presence and demand his immediate intervention so that, according to our judgment, a disaster can be avoided. In such instances we are tempted to act on our own and according to our limited outlook, and then we are surprised when failure and grief are the final products.

This is a lesson which every Christian should learn: synchronise your timing with that of God. This is possible if you maintain a close and living relationship with Christ. If his will is all-important in your life and you are led by his Spirit, you will see God's perfect plan with your life and you will find peace.

Father, help me to forget about my own inadequate will and to focus on your perfect will and timing in my life.

The world around us will recognise us as disciples of Jesus when they observe our prayers being answered
— COLIN URQUHART.

Make Christ your partner

Sometimes one's daily tasks become very demanding and perhaps even boring. Inspiration and joy no longer fill your life and your attitude to life becomes negative. Perhaps you don't allow yourself the necessary sleep and relaxation; maybe you simply have too much on your plate; you cannot deal with it all, you become tense and you build up resentment against your job.

> *If a man remains in me and I in him, he will bear much fruit; apart from me you can do nothing.*
>
> JN 15:5

Do you feel that way? Ask yourself: Are you busy living and working without the sustaining power of Jesus Christ? Has your job become more important than your relationship with him? If that is the case, your life will be like an automaton: cold, callous and mere routine.

The answer to this problem is rooted in Christ. Make him your partner in life, then you will reach the peak of your productivity. Put every aspect of your life under his omniscient control. He has a better understanding of life than you have. Start each day in prayer. You will be assured of his presence. Go out and take charge of your job with confidence. Look up to your Guide and Friend – and discover the wonder of having joy and pride in your work.

Thank you that I can trust you, even for my daily task, o Lord! Help me to do my job every day as if I am working for you and not for people.

Talk to him in prayer about all your needs, your problems – even about your slackness in his service. You can never be too familiar or confidential with him – FRANCOIS FÉNELON.

God of comfort

Nobody can escape grief. We live in a world full of pain, suffering, disaster, distress and death. Against this background only One can change darkness into light; only One can heal a broken heart, bring peace in our hearts and put our minds at rest.

God does not guarantee that his children will be spared grief, but he does guarantee his loving comfort for those who are willing to open their hearts to him.

Faith in him is the gift of grace to make us strong enough to face life's challenges. Faith does not relieve us of the burden, but it gives us the strength to carry the burden and to triumph over any loss. This knowledge makes us worthy of carrying our own cross and it gives us the power to carry it joyfully, following the example of the One who bore the Cross.

> *The eternal God is your refuge, and underneath are the everlasting arms.*
> DEUT 33:27

We worship a God who is aware of our grief, who cares when we suffer and who has the power to do something about it. We may never doubt God's involvement in our suffering, otherwise we shall not gain anything from the dark periods in our lives.

God of comfort, comfort us in our suffering through the work of the Comforter whom you have sent us.

We are the extension lead. God is the power. We can only be strong if his power flows through us – CARLO CARETTO.

With God it is never too late

Have you ever wanted something to happen before a certain date? At the time, did you spend much time in prayer, imploring God to do something before that particular point in time, otherwise it would be too late? Nothing happened! You have learnt the painful lesson that you cannot force God to act, neither can you make him subject to your desires.

When Jesus heard that his friend Lazarus was dying, he did not hasten to go to him. When he eventually arrived in Bethany, he converted the tragedy of Lazarus's death into a triumphant glorification of God.

> *Jesus loved Martha and her sister and Lazarus.*
> *Yet when he heard that Lazarus was sick,*
> *he stayed where he was two more days.*
> *Then he said to his disciples, "Let us go back to Judea."*
> JN 11:5-7

At certain times in your life you might have felt that God did not act according to your time-table; at that time you really thought that God acted too late. However, God's timing is never out. His timing is perfect. He sees your life from an eternal perspective and in his omniscience he acts for your own good. Therefore, never stop him from moulding your life according to his perfect will. You will then live in harmony with him and you will find peace.

Forgive me, dear Lord, that I sometimes urge you in blind ignorance to act immediately. I lay my life and desires in your hands and resign myself to your perfect timing.

Luther spent the best of three hours a day in prayer
— ROBERT MURRAY MCCHEYNE.

24 JULY

Read JOHN 14:1-14

Human and Godly sympathy

True sympathy between people lies not so much in words, but rather in a deep, quiet togetherness. We can be with a person without saying a word, but he or she will know that you are a friend who is willing to listen, who understands and cares.

Few things in life can be more comforting than the sympathetic touch of a friendly hand. Tennyson wrote to a friend who had suffered a great loss through death, "Recently I attended a funeral and in silence I joined hands with one of the deeply bereaved as if spanning the grave. Speech seemed quite out of place and unnecessary. This letter cannot take away your grief, but it resembles the joining of hands across the grave. May it temper your grief."

> *I tell you the truth, anyone who has faith in me will do what I have been doing.*
> JN 14:12

However precious human sympathy might be, it will remain limited. God, in turn, understands perfectly. His sympathy is endless and miraculous. Because Christ himself became man, he can understand our pain whenever ties with loved ones are broken. He is almighty and therefore he is able to help. The comfort which his heavenly sympathy gives us, makes it possible for us to comfort others in turn.

Father, help me not to collapse under the burden of my grief, but to live by trusting in your love and support.

Give of yourself, forget about yourself, don't focus all your attention on yourself.

Faith in temptation

We are so often on the losing side where sin is concerned that we start doubting whether we shall ever be able to be what God has called us to be. We doubt whether victory will ever come our way. Is that how you feel? I can assure you that Christ can help you because he himself was tempted.

Perhaps you have been battling against a specific sinful habit or weakness for a long time. You are sincerely trying to break this habit, but time and again you fail to keep your promise to God and slowly but surely you become weaker and weaker spiritually. In the end you simply give up.

God, however, never gives up. He confirms over and over again that you can be saved. He has understanding for the power of temptation which clings to you like a burr. Christ was tempted just like you, in fact much worse. He resisted the temptations and expects you to do the same in his strength. He puts his power at your disposal. This will ensure that you triumph over your sin. Fight with perseverance, fight courageously and in steadfast faith in the name and power of Jesus Christ, then you will be sure to overcome your weakness.

> *Perseverance must finish its work*
> *so that you may be mature and complete, not lacking anything.*
> JAS 1:4

Thank you, dear Lord, that you enable me to resist temptations. Strengthen my faith in your omnipotence so that I can also have victory over sin in my life.

If you cannot believe in God when everything goes wrong, you still don't know the meaning of faith – SPURGEON.

Never lose courage

People often doubt whether they will ever be able to lead a good life, because they never seem to succeed in growing spiritually. They abandon their highest ideals because they feel so discouraged. Consequently their testimony loses its credibility, and the church of Christ eventually suffers.

As a Christian you should live according to Christ's commandments. This is not always easy, and you might even often be discouraged as a result of problems. Temptations will affect your perspective on life and at times you might feel like quit-

> *Trust in the Lord and do good.*
>
> PS 37:3

ting. Just remember, the heroes of faith portrayed in the Bible, could remain steadfast in faith because they put all their trust in God. Complete trust and faith in God made it possible for Jesus to conquer sin, Satan and death. Through faith the Christian church was established successfully and grew in spite of opposition.

Never lose courage in the face of hardship. Never stop testifying for Christ. Put all your trust in God, for he will never fail you even if you should fail him. Your faith will uphold you, in spite of all your problems. This is the unfathomable grace of God.

*H*oly Spirit, through your inspiration I shall keep trusting God and serve him in faith at all times.

Courage is to do what has to be done, inwardly inspired by the conviction that you can trust God to do the rest.

Praise the Lord

Praising the Lord is one of the most remarkable powers used by the Holy Spirit to lead us in our spiritual lives. Put this remedy to the test. Whenever our lives are threatened by dark clouds of trials and we become more and more depressed, we tend to doubt God's wisdom and his goodness. Then the time has come to exchange our doubts and self-pity for praise and thanksgiving.

It might sound silly to sing and be thankful when you feel depressed, but this is God's way of lifting us out of the depths of our sorrow and allowing him to reveal the glory of his presence.

> *Though you have made me see troubles, many and bitter, you will restore my life again . . .*
> *My tongue will tell of your righteous acts, all day long.*
>
> PS 71:20, 24

Don't tell yourself that there is nothing in your life for which you can praise God. God, for one, is still there; he has not deserted you; his love shines through your life too. As soon as you have realised this once again, you will discover God in nature, in the Holy Scriptures and in others. Life will smile at you just the same as before and you will revel in the fact that your faith in God has once again proved itself to be a dynamic force in your life.

Create in me a thankful heart and mind and help me to triumph over depression in the name of Jesus Christ. I praise you, Father, and remember all your wonderful acts.

Bow your heart before the Lord every minute of the day, then the once-a-day-worship will no longer simply be a habit-forming physical action – STELLA SEYFFERT.

Persevere in prayer

When we are grief stricken and need the healing power of prayer more than ever, we often find it difficult to pray. However, don't think that a sorrowful heart cannot find consolation in prayer. The deciding factor is not how well you can pray, but the fact that you pray. God desires you to direct your thoughts and emotions towards him.

> *We do not know what we ought to pray for, but the Spirit himself intercedes for us.*
>
> ROM 8:26

You thereby acknowledge that he is with you – even in the darkest moments. Simply whisper a prayer – amidst your pain – and implore God to comfort you and to grant you strength, wisdom, calm and peace. You will feel him touching you with a comforting hand and you will be blessed to see the light shining through the darkness again.

A sincere prayer means confessing your limitations, your distress, your willingness to be changed and your preparedness to be enriched by God's love. He never answers prayers because they are perfect, but because he reaches out to people in distress. Also, you don't pray in isolation. The Holy Spirit intercedes for you in his infinite wisdom, with insight which is beyond your understanding. Moreover, in your weakness and insecurity he prays for you according to the will of God.

Never rebel against God when you feel incapable of praying to him. Hold on to the eternal truth that God's love for you will never change!

Lord, teach me how to pray, and grant that I shall proceed from the dark valley of sorrow and step out into the blessed gift of your eternal light.

The person who has learnt to pray, has discovered the biggest secret of a dedicated and happy life on earth – WILLIAM LAW.

False peace

In countries where earthquakes are common there is often an ominous silence directly before the earthquake strikes. It is as if earth holds her breath in awe of the approaching disaster. All is quiet; however, everybody is facing extermination.

The same applies to God's silence regarding the false peace proclaimed in his name. Many people incorrectly interpret this silence of God as peace; this silence will, however, be followed by his final judgment.

> *'Peace, peace,' they say, when there is no peace.*
> JER 6:14

How can this false peace be turned into God's true peace? Obedience and a life of dedication will bring true peace. Those who have fully surrendered their will to the perfect will of God, will invariably find God's true peace, because he is the source of peace. The moment we start sharing in his peace, we learn the real meaning of the word. Christ's death and resurrection is our guarantee of true peace – which God confirms by saving us from our sins. When we repent and confess, true peace will fill our lives and we shall be able to proclaim, "Peace, peace!" because of our loving relationship with God and because we shall fully share in his peace.

*P*rotect me, dear Saviour, from becoming a partner to the false peace of this sinful world. Grant me the true peace which is only possible in a life fully surrendered to you.

A peace treaty is not worthy of its name if it carries the germ of renewed violence – *IMMANUEL KANT.*

God-given opportunities

One person can experience a particular situation as being a nightmare; while another person can regard it as a God-given opportunity. One person succumbs to his problems and refuses to sort them out; another gives her utmost and gains a victory. Which of these two are you?

Do not try to run away from your problems. A Christian faces his problems courageously and in faith, because he knows that the Lord will give him the power to be victorious.

> *No one will be able to stand up against you all the days of your life. As I was with Moses, so I will be with you; I will never leave you nor forsake you.*
>
> JOS 1:5

The Christian warrior is not oblivious of dangers and he or she often experiences fear. Faith does not imply the absence of fear, but the victory over fear in the powerful name of Jesus Christ. Our victory does not lie in escape or in despondency, but in our joining the battle and in being faithful in prayer. God is the conqueror in this battle. We may also appeal to the promise God made to Joshua, "Do not be terrified; do not be discouraged, for the LORD your God will be with you wherever you go" (Jos 1:9).

*B*lessed Redeemer, you overcame all obstacles because you trusted your Father unwaveringly. Help me to convert my problems into opportunities through the power which you grant me.

Don't lose courage! Never ever lose courage! Do not ever, ever, ever lose courage . . . not with regard to important matters, and especially not with regard to the insignificant ones
— WINSTON CHURCHILL.

Pursue love

These days there is so little love, so much jealousy and bitterness in the world, that we are often overcome by these negative and destructive powers. Unless we remain watchful and faithful in prayer, we shall likewise start thinking and acting in a negative manner. The words of the new commandment which Jesus gave us are therefore extremely important, "My command is this: Love each other as I have loved you" (Jn 15:12).

We need the inspiration and guidance of the Holy Spirit if we wish to counteract this lack of love. We need to truly love Christ and this love should spur us on to lead a positive life. Love must control our thoughts, words and deeds. Whatever we say and do will then be inspired by love and we shall lead a life which is good in the sight of the Lord.

> And he has given us this command:
> Whoever loves God must also love his brother.
> 1 JN 4:20

This is the formula which we must use if we wish to survive in this life so lacking in love. As exemplified in Jesus Christ we shall conquer hatred through love. Jesus demonstrated it to us when on the cross he prayed for those who had crucified him.

Holy God, I worship you as the source of love. I am not worthy of anything, yet you grant me love in abundance. Help me to follow your example and to share my love abundantly.

If I give of my possessions I give but little. It is when I am willing to sacrifice myself for the sake of others that I begin to understand the true meaning of love — KAHLIL GIBRAN.

Notes

AUGUST

PRAYER

*H*eavenly Father
In your grace guide me through this month.
Like Abraham and Enoch, Moses and every one
    in the gallery of great believers we learn about in Hebrews 11
    I want to believe unconditionally –
But all too often I am like a Thomas, who first wanted to touch
    and see.
My faith is often limited to what I experience through my senses
    my eyes and my fingertips.
I would dearly want to believe in what I cannot see
    and quietly acknowledge, "My Lord and my God!"
Through your Spirit guide me to an honest and practical faith
    which will form an unbreakable bond between me and Jesus
    Christ.
In my heart I desperately want to bear the inviolate hope:
    the expectation that all my secret ideals will be realised;
    that my spiritual life will improve and grow in love and
    knowledge and truth so that I can make the right decisions.
Keep the flame of optimism burning in my heart.
Lord, I want to love you.
In sincere honesty I want to be able to say, "Lord, you know
    everything, You know that I love you!"
I want to love others with a sincere, unselfish
    love which removes all barriers
    and makes reconciliation a reality.
In the month of August bring me to a new understanding
    of faith, hope and love.

*A*men

Grief in perspective

If we are sure that we are children of God we have a guarantee that trials, sorrow and pain cannot break us. It is not God's will that we should remain untouched by pain, but he expects us not to lose hope when we grieve and to see our trials in perspective. In spite of our sorrows, we must affirm our faith in life. Faith is not an insurance policy against grief – only the grace of God will see you through your sorrow.

> *Those who sow in tears will reap with songs of joy. He who goes out weeping, carrying seed to sow, will return with songs of joy, carrying sheaves with him.*
>
> PS 126:5-6

Remember, we never bear the burden of our pain on our own. Christ gives us the strength to bear our burden with dignity. We just need to ask what we must do and how we must act now that this pain has come into our lives. Then yesterday's trials become more bearable and we no longer fear tomorrow.

We go through the most deeply felt experiences in the darkest hours of grief and pain. We see God more clearly through a veil of tears than in peals of laughter. In this way we experience our sorrow and loss as a prelude to a fuller and richer life.

Dear Lord and Father, you have taught us that we shall find strength in quietness and trust. Give me that strength to gladden my heart in this dark hour.

The strangest truth of the Gospel is that redemption is born out of suffering – *MILO L CHAPMAN.*

2 AUGUST

Read COLOSSIANS 4:2-6

Wait on God's answer

ust we submit our desires to God and then leave him to answer them in his own good time, without our repeated reminders? Or should we constantly remind him of our needs and desires? This has been a point of debate for many decades. In fact, both arguments could be correct. True prayer is not controlled by rigid rules. It is the expression of God's holy Spirit at work in the hearts and lives of his children.

> *Devote yourselves to prayer, being watchful and thankful.*
>
> COL 4:2

The route prayer takes under the guidance of the Holy Spirit, is not always familar, but often it follows a path which God has chosen for you and your personal needs. The result is always surprising and encouraging.

On whichever path of prayer you find yourself, it is important for you to walk along that path purposefully and faithfully, always aware of God's holy and loving presence. Then you will recognise answered prayers and sing songs of praise about the way in which God has wrought his will in your life.

ord, I shall wait on you and when I impatiently want to act in my own strength, send your Holy Spirit to help me to wait patiently and prayerfully.

True prayer is a spiritual state which creates a channel between the almighty God and mere mortals. Only the sin of mankind can block this channel – GEORGE ALLEN.

Blessed are those who mourn

E verything that happens to us has a holy purpose in God's design for our lives – even grief. There is so much grief and pain in this world. When death strikes, there is an emptiness in our hearts, homes and our existence. When we, therefore, hear Christ say, "Blessed are those who mourn, for they will be comforted," it is balm for the soul (Mt 5:4).

The greatest loss in your life is if you pass through your time of grief without having gained anything, without having discovered God's love anew.

> *Blessed are those who mourn,*
> *for they will be comforted.*
> MT 5:4

Grief teaches us about God's tender comfort and his all embracing love. It also shows us the care and love of our neighbour. In our grief we again discover our God and our fellow human beings.

We may suddenly be driven to the dark depths of despair. But even in this desperate abyss we will be amazed to discover that, with God in our lives, a new beauty and power has been poured into our hearts. Grief teaches us that we have not been abandoned in our suffering and need for comfort and encouragement. God is there with us. Blessed indeed are those who mourn like this, for they shall be comforted.

H elp me Lord, stand by me in my suffering. I call on you and wait on your relief. Take my hand and comfort me through the dark hours.

God's promises are like the stars: the darker the night, the brighter they shine – DAVID NICHOLAS.

Faith and work satisfaction

Satan always tries to sabotage the spiritual life of God's children. He passes no one by and so Elijah, the warrior of faith, overnight becomes Elijah, the one who lacks faith and opts out to sit under a broom tree in abject despair.

A prophet on strike! Satan rendered him powerless by means of physical exhaustion and fear of the wicked Jezebel. Elijah complained to God and God strengthened him physically and spiritually, his rebelliousness abated and he was at peace.

> *"I have had enough, LORD",*
> *he said. "Take*
> *my life; I am no better than*
> *my ancestors."*
> 1 KINGS 19:4

Are you sitting under a broom tree? God also asks you, "What are you doing here?" (9, 13). When God asked Elijah this question, Elijah told him how hard he had worked for God, but no mention was made of taking time to meet with God and to hear his gentle whisper. That is the crux of the problem. After he had met with God, Elijah was given a new commandment, "Go back the way you came" (15). There is still much work to be done. With a renewed faith in God's omnipotence he could now tackle his task with new vigour and courage.

Be quiet before God. This will lead you to Christ, your perfect example who also sought to be quiet before God. He will give you rest and peace and strength to tackle the road ahead.

*H*eavenly Father, take my hand and lead me back to life with its many demands and give me strength and faith to do my duty according to Christ's example.

Sometimes happiness helps. Work always does
— JAPANESE SAYING.

AUGUST 5

Read ECCLESIASTES 2:4-11

Having everything and possessing nothing

The author of Ecclesiastes had everything that one could desire in life. He revelled in creative works; he built palaces and laid out gardens; he possessed many animals and had his own choir and orchestra; he could buy whatever he liked. Yet he concluded that "everything is meaningless, a chasing after the wind."

It is indeed true that one can have everything one desires and still be depressed and frustrated. It is also true the rich are not always happy or at peace. One of the biggest tragedies is that people regard the acquiring of earthly possessions as their sole objective in life. They often ignore the Giver of these abundant gifts. If these gifts impress you so much that you are unable to appreciate the omnipotence and generosity of the Giver, all your possessions will lose their charm and value.

> Yet when I surveyed all that my hands had done and what I had toiled to achieve, everything was meaningless, a chasing after the wind.
> ECCLES 2:11

We must realise that a loving and generous Father bestows every gift on us. Then we will develop a sense of appreciation which helps us to enjoy his gifts. When you have learnt appreciation you will also be able to say, thank you, Father! for every gift bestowed on me, the most precious of which is a thankful heart.

God of grace, place in my thankful heart an unlimited appreciation of all the wonderful gifts which you have bestowed on me.

To be satisfied when you possess very little, is difficult; but to be satisfied when you possess a lot, impossible
— *BARON ESCHENBACH.*

Read EPHESIANS 3:14-21

Do you have God in your heart?

The image of Christ knocking at the door of our hearts, is so well-known that it is in danger of losing its impact. Christ is never represented as someone who will force the door open – and that of course is true. However, we must remember that he does not stand in front of that door like a beggar, but as the One who has right of access to our lives.

Christ comes to you to change and inspire your whole life if you will allow him to do so. The single most important thing that you can do in life, is to invite him into your life as the most honoured guest.

> *I pray . . . that Christ may dwell in your hearts through faith . . . being rooted and established in love . . .*
>
> EPH 3:16-17

Joyfully accept the discipline which he will expect of you, because what he will do for you cannot be brought about in any other way. If you invite him into your life, he will reign in your heart. Even if you then still disappoint him, stumble and make mistakes, he will never leave you, because he will not abandon the work of his hands. His healing and restoring power will always lead you to a deeper and more faithful life.

*W*onderful Lord Jesus, enter my life as the most honoured guest. Thank you for the wonderful privilege of having you in my life. Through your grace help me to be worthy of your presence in my life.

I would quite easily be able to believe in the Redeemer, but then I must see a Christian who at least looks redeemed – *GANDHI.*

Christ is the key

We do not know what the future holds, but we do know Who holds the future in his hands. We do not know the road, but we do know him who shows the way. Although we do not have answers to every "why?" through faith we know the God who has all the answers in Jesus Christ.

That is why having a personal relationship with Christ is so important. If we, through God's grace, want to use his gifts of forgiveness and peace, we must be prepared to, in faith, step out courageously into the unknown. His presence will provide all the comfort we shall need.

> *Now we see but a poor reflection as in a mirror; then we shall see face to face.*
> 1 COR 13:12

Discuss your questions with God and accept the sovereignty of Christ. Then you will share in a God-given comprehension and will become the recipient of wisdom and power to comfort you and give you rest. One day we shall meet face to face with our Lord and we shall be given all the answers. Until that day, however, we shall have to live courageously and faithfully without all the answers, never letting go of him who can and will answer them in time.

Loving Lord, help me to accept and live within my limitations and to step out joyfully on the road which you have shown me.

If we could reach God solely along the path of knowledge and dispute, only the learned and gifted would be successful. God, however, has constructed the road into a "Via Regiam" – a royal highway – LANCELOT ANDREWS.

8 AUGUST

Read ROMANS 15:7-13

Peace in my heart

Peace is God's gift which he gives abundantly to all believers. However, we spend sleepless hours in fear and anxiety because we try to find that peace in other places. We punish ourselves unnecessarily by seeking calmness and peacefulness elsewhere. Instead of peace, we find tension.

Peace in your heart is the quiet but sure conviction that you are securely in God's care and for this reason life's opportunities are greater than its trials. When you accept God as the source of peace and joy and in faith are bound to him, you have taken the first step on the road which leads to peace of mind. If your spirit is in harmony with God, this attitude will affect your relationships with people and you will live in peace with others. When you are at odds with God, it is impossible to maintain good relationships with other people. Few things can so totally destroy your peace of mind as when you live in discord with God and people. To rectify this unhealty situation, you must heal your relationship with Christ and see to it that it remains sound.

> *May the God of hope fill you with*
> *all joy and peace as you trust in*
> *him, so that you may overflow with*
> *hope by the power of the Holy Spirit.*
> ROM 15:13

The wonder of the peace which you receive because of the merit of Christ, is that God himself leads you "beside quiet waters" where you will find peace.

Teach me, O Lord, how to nurture your peace in my heart and to pass it on to people around me.

The shortest route between two people is a smile.

Read ISAIAH 26:16-21

Living victoriously

Our spiritual life cannot survive on emotions. A positive and living faith exists independently of "feelings" or "atmosphere". Many people think that if they can live in a constant state of spiritual tension, they will develop spiritual "muscles" and their faith will be strong. They place their trust in a stimulating atmosphere and the quality of their spiritual experiences vacillates according to their state of mind. When the inspiration of the moment has passed, they experience a spiritual collapse and are often completely immobilised.

> *Your dew is like the dew of the morning;*
> *the earth will give birth to her dead.*
>
> IS 26:19

Isaiah 26:3 shows us the right road to spiritual well-being, "You will keep in perfect peace him whose mind is steadfast, because he trusts in you." For us to be able to live victoriously we cannot allow ourselves to be led by our emotions only. It is a far too shaky foundation for us to build on. A victorious life also does not depend on circumstances, but requires a heart and spirit that is at peace with God and lives under his grace.

The presence of Christ enables us to remain faithful even in the most desperate of circumstances. With this conviction Paul and Silas, bound in chains, could sing songs of praise in their cold cell. We too, can sing jubilantly when in faith we have an enduring relationship with God.

Lord, I thank you that I am a child of yours and that circumstances can never change this fact. Help me always to live close to you.

Our biggest mistake is that we often do nothing because we can only do so little. Just do what you can – SYDNEY SMITH.

Read MATTHEW 6:5-15

Forgive, for God forgives you

F orgiveness is a crucial requirement for being a Christian. Christ himself deemed it so important that he included it in the Our Father, the prayer he taught us.

If we are prepared to forgive others, God will forgive us. However, we tend to hoard and nurse grievances and find it difficult to forgive. It is then that God's love and grace must be able to work freely in our lives. What you are unable to do for yourself, the Spirit of God can do for and through you. If you find it difficult to forgive, allow the love of God to fill your heart and purify it of all bitterness and unforgivingness.

> *For if you forgive men when they sin against you, your heavenly Father will also forgive you.*
>
> MT 6:14

We often hear people say that they will forgive, but that they will never be able to forget. That is not forgiveness and does not contribute to your spiritual development. After all, God did not forgive only some of your sins, he forgave *all* of them. Therefore you cannot offer others only partial forgiveness. Forgive completely and forget all grievances which could have a negative influence on your life. Be a willing channel for God's forgiveness and experience the joy of being liberated from the bonds of an unforgiving attitude.

L ord Jesus, help me through the power of your love and your Spirit's purifying presence, to forgive because you have forgiven all my sins.

Forgiveness is man's deepest need and his greatest achievement — HORACE BUSHNELL.

Guard against bitterness

E mbittered people are never happy. The bitterness gnaws away at them and can eventually destroy them.

The only antidote for bitterness is to be purified by the love of Christ and to reflect his disposition. His nearness and love neutralises bitterness. He enables you to lead a reconciled life. Through God's grace the bitter waters of Marah in your life will become "sweet".

People who have suffered sometimes cling to their bitterness, only to drive the Light out of their lives, to stumble forward in the dark and eventually they become lonely people. To triumph over bitterness you must submit yourself to Jesus Christ. He has the ability to renew all things. If you live in harmony with his will, you will experience the liberating power of his love. You will continue on your way with a song in your heart and get more pleasure out of life.

> When they came to Marah, they could not drink its water because it was bitter. . . Then Moses cried out to the LORD . . . and the water became sweet.
>
> EX 15:23, 25

Remember, not far from Marah lies Elim with its seven springs and many palm trees. There your heart, free of bitterness, will sing songs of praise and you will see how sweet life can be.

H elp me, O Lord, to experience your presence in such a way that all bitterness is banished from my life. Give me more of your loving disposition in my life.

Bitterness is like burning down your own house to get rid of a rat — *HARRY EMERSON FOSDICK.*

Unanswered prayer

What a tragedy it would have been if Christ's prayer in the Garden of Gethsemane was answered! He became our Redeemer because this prayer was not answered.

Sometimes God does not answer because he has something better in store for us. Moses prayed for God to allow him to enter Canaan. God did not listen to him, because Moses had been disobedient at Kadesh. Nevertheless God gave him a heavenly Canaan which was immeasurably more than what he could have asked for or imagined (Deut 33:1-6). David pleaded with God in prayer for the life of his child, but God did not spare the child's life.

> *"My Father, if it is possible, may this cup be taken from me."*
> MT 26:39

But David was brought to confessing his sins and the result of this act he described in the unforgettable Psalm 51. Paul prayed that God should take away his affliction – God did not do this and he continued to suffer, but he experienced the truth of God's promise, "My grace is sufficient for you."

God answers all prayers directed to him in faith. He does not always answer in the way we would want him to, but at some time in God's loving dealings with us, we are given the answer after all. When we look back at a later stage, we shall be thankful that the answer was given according to his will and not our desires.

Jesus of Gethsemane, teach me to say as you did, "Yet, not as I will, but as you will."

Prayer is not a way of using God. Prayer is a method of dedicating ourselves to God so that he can use us
— WILLIAM BARCLAY.

From the bitter wells to the fountain of life

At some time in our life we all have to pass the bitter fountains of Marah. At such times Christ provides the only comfort in life and death: we belong to him for time and eternity.

At Marah God showed Moses a piece of wood which he was to use to sweeten the waters. For us this becomes a symbol of the cross – a cursed piece of wood where Christ healed the fountain of our bitterness and suffering. To Christ it meant death, but for us it brought life eternal.

When God adds this piece of wood to our life's cup, it becomes sweet and palatable and we exclaim gratefully, "Everything has been made new." Then we understand the purpose of our suffering, because we

> *The grass withers and the flowers fall, but the word of our God stands for ever.*
>
> IS 40:8

understand the reason why he had to suffer – to comfort all those who are grieving.

When the effect of this comfort wears off and your grief bears you down again, remember: Christ holds your hand in his! He is your Intercessor who died and rose again, ascended into heaven and intercedes for you with God. Marah is merely a stop along the road where we learn one of life's lessons. We continue our journey with our hand in his, bound for our ultimate destination – the heavenly Canaan and eternal rest.

*H*oly Lord Jesus, thank you for your consolation which gladdens our hearts. Thank you for your suffering so that our suffering will never be unbearable. Help me to be strong when I am tested.

When despair says, A cloud has obliterated the sun! faith tells us, Behind the clouds you will find the sun! – F VAN VLEDDER.

14 AUGUST

Read ISAIAH 61:1-11

Faith that inspires

Have all your dreams, ideals, ambitions and most promising prospects ever crumbled around you? Has a single incident wiped out everything that you have worked and prayed for and all you have left are the ashes of what was once a burning ambition? Rest assured that you are not alone, for many others have walked this road, perhaps carrying an even heavier burden.

However dark your prospects seem to be, don't wallow in self-pity. In faith, pick up the pieces and try to make sense of your disaster. If others could have persevered through God's grace and have been victorious, why can't you? Yes, you might say, it's easy for you to talk, but I have to face the stark reality and deal with it.

> *For as the soil makes the young plant come up and a garden causes seeds to grow, so the Sovereign LORD will make righteousness and praise spring up before all the nations.*
>
> IS 61:11

Then you must use all the means of grace that God has placed at your disposal: prayer, support and encouragement through the promises to be found in the Scriptures, the example of other children of God, the power of positive thinking. This brings you to the road of victory.

If you believe that you can be successful, God will give you the victory. Inspired by your faith, you will in turn be able to encourage and comfort others.

Lord, help me to be victorious through your presence and to believe in the future through Christ Jesus, the Victor.

Lord, give me strength to do what you ask of me; then ask of me what you will – ST AUGUSTINE.

Read GALATIANS 6:11-18

A new person versus new arguments

People can argue at length about religion, but the only criterion is whether it makes any difference to their lives. The best argument for the validity of Christianity is a Christian. Is that person easy to get on with, trustworthy, unselfish, pleasant, living a chaste life? It is no good to proclaim that you believe in God, if it is not demonstrated in your daily life.

An effective faith enriches your spiritual life, produces a more profound inner awareness and brings about a radical change in your life through the Holy Spirit who lives in you. You must never forget that the Christian faith is only effective when expressed through a dedicated life in the throes of the battles of every

> *Neither circumcision nor uncircumcision means anything; what counts is a new creation.*
> GAL 6:15

day. It does not mean running away from life, but to meet it head-on and winning the battle because you have been obedient to the will of God. This ideal can only be achieved in a life which has been radically changed through the power of the living God.

Our Lord and Saviour, may my life speak louder than all my words, through the work of your Holy Spirit in my life.

In heaven things are different, but here on earth "life" is synonymous with change. Perfection means having changed often. — *JOHN HENRY NEWMAN.*

16 AUGUST

Read 2 CORINTHIANS 5:11-21

Reconciled with God

The crux of being a Christian is that we know that Christ came into this world to reconcile us with God.

Man was separated from God when in his stubborn disobedience he wanted to be independent of God. Man thought that now he was free, but in fact he had become a slave to forces far stronger than he.

However, even though man turned away from God, God had not abandoned his creation. He reached down to touch us in the person of Jesus Christ. Through Christ's earthly ministry God demonstrated to us what we could become through his love and grace. We can be free of sin, we can have the enriching experience of his presence in us and share in the communion with him. This leads us to experience spiritual growth and become spiritually mature.

> All this is from God, who reconciled us to himself through Christ, and gave us the ministry of reconciliation.
>
> 2 COR 5:18

It is God's dearest wish that those who are far from him, should be drawn closer through the love of Jesus Christ. May you experience this in your life, whether it be for the first time or a repeated experience.

Thank you, Lord Jesus, that you have paid the price in order for all people, including me, to be reconciled with God.

God creates out of nothing. Therefore, until you become nothing, God cannot make of you a new creation
— MARTIN LUTHER.

Christist who never changes

When misfortune overtakes us, we realise how fragile, weak and transcient we are and how insignificant our mortal dwelling is. Our years pass by in the blink of an eye and we feel threatened and insecure.

However, in spite of all this we are assured of God's omnipotence and immortality. When we move out of the light into the darkness, God's light is always there – when we depart from this life and face death, God is there. With our hand in his we shall take our last steps. Because our faith is firmly anchored in the living and unchanging Christ, we can fearlessly face life and death.

> *Jesus Christ is the same yesterday and today and for ever.*
> HEB 13:8

We often feel powerless in our grief and loss, but then we are comforted by the support of our eternal God who in Jesus Christ assures us of his infallible love. May we, in his strength, bear our sorrow courageously.

I love you, O Lord, be my strength and power. Draw my attention from the mortal to the eternal and stay with me always.

We have the whole of eternity in which to celebrate our victories, but only one short hour before the sun sets to achieve them – *ROBERT MOFFAT.*

18 AUGUST

Read PHILIPPIANS 3:1-14

Making peace with my memories

Pleasant memories are precious and bring us much joy, but unpleasant memories can make us very unhappy and rob us of our peace of mind. Jesus Christ is the Prince of Peace. He can and wants to free you from those bad memories. In his grace he wants to strengthen and liberate you and bring you rest.

> *But one thing I do: Forgetting what is behind and straining towards what is ahead, I press on . . .*
> PHIL 3:13

In order for you to be freed from memories of the past, you must set aside time to be quiet and alone with God. Praise and thank him that in his grace he is there for you. Confess your sins and plead for your forgiveness. Proclaim Christ as your Redeemer and then resist all negative thoughts. Ask for the guidance of the Holy Spirit and earnestly pray that Christ will heal the pain through his love and forgiveness. Put those disturbing memories behind you. Perhaps a feeling of rejection, a divorce, lovelessness or feelings of guilt have left a scar. Jesus knows about it, he can heal you and give you peace of mind.

Dedicate each day to Christ, love yourself and your fellow human beings; and most important of all, love God. Thank him for the healing and peace abundantly poured out on you.

Thank you, heavenly Comforter, that you heal the scars of hurtful memories and that you give me peace of mind.

One cannot change the past but you can learn from it
— ENA MURRAY.

See the light

L ife does not only have a dark side. We must be sure of this fact when we become depressed and when it feels as if there is nothing left in life to lift our spirits and to spur us on to meet life's challenges.

Spiritual barrenness is not unknown in the lives of God's children. Initially people will sympathise with your negative attitude to life, but all too soon you will chase them away if you can't do anything about your negativity, because people are attracted by joy, beauty and a cheerful and loving attitude.

When life presents you with its dark side, remember that God's goodness is still there: you will find it in the smell of the freshly ploughed fields after the rain; the love in the eyes of a child; spontaneous laughter. The wonderful reality of God's love and his will for your life will lift you out of your depression, and singing triumphantly, you will rise above your circumstances.

> *How I long for the months gone by, for the days when God watched over me, when his lamp shone upon my head and by his light I walked through darkness!*
>
> JOB 29:2-3

J esus, thank you that I find the strength in you to live victoriously in spite of the clouds which sometimes darken my horizon.

As long as there is hope, only a coward loses courage
— BERTRAND RUSSEL.

20 AUGUST

Read JAMES 1:19-27

The road to happiness

Happiness is like a butterfly; as long as you try to catch it it will elude you, but when you sit down, it will come and sit on your shoulder. Happiness is not dependent on circumstances, but on your attitude towards God and life. The more we make others happy, the more happiness we experience ourselves.

The secret of happiness lies not in doing what you want to do, but in willingly doing what you must do. That means you must ask what you can put into life. Devote yourself to God, to others and to your life's task.

> *But the man who looks intently into the perfect law that gives freedom, and continues to do this, not forgetting what he has heard, but doing it – he will be blessed in what he does.*
>
> JAS 1:25

Above all, be thankful. Thankfulness goes hand in hand with happiness. A thankful person is inevitably a happy person, because he lives in the knowledge that God has given him infinitely more than he deserves.

God wants us all to be happy. Happiness is not within us or outside of us – happiness means being united with Jesus Christ and that type of happiness is eternal and timeless.

Source of all joy and happiness, help me to remain within you like the grafted shoot in the vine, so that through you I can find true happiness.

Man was created for happiness, and anyone who is completely happy has the right to say to himself, "I am busy doing God's will on earth" – *ANTON CHEKOV.*

Prayer alleviates stress

L ife makes heavy demands upon one. Tension mounts within you. You cannot sleep, you are irritable and depressed and do not always have the ability to do something about your condition.

Preventing stress is easier than curing it. To be able to do this, it is essential to develop a meaningful prayer life. Time spent with God brings calmness and restores our equilibrium. His holy presence saturates your life and you are blessed and enriched. Imperceptibly the tensions will disappear and you will be your old self again. In prayer you are renewed and you find rest, because God brings you into a holy communion with him.

> *In vain you rise early and stay up late, toiling for food to eat – for while they sleep he provides for those he loves.*
> PS 127:2

Don't neglect this experience because time spent in prayer and meditation is essential. It is there that the emotional wounds are healed by the liberating touch of his Spirit. You will then deal with tension and pressure like a true disciple of Jesus Christ. You will understand how God brings calmness in their sleep to those whom he loves.

T hank you, Heavenly Father, that in the eye of the hurricane there is a place of peace and quiet. Make me still in your presence, so that I can find trust, power and peace with you.

I have discovered that the true purpose of prayer is to place God at the centre of our thoughts and to forget ourselves and the impression we make on others – ROSALIND RINKER.

Earth is but a temporary dwelling

E very day we grow older. Slowly our bodies deteriorate and death becomes inevitable. However, Paul assures us of our immortality, for he never doubted the eternal life. He stated that it would be better for him to die and be with God. With this prospect in mind he joyfully continued with his work on earth day by day, always prepared to step over to his permanent dwelling.

If we live close to Christ we would not cling to our life in this world. We would know that we live but in an earthly tent and that our eternal house in heaven is not far off.

> *Now we know that if the earthly tent*
> *we live in is destroyed,*
> *we have a building*
> *from God,*
> *an eternal house in heaven,*
> *not built by human hands.*
> 2 COR 5:1

Jesus promised that he is going before us to prepare a place for us, a permanent place where we no longer would live in a fragile earthly dwelling. We shall live in heaven in houses built by God and which will be eternal. Then we shall forever be with our God.

*O*ur God who never changes, help me not to be so attached to
my temporary earthly dwelling that I no longer
eagerly look forward to the eternal home
which your Son has prepared for me.

---

*We should all be involved in the future, because we are going to
spend the rest of our lives there — CHARLES KETTERING.*

Faith in the future

Your experiences of the past will determine whether you approach the future with confidence and enthusiasm or hesitantly and fearfully. However, it is not your experiences which should determine your attitude towards the future, but your faith.

If you believe that nothing good will happen to you, that life is hostile, you will not be able to live confidently and happily. Nothing will convince you that the future will be better than the past. When you have such a negative attitude, you reject God's promise that he is always with you.

However, if you firmly believe in the goodness of your Father and allow him to work in your life through his Spirit, you are building a happy future for yourself. Wherever you may be, believe that God surrounds you with his love and grace. This knowledge banishes the fear of the unknown and fills you with courage and confidence to tackle whatever the future holds in

> *Be strong and courageous.*
> *Do not be terrified;*
> *do not be discouraged,*
> *for the LORD your God*
> *will be with you*
> *wherever you go.*
> JOSH 1:9

store for you. There is no situation in life which God cannot deal with. All he expects of you is a firm and unshakeable faith in him. Place him first in your life and you can approach the future with optimism.

Thank you, Father, that through my faith in you I need not fear the future. Take my hand in yours and lead me in your ways.

He who no longer believes in God, extinguishes the sun and stumbles through the dark by the light of his own lantern
— CHRISTIAN MORGENSTERN.

Where do we stand?

Many voices call to us throughout life, many of them seductive and misleading. However, in the midst of this confusion God's voice rises above the rest and clearly calls us to him. If we hear and obey his voice and dedicate ourselves to him, we are commanded to repent, to be ever watchful, to pray and witness for him.

God loves us. This love inspires us to live a holy life. People often shy away from the word "holy" because they do not know what it means. However, becoming holy is an essential part of our religious life. It is a daily continuation of our conversion.

> *To all in Rome who are loved by God and called to be saints.*
>
> ROM 1:7

To live a holy life is to fight the good fight to the bitter end, to flee from sin and to become a new person. Then we shall also be inspired to do good works, not to earn a reward, but out of gratitude and to honour God.

God's children are still in "Rome", the world where the temples of idols abound; where only earthly glory and fame is important; where the blood of the martyrs flowed. In the Rome of this world, we must be Christians even if we have to pay the highest price, because we have been called by God. We must be hallowed children of God because he loves us. Are you prepared to do this?

Father of grace, help me to be a faithful and dedicated witness in this world where you have placed me.

Our task as laymen is to experience our personal relationship with God so intensely that it will be passed on to others
— PAUL TOURNIER.

Live courageously

F or many people shyness is a painful embarrassment. You battle to find the right words when you should be eloquent; it forces you into the role of a follower when you could be the leader. Many gifted people are prevented from making their contribution to the community because they are shy. They are too frightened to state their opinion and this stifles the development of their personality.

If you are one of these unfortunate people, God wants to comfort and encourage you. It is possible to overcome this unfortunate condition.

One of the main reasons for shyness is self-centredness. When you allow your life to be filled with love for Christ and freely pass that love on to others, you will discover that your fear has disappeared. You will no longer be anxious about what

> *Therefore we are always confident.*
>
> 2 COR 5:6

other people think, but rather strive for Christ's approval. If you live for Christ you will overcome your fear of what other people will say and think. When your "self" becomes less important and Christ more important you will acquire the confidence which destroys shyness and self-consciousness and you will be able to tackle life with courage and conviction.

J esus, Lord of my life, take an ever more important place in my life and let me become less important, so that through your Spirit which lives in me, I can tackle life with courage and confidence.

If you radiate light the world around you will never be dark.

26 AUGUST

Read 2 CORINTHIANS 5:1-10

Our eternal home with God

P aul compares our life on earth with living in a tent – a temporary home only. When we rise from the dead we shall live in a house which has not been built by human hands, but by God. Only when we fully understand the resurrection shall we be able to see death in the right perspective. When we die we simply move out of the tent. When those who have accepted Christ into their lives die, they will inherit a full life, because worry, change and toil have gone forever. In the midst of this indescribable splendour they will live in a home prepared for them by God himself.

> *Now we know that the earthly tent we live in is destroyed, we have a building from God, an eternal house in heaven, not built by human hands.*
> 2 COR 5:1

That is why we can rejoice for our loved ones who have departed, because in heaven they have inherited something far more blessed than anything which we could ever imagine on earth. God wants to give us the ultimate gift: eternal life with him, and consequently the temporary must make way for the eternal. The tent must become a palace; the mortal body must be made immortal. In this way death actually expands the limited horizons of our existence.

T hank you, Jesus, that you overcame death and bequeathed to us the hope of the resurrection. Thank you that you went to prepare a place for us in God's eternal home.

Death is the golden key which unlocks the palace in eternal splendour.

Peace which transcends all understanding

To strive for peace is a worthy but demanding objective. Hate and enmity pervade the world and therefore it does not understand God's peace because it differs so radically from the false peace of this world.

God's peace develops out of the unique relationship between him and you. It is reliable and steadfast because God himself is at its source. His peace calms and heals troubled and anxious hearts (Jn 14:27). As many people have no contact with God they find it impossible to understand his peace. The fact that they have no peace is due to their unwillingness to make an effort to improve their relationship with the Prince of Peace. The peace which Paul refers to in Philippians 4:7 is a peace which is not dependent on circumstances. This peace has its origins in Christ and is nurtured by trust. It is the peace born out of the conviction that our Lord has arisen, that the future belongs to God and that his peace will be triumphant in the end.

> And the peace of God, which transcends all understanding, will guard your hearts and your minds in Christ Jesus.
>
> PHIL 4:7

God of peace, I don't always understand your peace, but by your grace I can experience that peace which comes from you. My heart is quiet before you in humble thankfulness.

The peace of God transcends all understanding – also misunderstanding – BULWER.

Use your time constructively

It is very difficult to wait. It is far easier to be active than to discipline yourself to engage in positive meditation. However, in order to live creatively, we must go through periods of planning.

Times, when out of necessity you must wait, can be a great blessing in your life. It gives you the opportunity of connecting with others so that you do not pass them and their needs by like the priest and the Levite. Previously you only took from life and now God gives you the opportunity of putting something back.

> I wait for the Lord, my soul waits,
> and in his word I put my hope.
> PS 130:5

You could use this period of waiting for reflecting on God and doing introspection. Wait on the Lord and ask him in prayer what it is that he wants to say to you. Perhaps the Holy Spirit wants to lead you to the darkest corners of your inner spiritual life. What you may find there might not be pretty or flattering, but it will bring you to God. God can make all things new again and put new vigour and growth into your life. Don't avoid or let such an opportunity to wait on the Lord pass you by.

*B*ring me to a standstill, Lord, so that I can hear what you want to say to me. Help me to discover within myself and around me what you want me to see.

Do you love life? Then don't waste time, for that is the substance from which life is made – BENJAMIN FRANKLIN.

He is not heavy – he is my brother

As Christians, we must care for one another. This is an inescapable Christian duty. Crises descend on people unexpectedly, in the form of an emergency, grief or pain and then it is our duty to help them carry that burden.

Sensitive people serve their fellow men best and bring light into lives where darkness reigns. They truly become the light of the world. To be sensitive to the needs of others is the basis of true Christian service. Helping our brother is no burden!

> *Carry each other's burdens, and in this way you will fulfil the law of Christ.*
> GAL 6:2

When you suffer because of the need and pain of others, thank Christ that you can identify with him in a very special way. His sensitive spirit knows about the pain and heartache *you* suffer when those you love are on the road to self-destruction.

The more you become aware of Christ's fortifying presence in your life, the more you become aware of the needs of others. That is the price of love. We who follow his holy example must be prepared to pay this price. Those who themselves have suffered are well-equipped to encourage others.

*J*esus, help me, through the intervention of your Holy Spirit, to develop a sensitive spirit and to care about the needs of others as you care about me.

We must not assess people in the light of what they do or don't do, but in the light of their suffering – *DIETRICH BONHOEFFER.*

Insight through prayer

Some people think that prayer is only for those who doubt their own capabilities and who lack the courage to face life's challenges. However, true prayer is infinitely more than just a panic button.

Prayer holds many blessings for those who make it a fundamental part of their lives. When we patiently become quiet in the presence of God, we experience something of his Holy Spirit and our prayer time fills us with new strength, calmness and a sense of equilibrium.

> *If any of you lacks wisdom, he should ask God, who gives generously to all without finding fault; and it will be given to him*
>
> JAS 1:5

When we look at life through prayerful eyes we develop a calmer outlook and start to understand God's plan for our lives more clearly. He also gives guidance to those who turn to him in prayer and who are obedient to what he tells them through his Spirit. Whether you are in doubt or confused; uncertain or frightened – the person who prays is given wisdom and insight and experiences God's guidance through his Holy Spirit. Prayer therefore reinforces our conviction about God and his love and gives us an understanding of life and its demands.

Father, I thank you for every time that you have given me wisdom and insight. I bow before you in prayer. Let your Spirit lead me towards the full truth about myself and life.

Prayer is not an useless attempt to try to change the will of God; it is a childlike desire to get to know God's will and to obey it – GEORGE A BUTTRICK.

Christ's resurrection is our guarantee

Darkness descended in the garden of Gethsemane and on Calvary when Christ died. The morning of the resurrection dawned and there was light, as there was light at God's command at the beginning of creation. The sun of righteousness rose and from the grave came new life; out of the darkness came light.

In her ignorance Mary Magdalene grieves at the empty tomb. Such devotion is touching, but we are constrained to ask, "Mary Magdalene, why are you crying?" If the grave was not empty then there would have been a reason to cry, but now we have a reason to rejoice! The Lord we lost, was found and in him we

> He is not here; he has risen, just as he said.
> MT 28:6

find eternal life! Now life has meaning, because death no longer is the ultimate end.

Christ's resurrection assures us that eternal death will pass us by because the Son of God was not spared! Heaven now becomes an exciting reality. Along with our loved ones we can now have eternal life, because Jesus Christ rose from the dead and assured us, "He who believes in me will live, even though he dies" (Jn 11:25).

Lord, help me not always to be bogged down by my circumstances, but let me look up to you, the One who guaranteed my salvation.

Death is not putting out the light; it is merely blowing out the lamp because day has dawned
— RABINDRANATH TAGORE.

Notes

SEPTEMBER

PRAYER

❖❖❖❖❖❖❖❖❖❖❖❖❖❖❖❖❖❖❖❖❖❖❖❖

*L*oving Father
Thank you for maintaining your creation.
Thank you for spring, for the new life
    which can be seen all around us.
Thank you for the trees which paint the heavens
    with their blossoms like giant bouquets –
    trees with tender, young leaves
    in numerous shades of green spreading in all directions.
The earth has awakened and rejoices in renewed life –
    winter has passed; the season of rejoicing has come.
Grant that all of us –
    farmer, painter, poet, economist, teacher alike –
    shall observe your handiwork and will not fail to know
    that you have touched the earth.
Saviour, touch my heart and life with your blessings;
    grant me renewed growth within my barren soul.
Grant that the grain of wheat which has fallen to the ground
    and has died, will germinate now, grow vigorously and bear
    fruit.
May I then rejoice and sing the jubilant, heartfelt song of
    spring:
Praise the Lord, o my soul!

*A*men

Confess that Christ is King

People often maintain, "I owe nobody anything" or "I do things my own way." Courageous words! However, people who argue that way, ignore one very important fact: apart from who or what we are, God created us. We belong to him, first of all. Through him we live, move and exist.

Ever since the time of Adam and Eve man has tried to obey his own impulses and desires. And time and time again he is faced by problems which he cannot solve, simply because as a human being with limitations he does not have all the answers. In spite of our rigid obstinacy of heart, God never fails to offer us his wonderful love and mercy. He is waiting to save us when we stray from him and find ourselves in trouble.

> *If we live, we live to the Lord;*
> *and if we die, we die to the Lord.*
> ROM 14:8

If you sincerely desire to lead a meaningful life, get rid of your human pride and self-sufficiency. Confess your dependence on Christ and follow him in obedience. You can do everything through him who gives you strength.

Before you make a decision or initiate a project, seek first of all God's will and plan for you. He will lead you in truth through his Holy Spirit. No one has been more successful than the one who lives through and in Christ!

I praise you, Lord Jesus, that I may put my trust in you as the Lord of my life and that you inspire me and make life purposeful and worth living.

Unless we are rooted in God as a Person and Being, he cannot grant us joy and peace. That is simply impossible – *C S LEWIS.*

Follow him

I n life all of us experience both prosperity *and* adversity. The times of prosperity seem to pass in a flash; the dark moments, however, seem to last forever. We become depressed and discouraged and we cannot experience Christ's presence in our lives.

Micha 4:2 offers us good advice, "Come, let us go up to the mountain of the LORD, to the house of the God of Jacob. He will teach us his ways, so that we may walk in his paths."

You are well aware of all the things that cast a shadow on your life. Yet you don't have to keep walking in the shadows. Focus on the mountain tops, then the way through the dark valley will not seem so endless. Keep on praying. Perseverance and enthusiasm in difficult times will lead you through the darkness and you will gaze at the sun-tinted peaks of the Lord's mountain tops.

> *The LORD said to him, "Go back the way you came . . ."*
> 1 KINGS 19:15

There is no other way to God and his power than through Jesus Christ, prayer and meditation. This will give you courage and will enable you to sing songs of praise to God, even when life seems dark. In the morning of God's grace you will rejoice again, your faith will be renewed and you will fully trust your God.

/ worship you as the God of light, but also as my Father who always takes my hand when the days are dark and guides me along your way with loving care.

Dear God, rather allow me to become the prey of lions before I prey upon the hare – KAHLIL GIBRAN.

Love drives out fear

When a loved one dies, we experience a paralysing fear. Everything changes, and we are all inclined to anxiety when things change. We are afraid of what might happen to us; we are anxious about the arrangements for the funeral; we fear the long, lonely years that lie ahead.

The wise man prays to God in the midst of such a storm – not imploring him to relieve him of all danger, but asking to be freed from anxiety. Throughout the Lord's ministry he proclaimed that he had come to save us from the slavery of fear.

> *For God did not give us a spirit of timidity, but a spirit of power, of love and self-discipline.*
>
> 2 TIM 1:7

Fear weakens our faith in our Saviour. Love is the antidote for the paralysing effects of fear. "There is no fear in love. But perfect love drives out fear . . ." (1 Jn 4:18). Love strengthens our faith and trust in the One who leads us along the dark path. The love of Christ assures us that we are safe in his hands.

In our distress we must therefore fix our eyes on Jesus Christ, the author and perfecter of our faith. We shall be released from the chains of fear and we shall be delivered from all anxiety.

Mighty Redeemer, I put my life into your hands. I shall fear neither people, nor circumstances, because I love you with all my heart!

Fear nothing except sin – GEORGE HERBERT.

4 SEPTEMBER

Read JOHN 16:25-33

So that you may find peace

All of us yearn to find peace: in ourselves, in our circumstances and especially with God. Jesus promised us that we would find peace. He calls upon us to find peace and he empowers us to spread his peace on earth. If we can spread this peace, we shall contribute to the glory of our Creator; moreover, we shall be fulfilling the high purpose for which God has created us.

Jesus, our Prince of Peace, came as our guide on the road to peace. The Spirit of God removes all the barriers which cause us to be continually at odds with others. He helps us to build bridges which reach into the hearts of others. We must therefore commit ourselves to be instruments of peace in his hands.

> *"I have told you these things, so that in me you may have peace. In this world you will have trouble. But take heart! I have overcome the world.*
> JN 16:33

God's gift of peace is offered in abundance to those who are willing to grant others forgiveness. We find peace when we liberate the oppressed; when we give food to the hungry; when we pursue righteousness and when we allow the love of God to be triumphant.

Redemption and peace are inextricably bound together. If we believe in Christ as our Saviour, we are called upon to be peacemakers. If we obey, we shall share in the abundant harvest of all those who have sown the seeds of peace in the world.

Heavenly Father, I thank you that, despite the difficulties of life, I can always find peace with you.

There is no abstract reality called "peace"; there are only people who pursue peace – DAG HAMMERSKJÖLD.

Self-examination

At times we are so dejected that we are on the verge of calling out in despair: "I cannot go on. I have reached breaking point!" After all, we are living in times where the stress and pressure of modern society can become overwhelming. Human relationships are placed under strain all the time. Sometimes everything you try your hand at seems to be a failure. Nothing goes according to plan and faith often suffers a serious blow. Suddenly prayer is no longer a guiding force in your life and you feel that life is not worth while.

You must have the courage to try and find the reason for this situation without mulling over the symptoms. Maybe you are making too many demands on your own physical strength; perhaps you are tackling too many projects all at once and fail at all of them.

> *"I have had enough, LORD,"*
> *he said.*
> *"Take my life, I am no*
> *better than my ancestors."*
> 1 KINGS 19:4

Time is never wasted on honest introspection. Moreover, it can even prove to be a valuable opportunity for a fresh meeting with the Lord. In God's Word and through prayer you will find many promises of a full and rich, fruitful and powerful life. Your restless soul will be calmed. Life will have a new meaning again and you will sing joyful hymns of victory.

Lord Jesus, please allow your Spirit to lead me to a new discovery of your wonderful, renewing power.

Who am I? Who am I? These solitary questions are driving me mad. However, whoever I may be, o God, I know: I AM YOURS!
— DIETRICH BONHOEFFER.

---

6 SEPTEMBER

Read PSALM 42:1-12

Hope when you are downcast

When you are downcast and look upon yourself as a complete failure, it is difficult to keep your hope alive. However, try to counteract these negative feelings by taking the following action in faith:

* Believe that God is bigger than all your depressing circumstances and your problems; furthermore, claim victory in his holy name.

* Commit your stress and problems to your heavenly Father in prayer. Pray specifically and list each of your problems.

> *Why are you downcast,*
> *O my soul?*
> *Why so disturbed within me?*
> *Put your hope in God,*
> *for I will yet praise him,*
> *my Saviour and my God.*
> PS 42:6

* Firmly believe that God has a special plan for your life right now. Don't resist him if he is trying to teach you his will by subjecting you to grief.

* Identify the causes of your condition. Visit people. Isolation can be the cause of acute depression. Go out and face life – even if it requires some battling.

* Turn to a world full of distressed people and you will forget your own problems and sorrows. Observe God's hand in everything around you. Face life cheerfully. God is still in control, you are his child and he loves you. Believe that in all things God is working for your good.

*E*ternal God, your presence drives away my depression and renews my spirit. I thank you for this gift through Jesus Christ.

If ever you hope to find happiness by searching for it, you will find it just like the lady who found her precious spectacles: safely on her nose – JOSH BILLINGS.

Read MARK 1:32-39

Jesus prays in solitude

When Christ was baptised, he prayed and the Holy Spirit descended on him (Lk 3:21-22) and equipped him for his task. Nobody can perform a task successfully unless he has spent some time in prayer with God.

When Jesus had to choose his disciples, he spent the entire night in prayer, wrestling with God (Lk 6:12-13). Whenever we, with our limited capabilities, have to make important decisions in life, we need contact with God in prayer even more.

When we are disappointed and upset, we must know and use the power of prayer.

When Jesus contemplated the cross, he was wrestling with God in prayer in Gethsemane (Lk 22:39-46). When we find ourselves in crisis situations, we must also be able to wrestle with God in prayer so that the way ahead can become clear to us.

> *Very early in the morning, while it was still dark, Jesus got up, left the house and went off to a solitary place, where he prayed .*
>
> MK 1:35

Even on the cross Jesus prayed for those who had nailed him to the cross. When we despair in the midst of distorted relationships and when an injustice has been done to us we must know the power of prayer.

Jesus prayed to God continually. He prayed for his disciples and he also prayed for us (Jn 17:20). If Christ was so faithful in prayer and is still praying for us, how can we condone less prayer commitment with regard to ourselves?

/ thank you, dear Lord, for your perfect example in prayer. Help me to grow in my ability to converse with you in prayer.

Prayer as a process is the highest form of energy of which the human mind is capable – COLERIDGE.

Read JOHN 20:11-18

A tragic loss

C hrist always makes himself known to persons in distress who wait upon him in prayer. He then comforts and strengthens them – just as he did with Mary Magdalene.

When the angels found the grief-stricken Mary Magdalene at the grave, they asked her why she was weeping. She answered, "They have taken my Lord away, and I don't know where they have put him" (Jn 20:13).

Love had inextricably bound Mary to Jesus. Even death could not separate her from him and that was why she was weeping at the grave. Tears are a gift of grace from God and they alleviate our grief. Mary's tears, however, were proof of despair and desperation. She was convinced that she had lost everything when her Lord died. In her grief she did not recognise the risen Saviour, because her eyes were filled with tears. We should never allow our tears to blind us to the glory of his resurrection and life eternal.

> *"Woman," he said,*
> *"why are you crying?"*
> JN 20:15

Mary could not take her eyes off the grave. Her back was therefore turned on her Lord who had told her before that he was the resurrection and the life. Our loved ones are not in the grave. Through the resurrection of Jesus they are with God. Allow the Conqueror of death to be the central figure in your grief.

L ord, help me to look past the grave and to see you in your full resurrected glory.

Most of the time we walk around with the wrong question in our hearts: What will happen to my earthly possessions when I die? The question should rather be: What will happen to me?
— ENA MURRAY.

You have a loving duty to fulfil

The world today is a divided place. War, unrest and violence increase and shake the foundations of society. Moreover, instead of being united, the church is also divided and this is destructive. We waste our time trying to settle quarrels among ourselves. The various denominations disagree on insignificant issues. We occupy ourselves with trifling disagreements, we allow jealousy and even hatred to enter into our hearts. We fail to obey God's command that we should work together to oppose Satan and to let God's kingdom come.

> *Dear friends, let us love one another, for love comes from God. Everyone who loves has been born of God and loves God.*
>
> 1 JN 4:7

The main reason for this disunity can be traced to the fact that Christians refuse to obey the command of love. "My command is this: Love each other as I have loved you" (Jn 15:12). We could solve most of our problems if we would obey this command of the Lord.

The point of departure to finding a solution is in our own hearts. All Christians are called upon to love, to show sympathy, to understand, to be accommodating and tolerant towards one another and to put all pride aside and refrain from judging others. Your demonstration of Christian love could be the beginning of a wave of love filling the entire country. Wouldn't you like to try it?

Purify my love, Father. Help me to serve others with Christian love because your love fills my heart.

True love begins where you truly don't expect any reward
— ANTOINE DE SAINT-EXUPERY.

Live for God alone

Some people express their Christain faith in a very exuberant manner, rejoicing openly as they go through life. Others serve God in reticence. Whatever the nature of your Christian experience, you must make allowances for the fact that other people can experience their faith in a way quite different from yours. Therefore, never be critical or judgmental or think that your relationship with Christ is superior to theirs.

The Christian with a quiet disposition is often misunderstood and accused by others of being lukewarm. Because he or she is reserved they do not find it easy to talk to others. When they are with other Christians they often feel they are lacking a spiritual asset. However, this is not the case at all.

> *God . . . has saved us and called us to a holy life.*
> 2 TIM 1:9

True Christian experience is something that happens in our hearts and this fact is then demonstrated in our lives. How exactly a person witnesses to this experience depends on the particular person's personality and background.

If you truly want to live for Christ alone, you need not compare your life with the lives of other Christians. You need not envy others who are "on their toes" and "vibrant" in their spiritual fervour. You can admire their keen activity and enthusiasm, but through devoting yourself to Christ you will become more and more what he intended you to be.

Take my personality and nature, dear Lord, and use me to your glory and towards building your immortal kingdom.

There is no true freedom except the freedom of those who cling to God – ST AUGUSTINE.

Read JOHN 15:1-8

The pruning-shears and growth

Our sorrows often lead us to the great Healer in a singular way. And his treatment helps us to get well again.

God often uses trials and afflictions to teach his children important lessons in life. In addition he strengthens our character and our faith and offers us space in which to grow spiritually. God plans our problems to become opportunities through which we can grow spiritually; provided, however, that we accept our afflictions with the right attitude.

Christ tells us that God is the great Gardener who prunes our lives in love. The results of the correct pruning methods are that vines, shrubs and trees grow better and bear more fruit. There are many "useless branches", bad habits and sinful thoughts in our lives that need to be pruned away. We can be sure that our Father is a Master Gardener. He knows our shortcomings. He also knows when the time is ripe for pruning and his pruning

> *He cuts off every branch in me*
> *that bears no fruit,*
> *while every branch*
> *that does bear fruit*
> *he prunes*
> *so that it will be even*
> *more fruitful.*
>
> JN 15:2

methods are perfect. If we allow God to do his pruning in our lives according to his plan, he promises a rich harvest of fruit in his kingdom.

The tender care of the Gardener heals the wounds he has inflicted and all over we shall observe new life. Pass through your period of affliction with this attitude and you can be sure that God will help you to accept his own special healing and consolation.

Father, I ask of you to help me accept pain in my life as part of your loving pruning, so that I shall be able to bear fruit for you.

Nobody in heaven will wear a crown, except those who carried a cross on earth.

The roots of peace

When Christ is the centre of your life, you will know true peace. Therefore, stay close to him, the guarantee of peace. Fully accept dominion, for he is the One who protects you against Satan who continually tries to rob you of your peace.

Strive for a life which is free of sin. Confess your sins, oppose sin and you will be victorious through the power of the Spirit of God. Then you will find peace.

Change your attitude. Set aside your pride and self-righteousness. Humbly reflect the attitude of Jesus Christ (Phil 2:1-11).

> *Therefore, since we have been justified through faith, we have peace with God through our Lord Jesus Christ.*
>
> ROM 5:1

Ensure that your life and testimony complement each other. Be prepared to grow unto spiritual maturity through the work of the Holy Spirit within you.

Pursue God's peace with perseverance and enthusiasm because peace with God and others is more valuable than gold.

If you commit yourself to these objectives in prayer and faith, the peace of God will fill your life. Furthermore, through his grace you will become a messenger of peace in this world.

*D*ear God, make me willing to exert myself spiritually so that I can joyfully share in the rich blessing of your peace through the sacrifice of Jesus Christ.

Before we can experience the peace of forgiveness we must first experience the grief of penitence – ROBERT M HEROLD.

Though . . . yet!

Many people find it difficult to reconcile their Christian faith with joyous living. They associate stateliness, dignity and solemnity with their religion. That way they miss so many of the rich dimensions of a balanced Christian life.

The Word teaches us that there is joy in the presence of God. To experience this, however, we must live in complete harmony with him. This harmony is the result of a daily walk with Christ and a steadfast love for him, both of which serve as the motivating factor and driving-force in our lives and add joy to our hearts.

> *Though . . . yet I will rejoice in the LORD,*
> *I will be joyful in God my Saviour.*
>
> HAB 3:17-18

The most important consideration is not how this Christian joy manifests itself in your live. Whether you loudly profess your joyous faith and wonder at being a child of God, or whether your joy finds expression in a quiet warming of your heart – the most important thing is that you should praise him with a thankful heart.

Jesus, source of my joy, thank you that my joy is not dependent on circumstances, but on your continuous commitment to me.

Joy is a light that fills you with hope and faith and love
— A R ST JOHN.

14 SEPTEMBER

Read JAMES 4:1-10

Stumbling-blocks in prayer

Various stumbling-blocks can seriously harm the effectiveness of our prayer life. A few of these are:

Sin: Sometimes we are quite unaware of a particular sin in our lives. In trying to make us realise this, God does not answer our prayers. However, do not make the mistake of equating all unanswered prayers with sin.

Lack of faith: The feathers in the arrow of prayer is faith. The prayer of an unbelieving heart is an ineffective prayer. Faith in prayer is a faith based on the wonderful promises which God grants believers.

> *You do not have, because you do not ask God. When you ask, you do not receive, because you ask with wrong motives, that you may spend what you get on your pleasures.*
>
> JAS 4:2-3

Worldliness: Friendship with the world is being at odds with God (Jas 4:4). If the world becomes too important in our lives, our yearning for prayer is smothered and eventually we turn away from God.

Selfishness: A selfish prayer has no power and is never answered. We must serve the Lord with that which we have received from him through his grace and never expect preferential treatment.

Wealth: Our possessions can play such a major role in our lives that we tend to forget God and stop bearing fruit (Mt 6:19, 21; 13:22). We must be willing to serve God with all that we possess and we must confess our dedication in prayer.

Ask God through his Holy Spirit to help you overcome these stumbling-blocks and you will experience a meaningful prayer life.

Lord God, please help me to overcome the stumbling-blocks in my prayer life so that I shall be able to pray according to your will.

If I should fail to pray but for a single day, the ardour of my faith would be greatly diminished – *MARTIN LUTHER.*

Read JOHN 11:1-14, 23-27

All the deceased ones

Life is one long battle. It is therefore a comforting thought that we shall rest in death at the end of our life on earth.

On earth we are servants who toil in the vineyard of the Lord. In heaven we shall rest from our laborious efforts.

On earth we press on towards the goal to win the crown which will fade away; in heaven we shall receive from God's hand the crown of glory which will never fade away.

Here we are pilgrims on an uneven road; there our journey will end in the eternal home which Christ has prepared for us.

Here we are soldiers fighting the battle against the attacks of Satan; there we shall savour victory over sin, death and Satan.

In death we shall be unaware of earthly sorrows. We shall know no sickness, suffering, fear, loneliness or desolation. Death is a temporary con-

> *I am the resurrection and the life. He who believes in me will live, even though he dies; and whoever lives and believes in me will never die.*
>
> JN 11:25-26

dition. A new, endless morning will dawn when we are raised from the grave. Our graves will be as empty as Christ's grave was.

Those who have died in Christ, will be awakened by him to see him face to face. What an indescribable joy and grace!

Redeemer and Lord, thank you that the horror of death will be converted into a triumphant resurrection when we shall be awakened from the sleep of death.

Music is the only thing from this earth which we shall find again in heaven – *J S BACH.*

Spiritual maturity

To become a new person in Christ is one of the most enriching experiences in life. However, what you should not forget, is that this experience is only the beginning of a life that must constantly be enriched through Christ, who is with you through the Holy Spirit. If he becomes the focal point in your life, you will increasingly become united with him. Your desire to know him better and to love him more will grow from day to day.

Your feeling of reverence towards God, your yearning for him and your meaningful communion with him, are all signs that you are growing towards spiritual maturity. Some of the practical results which this growth will hold for you personally will be that you will begin to apply Christ's teachings in your life and that you will seek his guidance in all you do. For this purpose he gave his Spirit as Guide as well as the gifts of grace such as prayer, his Word and communion with other believers.

> *But grow in the grace and knowledge*
> *of our Lord and Saviour Jesus Christ.*
>
> 2 PET 3:18

To grow towards the image of Christ is to become spiritually mature. You strive to be and to give your utmost for him. Your spiritual maturity will also afford you a clear understanding of life itself. Therefore, choose Christ today; choose life!

I worship you, Lord Jesus, as the true vine in whom, through your grace, I can be a growing and fruit-bearing branch.

To be a Christian entails more than an instantaneous conversion – it is a daily process through which you grow to become more and more like Christ – BILLY GRAHAM.

Your utmost for his highest

Our second best can never be good enough for God, because he gave his utmost for us: "For God so loved the world, that he gave his one and only son, that whoever believes in him shall not perish but have eternal life" (Jn 3:16).

If we put God at the end of our list of priorities, we must expect our lives to be without any meaning and to lack real depth. If you give him the worthless leftovers in your life, the mere dregs of your love, your time, your possessions and your strength, don't complain if your blessings are just as meagre as your offerings.

If you are satisfied to give less than your best to the Lord, it implies that you regard other things as more important than God; that you

> *"When you bring injured, crippled or diseased animals and offer them as sacrifices, should I accept them from your hands?"* *says the Lord.*
>
> MAL 1:13

prefer this life to life everlasting. You are trying to gain the whole world, but your soul is suffering. If you backslide in your relationship with the Lord you will discover at a later stage that your life has suffered. Values become distorted if your life is not built on the Rock. However, if you give your utmost to his highest, you will enjoy spiritual growth undreamt of. This is brought about solely by the Holy Spirit and the love of God.

From what I have, dear Lord, take only the best, each day of my life, because for you, my Saviour, only the best is good enough.

It is not that which we accumulate on earth that makes us rich, but that which we are willing to sacrifice – HENRY WARD BEECHER.

Read PHILIPPIANS 4:2-9

The therapy of thankfulness

All of us find it difficult to give thanks to God in times of suffering. However, Paul, who himself was often faced by setbacks, stressed, "Be joyful always; pray continually; give thanks in all circumstances, for this is God's will for you in Christ Jesus" (1 Thess 5:18). We need not be grateful *for* everything, but we must be grateful *in* everything and in all circumstances. In difficult times God expects us to focus on his goodness and blessings and on the support and love of our friends.

> *Do not be anxious about anything . . . And the peace of God, which transcends all understanding, will guard your hearts and your minds in Christ Jesus.*
>
> PHIL 4:6-7

Job continued to worship God and he overcame his grief with the words, "The LORD gave and the LORD has taken away; may the name of the LORD be praised" (1:21). His consuming sorrow could not prevent him from giving thanks to God.

Remember, the Lord who "takes" also "gives" abundantly. Our loss will never exceed our gain, therefore our thankfulness must exceed our grief. The result of our thankfulness is that God's love and grace will fill us, and we will receive his peace which exceeds all understanding.

Lord, thank you that you always abundantly meet my greatest need. Help me to be joyful despite my sorrow.

A true Christian is a person who never forgets for one moment what God has done for him in Jesus Christ; his attitude and all the activities of his life are focused on giving thanks to the Lord
— JOHN BAILLIE.

Peace – when we obey God

All those who obey God find peace and are liberated. It applies particularly to those in distress, for God is the One who encourages those who have given up hope; the One who releases those who are in chains; who comforts the grief-stricken and who honours those who are battling to come to terms with grief. Only the grace of God can bring peace to a broken heart torn apart by unhappy circumstances, worry, rejection, setbacks . . .

God never intended his peace to be a ticket on a journey towards security and away from the storms of life. If you wish to find peace you have to face your circumstances and deal with them courageously. Whatever these circumstances, only God can give you inner peace. Because he makes all things new he alone can restore you to being a whole person in a broken world. Only the gospel of Jesus Christ can give us peace because it guarantees that we shall be saved from our sins. Only Christ can protect us against Satan who continually tries to rob us of our peace; only Christ can make us new.

> *He (provides) for those who grieve in Zion*
> *– to bestow on them a crown of beauty instead of ashes, the oil of gladness instead of mourning . . .*
> IS 61:3

*H*oly Lord, open my ears so that my heart will be open to receive you. I desire to live near you so that peace can control my heart and mind day after day.

Sometimes we pray that God would give us things which in our hearts we hope would not be granted – simply because the price of an answered prayer will be too high for us. That is often the way in which we pray for more love, for reconciliation, for peace – D J SMIT.

Chained to the past?

Never allow self-reproach about the past to dominate your thoughts. It can handicap your spiritual growth and can rob you of the joy which God intended you to experience.

Perhaps worldliness or a lack of enthusiasm has robbed you of your noblest ideals. These memories can cast unnecessary shadows over your life. If you keep on moping about what could have been, you allow the exciting present to slip through your fingers. The past is history; the present is the only thing you really have.

> *To be made new in the attitude of your minds; and to put on the new self . . .*
> EPH 4:23-24

A living faith in Christ always requires new adjustments in life. Mistakes of the past no longer have a paralysing effect on your life. Your former fear of the past and the future is replaced by faith and courage. Your reluctance to forgive is converted into the will to forgive and to forget. Your life passes through an invigorating growth phase and you develop constructive habits.

Allow your spirit to be controlled by the Spirit of the living God. He will lead you to see the wonderful potential for blossoming in your personality.

I praise you, holy God for the past. I rejoice in the challenging present and I trust you for the unknown future.

Commit the past to God's grace; the present to his love, and the future to his providence – ST AUGUSTINE.

Prayer in times of trial

The person who prays, surrounds his life with protection stronger than steel. Prayer is the way through which the power and grace of God comes into operation in all areas of life. This applies particularly when we have to face trials which test our faith.

Our hearts must be in harmony with God if we want to come to terms with our afflictions. A disciplined prayer life is the answer. There is but one road out of the distress, failures, disappointments and problems which come our way: the road

> *Is any one of you in trouble? He should pray.*
> JAS 5:13

to God is through prayer! God is always available and Jesus Christ died so that we can go directly to God; unhindered.

Perhaps you are carrying a heavy burden of which only you and God are aware. Take it to your Saviour in prayer. He will listen and will be able to help. If you pray in faith, the Lord will grant you whatever he knows in his wisdom will be best for you. Moreover, he will also grant you his grace which is always sufficient for the believer who prays in faith.

Persevere in prayer and follow obediently and with a believing heart wherever God may lead you. Your trials will become blessed experiences which will bring you in closer harmony with the Lord.

I praise you, my God and I testify to my love for you. Thank you that you listen to me. I need you so desperately, particularly when my faith is tried.

No argument is required to prove that prayer is the universal reaction to every crisis and every desperate situation in life
— WILLIAM BARCLAY.

22 SEPTEMBER

Read JOHN 17:9-25

The communion of believers

Through grief we as Christians may experience one of the richest blessings possible – the communion of believers. This is a steadfast source of love and joy because it proves to us that we are never left to cope on our own.

The disciples despaired when the Lord was no longer visible to them in an earthly body. However, when they discovered that he would be with them forever through his Holy Spirit, their despair gave way to joy. When we discover this secret in life, we joyfully begin to understand the meaning of the communion of saints. Christ himself brings about and guarantees this joy.

> *My prayer is . . . that all of them may be one, Father, just as you are in me and I am in you. May they also be in us so that the world may believe that you have sent me.*
>
> JN 17:21

God also guarantees that we shall become one with our loved ones who have died. Through his Word and Spirit we know that they live with him. Each time when we confess this communion of believers, we remember those who have gone before us.

We must always believe that we never stand alone. The communion of believers on earth is our spiritual support. Even in our grief we must still be God's witnesses, for it will help others who are also suffering. In this way the communion of saints is expressed in our lives.

God of love, I thank you for the communion of believers which is a comfort to me in days of darkness.

All of us are strings in the orchestra of God's joy
— JACOB BOEHME.

Read HEBREWS 3:12-19

Trust God for the future

If you believe in God, you can enter and take possession of the promised land which he has prepared for you. However, your present situation can be so comfortable and familiar that you won't even consider adopting a new way of life. You try to convince yourself that the possessions which clog up your life are indispensable for your happiness and wealth. You therefore remain satisfied with the second best. God, on the other hand, is always prepared to give you his best.

God will never let you have a vision of a richer life unless it is his will that you should see its fulfilment. You have seen something of his promised land and nothing should prevent you from entering this land. God wants you to accept from him what he deems good for you.

> *So we see that they were not able to enter, because of their unbelief.*
> HEB 3:19

Put your trust in God and embrace the future. Be attuned to his guidance through the Holy Spirit. Never abandon the things in which you believe and stay true to the noblest ideals God has kindled in your heart. Live according to his will and life will yield you its abundant fruit. God will prepare the way for you until you have reached the promised land through his grace.

Lord God, being obedient to your will is far better than travelling on a safe and familiar road. Strengthen my faith in your omnipotent guidance until I reach the promised land.

The best thing about the future is that it comes one day at a time – ABRAHAM LINCOLN.

God is always near us

I may be far from God, but God is never far from me. This is the most comforting thought for any child of God.

Whenever we feel deserted by God, we only have ourselves to blame, never God. We must remember this when we feel depressed and powerless, and when our love for our heavenly Father seems to be fading. When your faith has lost its spark and is no longer a source of support, but an obstacle, know that the time has come for an honest self-examination. Identify those things which separate you from God.

> *You hem me in –*
> *behind and before;*
> *you have laid your hand*
> *upon me.*
>
> PS 139:5

When God is relegated into an inferior position in your live you cannot expect your faith to be vigorous and sparkling. Without really noticing it you may be trying to side-track God – no longer allowing him in your live and mind. But God cannot be side-tracked in such a way! He is still there!

Even though you might not want to accept his living presence and might slowly be drifting away from God's love and grace, he wants you to have only the best. Accept his love and goodness and enjoy the full life he is longing to share with you. Life without God has a hopeless end; a life with God is an endless hope.

Thank you, Father, that your love never lets go of me, even though, in my wilfulness, I may try to leave you. Thank you that your fatherly heart is always open to me.

God made us for himself, and our hearts remain restless until they find rest in him – ST AUGUSTINE.

Springs in the desert

The believer who desires to grow spiritually needs fresh water from a spring, particularly when he passes through a drought-stricken valley of grief. These are the times when he must find his strength in God who provides springs of comfort and hope to all believers in need.

Jesus Christ became our fountain of living water. Even now he quenches every form of thirst. We shall never have to pass through dry valleys without his comfort, because God will help us to discover his wells and allow us to drink from his fountains. The more we trust him in our tribulations, the more we shall experience the true relief of his comfort, invigoration and strength; with renewed power we shall then be able to proceed.

> *Blessed are those whose strength is in you,*
> *who have set their hearts on pilgrimage.*
> *As they pass through the Valley of Baca,*
> *they make it a place of springs; the autumn rains also cover it with pools.*
>
> PS 84:5-6

None of us would choose to be left in the desert of grief. Let us therefore focus on Jesus Christ for our strength and victory. In his life he was an example in all respects; in his death he was a sacrifice; in his resurrection he was a victor; in his ascension he was a king and in his intercession with God for us, a high priest!

Holy Lord, you know that I did not choose to be grief-stricken.
However, help me to be a witness for you,
even in this difficult time.

Growth is the only visible proof of life — *JOHN HENRY NEWMAN.*

26 SEPTEMBER

Read REVELATION 21:1-8

Peace in God's dwelling-place

Fear casts a dark shadow over the future. All over the world tension is mounting. We ourselves are experiencing it.

However, communion with Christ allows you to look past earthly things. It makes you realise that God is still in control of the times in which you live – full of anxiety and unrest as it may be. The almighty Creator will not abandon the work of his hands.

If you believe in God's omniscience and omnipotence you will acquire a positive attitude towards life. You will be convinced that he can recreate people. You will convey this message to the world with devotion and you will make it your calling in life to work towards peace amidst the storms of life.

> *Now the dwelling-place of God is with men, and he will live with them. They will be his people.*
> REV 21:3

If you are convinced that God is unfolding his godly purpose for this world, you will lead a peaceful and balanced life. The panic and fear of those who don't believe will not affect you. The choice is yours: you can either look at the future without God and never experience the joy of his peace; or you can truly believe that God's plan for humanity is unfolding. Than you can face the future with courage and confidence in your heart.

Thank you, heavenly Father, that you walk the pilgrim's path with me and make my heart your dwelling-place.

I feel safer when God is with me in unfamiliar surroundings than when I am without God in my own home
— ALBERT SCHWEITZER.

God in the dark valley

All of us experience setbacks in life. The times of prosperity seem to fly whilst the dark moments seem to last forever.

In times like these we must go to God in prayer. Nowhere else can we expect to find peace or answers. The cause of our distress lies in the fact that there has been a short-circuit in the contact between us and God. Do something about it and you will feel the peace of God entering your life.

Persevere in prayer and meditation and strengthen your communion with the Lord. Perseverance and enthusiasm in difficult times will guide you through the dark valleys to the sun-drenched mountain tops of God's grace and love.

> *Restore to me the joy of your salvation . . . and my mouth will declare your praise.*
> PS 51:12, 15

The only way to God is through Christ. He will enable you to sing his praises during the darkest times of your life. At the daybreak of God's love and grace you will once again know happiness. You will conquer the dark depths and leave it behind; your faith will be stronger and you will trust the Lord completely.

God of light, I worship you as the God who has healing power in our dark moments in life. Even though I walk through the valley of the shadow of death, I will fear no evil, for you are with me; your rod and your staff comfort me.

God expects us to face life with a heart filled with expectation. We must have faith that he will guide us in every situation, whilst we place our faith in him – COLIN URQUHART.

A silent God

Job lost everything; he was covered in sores and subjected to listening to those who could not offer him any comfort. However, his deepest suffering lay in the fact that he called to God in his most profound distress and appeared not to receive any answer from him. In his humiliation and suffering Job felt that God had deserted him and in this lies the worst suffering.

> *I cry out to you , O God, but you do not answer;*
> *I stand up, but you merely look at me . . .*
> *Yet when I hoped for good, evil came;*
> *when I looked for light, then came darkness.*
>
> JOB 30:20, 26

However, you and I see but a poor reflection as in a mirror. God was not playing a cruel game with Job, for just as gold is refined, God was testing him to make his faith invincible.

You cannot drift from the sphere of God's love. He knows you and cares about you. In his own good time, as in the case of Job, he will crown you with his grace and bless you abundantly – far more than you could imagine in your wildest dreams. Remember, he kept silent once – when his son had to die on the cross – but never was there a closer relationship between them than at that particular moment. If you trust God faithfully, you will have a similar experience.

My Redeemer, I praise you because I shall never be forsaken by God. I joyfully confess: I know that my Redeemer lives!

Prayer is not escapism – prayer is victory. Prayer is not despair – prayer is power. Prayer does not save one from a frightening experience – prayer enables one to deal with every situation
– WILLIAM BARCLAY.

The road ahead

All of us who have lost a loved one through death and have had to return to face life with all its demands, can find comfort in Psalm 23, the Psalm of the Shepherd and a source of consolation and inspiration.

"The LORD is my shepherd, I shall not be in want" (1). He does not promise us pastures which will forever be green or waters which will always be calm, but he did promises us that he will grant us his comfort and peace.

The Lord is my shepherd in life! There is indeed Someone who will see to it that I shall not want anything which I might require for my spiritual well-being and comfort. He is with me in my loneliness and longing.

> *The LORD is my shepherd . . .*
> PS 23:1

The Lord is my shepherd in death! "Even though I walk through the valley of the shadow of death, I will fear no evil, for you are with me; your rod and your staff, they comfort me" (4).

The Lord is my shepherd in eternity. My shepherd makes it possible for me to say, "and I will dwell in the house of the LORD for ever" (6).

He is the resurrection and the life and declares that those who believe in him will never die. If we know the shepherd of this psalm, we know that in eternity there will be no more separation, grief, tears or death.

Father, you are the Alpha and the Omega. You will come and all people will see you. The whole of creation will serve you.

Take heart! Remember: today is the tomorrow about which you had so many worries yesterday — VICTOR HUGO.

God is greater than your problems

The course of our lives is sometimes cruelly disrupted. None of us are exempted from problems. Christ never guaranteed us a problem-free life; nor did he promise us that the Christian's journey on earth would always be smooth. However, if we tackle our problems in a positive way, God can use them to motivate us to serve him more effectively and to treat others with compassion.

> *Therefore, since through God's mercy we have this ministry, we do not lose heart.*
>
> 2 COR 4:1

Whenever you face difficulties, wait quietly upon the Lord and try to determine what he is trying to teach you. Never allow your problems to dominate your life. Don't panic. Remember that God is greater than any problem you may have to face.

When problems bombard you, trust in God. A living faith in him will enable you to triumph over your problems and you will be able to walk along this road courageously. Faith in the goodness of God and the conviction that he has a purpose with your life will help you to face the future with confidence. Nothing can separate you from the love of God which is in Christ Jesus, our Lord.

Heavenly Father, grant me your grace to enable me to realise what lessons you wish to teach me through my problems.

I try not to look too far ahead or at what lies behind – but I always look up – CHARLOTTE BRONTË.

OCTOBER

PRAYER

Unchangeable God

Among us there are many elderly people –
  people whose earthly tents become weaker day by day,
  yet who continue to grow spiritually and become stronger.
Thank you that you have confirmed yourself as the Unchangeable – particularly since we observe the change and
  deterioration around and within us.
We worship you as the God who fully controls our lives:
  youth with its strength and invincibility,
  its expectations and its fearlessness.
We worship you as the One who shows us your grace
  as we grow older,
  granting us years which bring with them maturity
  and experience, calm, peace and wisdom.
We thank you that you made life in its entirety so beautiful:
  the daybreak and the sunrise;
  the fullness of the noon;
  the lustre of the sunset;
  the magic of dusk and the quiet of the night.
Thank you that you will be with us during the last phase
  of our earthly pilgrimage.
Thank you that you will not forsake us in old age,
  nor will you leave us;
  that you are with us, just as when we were young,
and that we may be constantly aware of your eternal
  arms under us.

Amen

Read ZECHARIAH 13:1-9

Growth through suffering

Coal and gold are both minerals, but while coal is consumed by fire, gold is purified by it. In the same way people react differently when they pass through the crucible of affliction.

Those who trust in the Lord are purified and strengthened. They are blessed and prove themselves able to meet the demands made upon them. Those who do not trust in God, are torn by bitterness and become rebellious. The believers who survive God's furnace are strengthened by their afflictions, their characters are moulded according to God's will and in the end they are victorious. The sceptics become depressed and head for destruction.

How do you react when you are confronted by trials? Do you curse God, turn your back on him, or do trials bring you into closer contact with him and allow you to share in his comfort and grace? If you seek God's love in prayer and worship in

> *I will refine them like silver and test them like gold. They will call on my name and I will answer them . . .*
> ZECH 13:9

times of trial your suffering will be tempered and you will grow in joy and peace. If you trust in him and love him, you will be purified to become spiritually mature.

May the crucible in which I am being refined draw me nearer to you, Father, so that pure gold will be produced which will make your image visible to all around me.

The person who has learnt to suffer, will enjoy great peace. He is conqueror over his own self and ruler of the world; he is Christ's friend and heir to heaven – *THOMAS À KEMPIS.*

Resting in God

M any people don't apply themselves long enough to any one thing to gain something from it. This leads to restlessness, spiritual and intellectual weariness and confusion. They lack inner peace.

Inner peace is the product of a dedicated relationship with God. If you identify your objectives in life and pursue them with dedication, direction and stability will be added to your existence. Choosing a purpose in life is not always easy, yet without it you will never experience the joy of inner peace and calmness.

> You will keep in perfect peace him whose mind is steadfast, because he trusts in you.
> IS 26:3

If you allow the Holy Spirit to enter into your life to define your purpose in life, he will not fail you. If you ask God in all honesty to reveal to you a purpose in life to which you can dedicate your time, your efforts and talents and you follow the road he opens up for you, you will experience the joy of fulfilment. Your life will be fruitful. All you actions will be characterised by a renewed drive. You will know peace and will be able to rest in the Lord, because your life will be controlled by his Spirit.

M y soul is quiet within me, o Lord, because I know that you will continue to guide me as before. Do not allow doubt to rob me of this certainty.

I searched for God until he found me – BLAISE PASCAL.

Perplexed . . . but not in despair

A ship is safe in a harbour where it is anchored securely. That is, however, not what ships are made for. They have to go out into the open sea to transport passengers or deliver their freight. In the same way we have to go out into life and face our problems with courage and in faith. If we face our problems with a positive attitude, God can use them to motivate us to serve him more effectively and to have compassion with others.

Whenever you encounter difficult times, wait upon the Lord in silence and pray to him. Ask him what he is trying to teach you. Don't let your problems dominate your life. God is greater than any problem you may be confronted with and he has the power to use it for your own good.

> *We are hard pressed on every side, but not crushed; perplexed, but not in despair; persecuted, but not abandoned; struck down, but not destroyed.*
>
> 2 COR 4:8-9

A problem can suddenly arise out of the blue or it can quietly creep into your life. If you lack a living faith which enables you to triumph over your problems, it will become impossible to carry on. Faith in the goodness of God and the sure knowledge that he has a purpose for your life will equip you to meet the future with confidence and courage. Nothing can separate you from the love of God.

*H*eavenly Father, grant that I may learn the lessons you are trying to teach me through my trials and problems. Do it through your Spirit which is able to comfort me.

The only light that illuminates the future is faith
— *THEODOR HOECKER.*

The earth still belongs to the Lord

Depression is one of the human weaknesses to which all of us succumb. When life's setbacks rest heavily upon us and everything at which we try our hand seems doomed, we all find it extremely difficult to keep a spirit of hope and expectancy alive. What is more, we cannot hide our depression. People notice it and it even has a negative effect on the lives of those who are close to us.

> *Why are you downcast,*
> *O my soul?*
> *Why so disturbed*
> *within me?*
> *Put your hope in God,*
> *for I will yet praise him,*
> *my Saviour and my God.*
> PS 42:5-6

There is, however, a wonderful antidote against depression, which you will find helpful for the rest of your life. Trust in God. Sing songs of praise to his glorious name, for he is your help and your God

If you yearn to raise your spirit and overcome your depression, set about your relationship with the living God in earnest. Convince yourself that the earth still belongs to the Lord, although it might look as if the Evil One triumphs over it. Ask God to assure you again that he loves you, that you are his child and that in all things God works for the good of those who love him.

*T*hank you, heavenly Father, that you will allow your goodness to fill my life and that you will be with me. Protect me against depression by strengthening my faith and by assuring me that you are in control of my life.

It is claimed that the highest praise of God lies in the denial of his existence as proclaimed by the atheist who finds the creation so perfect that he can dispense with its Creator
— MARCEL PROUST.

Concentration

We meet God in our quiet time with the firm resolution to devote all our attention to him, but before we know what has happened we get distracted. Don't be discouraged or stop praying because you sometimes find it difficult to concentrate. We must persevere in seeking, knocking and in asking (Mt 7:7-11).

Effective prayer does not depend on the length of the prayer. A few sentences spoken in sincerity has more value than a repetition of empty phrases and words that do not come from your heart. A silent prayer is of incalculable value, but it sometimes helps your concentration

> *Therefore, prepare your minds for action; be self-controlled . . .*
> 1 PET 1:13

to voice your prayer loudly. It focuses your mind on Christ, particularly if you are intellectually tired.

Many people have a God-given talent to write beautiful prayers. If your concentration has waned, read one of these prayers out loud. In the Bible you can also find meaningful prayers which you can use.

Always depend on the Holy Spirit, because he is there to strengthen us when our human weaknesses become stumbling-blocks in the way of prayer.

Father, you are so patient with me when I am weak! Thank you for the intercession of your Holy Spirit when I pray.
Thank you that the prayers I offer you reach you in a purified form through the grace of Jesus Christ.

All wise parents realise that true parenthood does not imply that you do things for your child; it means that you enable your child to do things for himself. God works in the same way through prayer – BILLY GRAHAM.

OCTOBER

Read PROVERBS 3:1-10

God will help you

Life is full of problems. Some undeserved; others are the product of your own foolish conduct and if you don't find solutions for them, they will dominate your life and thoughts.

If you talk to a reliable and sympathetic friend about your problems, they are put into perspective and you will probably no longer find them so intimidating. Granted, there are people who enjoy dwelling on their problems and secretly hope that a solution will never be found. They thrive on the sympathy of others and wallow in self-pity.

> *In all your ways acknowledge him, and he will make your paths straight.*
>
> PROV 3:6

If you have a problem which you really want solved, lay it before your heavenly Father. Make him the centre of your thoughts and move your problem over to take second place. If you are only vaguely aware of God and focus all your concentration on your problem, it will be all the more difficult to find a solution. Trust God to deal with your problems. Acknowledge God's sovereignty within your heart and mind and allow him to create order in your confuson. In his own good time and in his own way he will solve your problem. You will experience a profound peace and renewed spiritual strength, because you have given God his rightful place in your life.

*E*ven though I may experience the darkest of times, holy Father, I will not despair, for you are with me. Let me always remember that you are superior to and more powerful than any problem that may come my way.

If we put our hands together in prayer, God opens his hands
— GERMAN SAYING.

Hope, patience and prayer

To be patient when your life is unexpectedly overshadowed by grief, and to keep on trusting in the Lord despite the shadows, speak of a special relationship with Christ. The meaning of our hope as a Christian, our steadfastness in times of affliction and our perseverance in prayer all become evident in a special way when we are grief-stricken. In times like these we live fully surrendered to God and our deeply-seated religious relationship with him becomes evident.

Through the intervention of the Holy Spirit we are protected against succumbing to the burden of our afflictions. We know that our faith will not prevent us from suffering, it will, however, help us to convert our suffering into victory.

> *Be joyful in hope, patient in affliction, faithful in prayer.*
> ROM 12:12

Patience is a firm belief that, regardless of circumstances, our faith will triumph in the end. By remaining steadfast amidst our afflictions, by continuing to rejoice in hope, and by persevering in prayer, we take the sting out of our grief, even though the pain may persist. In Christ we are not only assured of the final victory, but also that we shall walk in the sunshine of God's love again.

Lord, keep me patient, grant that I may persevere so that I can share in your victory. I thank you that I shall always find the door of prayer open to me.

No arguments are required to prove that prayer is the universal reaction to every crisis and every desperate situation
— WILLIAM BARCLAY.

Messenger of peace

The Bible can be regarded as God's last will and testament, bequeathing peace, as fulfilled through Jesus Christ, as an inheritance to humanity (Jn 14:27). The Word refers to the "peace of God" (Phil 4:7) – the gift offered us by the joyous message, but also to "peace with God" (Rom 5:1) – the condition for sharing in the peace of God.

If we don't accept the redemption through Jesus Christ's sacrifice of atonement, we cannot possibly expect to experience God's peace.

> *He came and preached peace*
> *to you who were far away*
> *and*
> *peace to those who were near.*
> EPH 2:17

He is the Prince of Peace whose death and resurrection made it possibe for us to share in his peace. He is God's messenger sent to proclaim God's peace on earth.

God the Holy Spirit produces the fruit of peace in our lives (Gal 5:22-23). Through our obedience to the will of the Father he allows peace to grow in us. He urges us to become messengers of this peace and in this way we become part of God's peace plan for the world. If we have peace in our own hearts and minds, we shall be worthy messengers in a world yearning for peace.

*P*rince of Peace, make me a worthy messenger of your message of peace. Through you I have found peace and I desire to share the glory of this peace with others who are yearning for it.

The world is always far more anxious to receive the gospel than Christians are to preach it – GEORGE W PETERS.

A motto for life

On our earthly pilgrimage we are constantly afflicted by uncertainties. We do, however, have the indescribable privilege of Psalm 37:5 as our motto for life.

Our life on earth is often difficult. There are times when we seem to have landed in a dead-end; as though we are continually travelling uphill – always a struggle. Sometimes our road winds through dark valleys of suffering and sorrow. At other times we have to travel across barren plains of intense longing. Perhaps you are weary and burdened; you may be suffering a long illness and the road ahead may look impossible and uncertain.

> *Commit your way to the LORD;*
> *trust in him*
> *and he will do this.*
>
> PS 37:5

At times like these we are tempted to say: I give up. I cannot endure this suffering any longer. Ahead of me I see only darkness.

Is that how you feel right now? Remember: You have a loving heavenly Father to whom you can surrender this road which is humanly impossible for you to travel, a Father whom you can trust and who will bless the road that lies ahead.

Father in heaven, thank you that my destiny is under your almighty control and that I shall therefore never be a traveller to nowhere. I lay my life in you hands, fully trusting you like a child.

Every moment of resistance against temptation is a victory
— FREDERICK W FABER.

10 OCTOBER

Read PSALM 34:26-23

Grief can be shared

Grief can be shared. This is a wonderful heavenly grace, for shared grief is divided grief, a bearable grief. As we all have to suffer grief, it is good to know that in Christ we can triumph over our grief. However, to ensure this, it is necessary to share our grief with God. He has compassion with us and is the great Comforter. Do not be afraid to share your afflictions with him – he is waiting to embrace you with his love.

Call upon God in your distress in the words of Psalm 31:9, "Be merciful to me, O LORD, for I am in distress; my eyes grow weak with sorrow, my soul and my body with grief." Don't pity yourself. Remember that life must go on and that you must fulfil your responsibilities as a Christian. Never try to blame God or call him to account. Because Christ has suffered for your sake, he is full of compassion for you, and he desires to embrace you with his love. This assurance is your protection when you are assailed by grief and sorrow.

> *The LORD is close to the brokenhearted and saves those who are chrushed in spirit.*
> PS 34:18

Holy Spirit of God, sent by the Father to comfort us, I praise you for your tender support in my deepest moments of grief.

O my soul, never despise the classroom of grief – it will make you an unique participator in the universal praise
– GEORGE MATHERSON.

The spirit of true prayer

S ome people find prayer a dreary duty. If time allows it, they quickly ask God's blessing and protection for themselves and their loved ones. Fully convinced and reassured that they have finished praying, they go on with life.

A prayer offered with this attitude has no power, since prayer comprises far more than confronting God with a list of requests. Prayer is a powerful action which can enrich every area of your life.

> *Praise awaits you, O God, in Zion; to you our vows will be fulfilled, o you who hears prayer.*
>
> PS 65:2

When you enter into the presence of God, your heart should overflow with praise. You must learn to focus your mind on God and to praise and gratefully honour him. Joy will fill your entire life and you will thank God for all his blessings.

In this spirit you will find it easy to deal with the difficult side of prayer: to pray for your enemies; to forgive those who have trespassed against you. You will be liberated and you will become a disciple of God, forever praising him.

/ come with grateful praises before you, eternal Father, and I thank you that your Holy Spirit teaches me to pray in a spirit of rejoicing thankfulness. You uplift my soul!

If God is your friend for life, you will want to talk to him unceasingly — WILLIAM BARCLAY.

God's training

If we had God's insight, no affliction would have upset us. Being human, though, we always look for an answer. Our first reaction is usually: *Why did this happen?* Because we are so inclined to see only the negative side of things, the loving countenance of our Lord is hidden from us. The light which he radiates is dimmed and we continue to stumble in the dark.

Both the righteous and the unrighteous encounter setbacks and afflictions. The Word of God, however, assures us that God will save those who believe in him. We have but an imperfect and meagre conception of his purpose for our lives, but God is omniscient. In our lives he can convert good as well as bad fortune into the best opportunities. Because we now only know in part, we find it trying to understand what God is planning for our lives, to understand his deeds and to assess his ways. However, take a moment to admire the wonders of his creations and allow the Master Artist to paint according to his will.

> *It was good for me to be afflicted*
> *so that I might learn your decrees.*
> PS 119:71

Christ passed God's test with distinction in Gethsemane and left us a perfect model. Be prepared to be trained by him and you will find peace, comfort and peace of mind.

Lord, our Creator, I put my trust in you to create beauty out of my suffering; and to convert my chaotic life into a life of loving orderliness. Grant me patience until you have revealed your plan for my life to me.

Long sick-beds are training-schools of grace for those who care for the sick and train those who suffer to find patience in love
— JEAN PIERRE CAMUS.

Peace through prayer

S tress, anxiety and worry have become part of our lives and rob us of our peace with God. Let's look at the example that Jesus set for us: He always isolated himself to have communion with his Father in prayer, thereby gaining inner calm and power which enabled him to face all the demands of his day.

God does not want us to be overcome by tension and worry. That is why he gave us the power of prayer. If we do not pray, we limit God's work of grace in our lives.

Our spirit yearns for an experience of complete calmness, of total peace of mind. It is therefore essential to set some time apart each day for prayer and meditation. This is the God-given way through which we shall find permanent peace. If we are worried or under stress because we can only think about our burdens and worries, the time has come to

> *Very early in the morning, while it was still dark, Jesus got up, left the house and went off to a solitary place, where he prayed.*
> MK 1:35

say to ourselves: Be calm! Relax! Leave everything to God! Allow your thoughts and mind to be controlled by the peace of God! Actively seek peace. Support this search with prayer and faith. In this way we glorify God and enhance the quality of our peace.

/ thank you, God, for comforting me through your Word. Thank you for casting out all the tension and fear in my life, and for granting me your peace.

God will hear the prayer of a sincere heart – even without a single word being spoken – IRISH SAYING.

14 OCTOBER

Read PHILIPPIANS 4:2-9

The glory of rejoicing

We can face life with a rejoicing spirit because we are God's children and followers. Let us share the glory of this joy with all whom we may meet along life's way today. After all, if your faith makes you happy, you will not be able to keep this joy to yourself.

To share joy is an outstanding privilege. Sincere appreciation, a friendly gesture, a word of encouragement, time spent with someone who is sad, all these things will prove that we have a deep and sincere joy in our hearts.

To abundantly share friendliness and joy is a way of life which makes our existence worthwhile. It builds friendships, makes us sensitive to the needs of others and honours God.

> *Rejoice in the Lord always. I will say it again: Rejoice !*
> PHIL 4:4

God in his love wants us to rejoice. Christ promised that nobody would rob us of our joy if it is rooted in him. If he is the focal point in your life, you will rejoice and always see the positive side of life. Happiness and joy are gifts of love from God to his believing children. Take these gifts and share them with others.

Loving Redeemer, help me to rejoice under all circumstances. Grant me the grace to share my joy with others.

Not what is around me, but what is in me is the thing that counts. Not what I possess, but what I am makes me happy or unhappy – GOETHE.

God will satisfy your needs

Each day we realise that we have diverse and numerous needs with regard to body, soul and spirit. To these needs are added our problems in life, temptations, bad habits, our intellectual limitations, and many others. Whenever we feel overcome by these needs, let us accept God's promise as formulated in Philippians 4:19.

There is no need which God cannot satisfy. If only we would believe it and act according to this good news!

God satisfies our needs through Jesus Christ. He unlocks the treasure troves of God's blessings and allows us free access. If only we would enter! Our God is the Almighty, the All-Sufficient. He is the God of heaven and earth. Everything is the Lord's. And in

> *And my God will meet all your needs according to his glorious riches in Christ Jesus.*
>
> PHIL 4:19

Jesus Christ we are his children, able to share in his riches. Moreover, he desires us to share in this abundance.

Never allow yourself to become spiritually poor. Accept the abundance offered to you by God.

How wonderful is your grace, Lord. Through Christ Jesus I shall receive everything because I am heir to God's riches.
I accept this in faith and thank you in the name
of my Redeemer.

"Poor in spirit" does not so much refer to humbleness as to a spirit of dependence on God and not being dependent on earthly support — RONALD KNOX.

Read MATTHEW 6:1-15

Powerless prayer

Prayer can easily become a sheer formality without any real depth or meaning. We can say, "Our Father", without experiencing the wonder of having the right to utter these words. Saying grace at a meal can be just an empty gesture and our quiet time can be a waste of time because we have got into a rut.

It is good habit to discipline yourself and set aside a specific time for prayer. But as soon as the time aspect becomes too important, the habit can also be detrimental to our spiritual life. Eventually the time set aside might appear to have magic power.

> *"And when you pray, do not be like the hypocrites."*

We could even get the idea that prayers said in a specific place will be particularly powerful. However, any place can be converted into a Bethel should circumstances require it and provided our hearts are suitably attuned to God.

Some people attach special value to lengthy prayers. However, few, but sincere words are much more important. Christ also warned against the danger of praying merely for the sake of being seen by the people. It is not important *how* we pray, but *what* we pray about. If we seek God in all sincerity and honesty, he will give power and vitality to our prayer life.

Almighty God, help me to do away with all the things that make my prayer life powerless and grant that I may be able to discern what is best.

More things are wrought by prayer than this world dreams of
— TENNYSON.

Read MATTHEW 5:3-12

No growth without suffering

The greatest loss which you can experience in life is if after your hour of suffering you cannot testify to increased spiritual growth.

Grief *can* be of great value. It often leads to a more intimate relationship with God. Those who have suffered most, are often those who know God best, because he bends down in compassion to those who need him most.

> *Blessed are those who mourn,*
> *for they will be comforted.*
> MT 5:4

Grief has a purifying power: it is like a fire which consumes our weaknesses and like refreshing rain which helps us to grow. Grief helps us to experience the comfort and love of God. At the same time we discover the love and goodness of others and renewed strength is born in our hearts.

In every form of suffering to which we are subjected there is a hidden blessing. We must simply pray for the grace to see it and share it with others. Our grief will be tempered and we shall become instruments of comfort in the hands of the great Comforter. Through our grief we continue to grow, to become more and more like the image of our Lord and Master.

Holy God, keep me from experiencing only loss through my grief. Teach me to be just as gentle towards the suffering of others as you are towards mine.

Is life really so miserable? Are not perhaps your hands too small, your vision obscured? Are you not the one who must grow? — DAG HAMMERSKJÖLD.

18 OCTOBER

Read PSALM 127

The tender footsteps of peace

Peace is like a beautiful butterfly: while you are chasing it, it will evade you. As soon as you sit down peacefully, it will settle on your shoulder. It is quite clear that circumstances do not determine whether or not you will have peace in life. What is important, is your attitude to your Creator and life as such. The secret of peace does not lie in being able to do what you want to do, but in gladly doing what you have to do. This means that you *put* as much as you can *into* life, instead of trying to *get* as much as you can *out of* life. Learn to give as much of yourself as you possibly can to God, to others and to your task in life.

> *In vain you rise early and stay up late, toiling for food to eat – for while they sleep, he provides for those he loves.*
> PS 127:2

Thankfulness goes hand in hand with peace. A thankful person lives in peace with God, with himself and with others. He lives, knowing that from God's hand he receives far more than he could ever deserve.

If we wish to walk the road to peace, we need not try to change our circumstances, we need to adopt a new mindset. God wants us all to be heirs to his peace. It is not necessary for us to perform great and powerful deeds so that others will notice us. It is only essential that we surrender ourselves quietly to the love of God. Then he will lovingly pour his peace upon us as we sleep. For our strength lies in finding rest in the Lord alone and in trusting him.

Father, help me to remain in the Son as the branch remains in the vine so that your perfect peace can flow through me.

If you bring sunshine into the hearts of others, you will not be able to withhold it from yourself – J M BARRIE.

A unique creation

At some stage in our lives all of us experience a lack of self-confidence. When that happens to you, remember: God created you as a unique person. You were created in his own image.

You can make a list of all your shortcomings, you can think about them and start pitying yourself. But if you want to be sensible, don't allow yourself to sink into despair when judging yourself or when you listen to others criticise you. Accept yourself – that is the only way you will be able to live with yourself.

To accept and respect ourselves *with* our shortcomings, we need the grace of God.

Perform your duties conscientiously and God will grant you his merciful support. Remember the

> *So God created man in his own image, in the image of God he created him.*
>
> GEN 1:27

encouraging words of Philippians 4:13, "I can do everything through him who gives me strength."

Keep on praying to your heavenly Father. Pray and remember that you will always be his child and that he loves you, sees great potential within you and has great expectations for you.

If you live for God, he will endow you with a dignity which will ennoble everything you lay your hands on.

God, our Creator, thank you that you have a plan for my life. Protect me against self-pity and despair and inspire me with a sanctified idealism, to the glory of your name.

Every person knows that he is unique. There is no possibility that there will be a duplication of such a marvellous creation
— *FRIEDRICH NIETZSCHE.*

Prayer unites

Many people are so self-centred that they take no interest in others. They are lonely but do not realise that, if they showed interest in others, a mutual interest could be established and friendship and love could grow.

If we as Christians take a genuine interest in others, we need to pray for them. Genuine interest in others break down the walls of isolation, but it does require prayer and self-sacrifice. Through mutual prayer we become aware of the communion of believers. The moment you pray for a person, you cannot help but take an interest in him or her.

> *Our Father in heaven, hallowed be your name.*
> MT 6:9

When you say, "Our Father", you commit the individual for whom you are praying to the sphere of influence of God's love. You become involved with that person, because you cannot call God "Father" and distance yourself from the family ties of God. If you say "Our Father", you experience an emotion of being united with God and others, and loneliness and selfishness are dispelled from your life.

Prayer unites and enriches our lives beyond description. Thank and praise God unceasingly for this precious gift.

Thank you, heavenly Father, for the privilege and experience of being safe within your family. Your Holy Spirit now enables me to look at the people around me with new eyes.

You know the value of prayer. It is precious and priceless. You must never, yes, never, neglect it – SIR THOMAS BUXTON.

Read JOB 1:13-22

Healing worship

After Job had lost his children and his possessions, he tore his clothes and shaved his head – a symbol of his shock and mourning. In performing this act he paid tribute to those who had died, but he also showed his humility before God. Even in his deepest grief Job clung to God with a believing heart. Even in his grief he fell to the ground in worship before God.

A time of mourning and grief should culminate in worship, because this brings resignation with regard to God's actions and it results in a cheerful view of life. When we worship we focus our entire being on God, meditating on his majesty and praising him. When we meet him in worship our soul is healed and our heart is comforted.

> *The LORD gave and the LORD has taken away; may the name of the LORD be praised.*
> JOB 1:21

Worship frees us from the pain associated with our grief. We find the One whose ways are not our ways and whose thoughts are not our thoughts. God's grace broadens our perspective and our concept of life and death. This will enable us to sing praises to him, our Redeemer – regardless of our pain and grief. The healing balm of God's grace will soothe our wounds through our worship of him.

Loving Lord, open my eyes so that I can worship you;
open my heart so that I can love you;
open my lips so that I can praise you.

The happiest person is he whom nature has taught the lesson of praise and worship – RALPH WALDO EMERSON.

God's peace imbues trust

A person who has been disobedient constantly fears that his sin will be exposed. This causes anxiety. Self-reproach and feelings of guilt rob such a person of his self-confidence – something which is essential for a life filled with purpose and cheerfulness.

If you are striving towards establishing a sound trust in God and wish to be at peace with your Creator, others and yourself, it is essential that you obey God. This obedience is a joyful acceptance of everything he might have ordained for you in his wisdom.

> *Now it is God who has made us*
> *for this very purpose and has given us the Spirit as a deposit, guaranteeing what is to come.*
> 2 COR 5:5

God gives you his Spirit as a gift. When you surrender yourself to him, your greatest desire will be to know God's will and to live according to it. Then your life will be filled with his peace and the confidence which you need to deal with life's problems.

Initially it may look difficult, but because his Spirit lives in you and controls your life, you will receive the strength which will enable you to live a life which pleases God. When you live within God's will, you may approach God with confidence. Your relationships with others will develop successfully. You will live in peace and harmony with God and will not succumb to despair.

Thank you, Lord Jesus, that I have found favour in your eyes. Protect me, so that I shall forever share in your peace and grace.

Find peace in the knowledge that if you have not yet lost God, you have lost nothing – J S HOLDEN.

Read GALATIANS 6:1-10

Honest appreciation

All of us like to be appreciated for what we do. Never, therefore, hesitate to express honest appreciation. We so easily take the work of others for granted; and consequently claim sacrifices made for our sake as a right and show no appreciation for it. Appreciation does not only gladden the hearts of those who are at the receiving end, but it also brings joy and fulfilment to those expressing it.

Guard against being self-centred and wanting to take more out of life than you are prepared to give. Be sensitively aware of all the things you can be grateful for. You will become aware of the many wonderful things people are continually doing for you and by showing your appreciation their love will increase. Always reward love by performing you own deeds of love.

> *Therefore, as we have opportunity,*
> *let us do good to all people,*
> *especially to those who belong to*
> *the family of believers.*
> GAL 6:10

God's love is the greatest love of all. Allow your thankfulness to be expressed in deeds of love towards others and it will become a source of blessing for you and all those around you.

Help me, dear Lord, always to be filled with appreciation for all the love and help I receive from so many people, but particularly from you. Humbly, and with a rejoicing heart, I thank you for all your blessings.

Thankfulness is the heart's way of remembering
— *FRENCH SAYING.*

24 OCTOBER

Read ISAIAH 62:1-9

The privilege of intercession

God's indescribable grace allows us to be intercessors. Through intercession we become the co-workers of the great Intercessor, Jesus Christ. Our prayers form part of his perfect prayers and through these prayers we serve a world which is not even aware of it, but on whose behalf we release the omnipotence of God.

> *You who call on the LORD, give yourselves no rest, and give him no rest . . .*
>
> IS 62:6-7

We pray in the name of Jesus Christ for his church on earth; for all those in need; for God's servants and their ministry; for unbelievers and unreached peoples of the world and God's workers in this field; for the preaching of the gospel that sets us free.

We are not isolated in this respect, but form a close union with millions of God's children throughout the world. It is an outstanding privilege to be united in prayer until we have gained the victory in his name. At the same time, however, it is a great responsibility.

We must therefore be prepared to give our utmost to fulfil this calling of intercession. The rich fruits in our own lives and in the lives of others will become evident.

Father, I thank you that, through prayer, I may be a co-worker of Jesus Christ. Grant that I shall be faithful and watchful in prayer. Open my eyes and ears to the suffering of others and make my heart sensitive to their needs.

Prayer opens up the heart until it has grown big enough to contain God's personal gift – God himself – MOTHER TERESA.

Prospering amidst affliction

S ome of Paul's most consolatory letters were written in jail. Can anything good be born out of affliction? Definitely! We are so shortsighted that we can only see pain and suffering, affliction and loneliness. We wonder how we shall ever be able to fill the emptiness left by the death of a loved one.

But life goes on. When we are confronted by death, we gain a new appreciation for life. The loss of a loved one bring us into closer contact with those who were left behind. Grief enriches us in such a way that we are better able to comfort others.

> *I have tested you in the furnace of affliction . . .*
> IS 48:10

Let us reach out in faith and gratefully take God's healing hand in our affliction. If we desperately hold onto grief it becomes an unbearable burden and we are blinded to the wonder of life. Let us, therefore, put aside our grief and try to discover what God is trying to teach us through our suffering.

Death and its effects can be counteracted by two joyous certainties: the triumph that is rooted in *faith* and the certainty of the *resurrection*. Both guarantee us the final victory – also over death. God uses these gifts to guide us through the darkness into the eternal light.

L ord Jesus, help me to recover from the grief of death with dignity. Help me to once again find meaning and joy in life.

Jesus Christ did not come to reason away suffering or to wave it away with a magic wand. He came to sanctify suffering and to allow his grace to shine through the darkness
– PAUL CLAUDELL.

God's peace as our companion

Y ou have been relieved of your burden of sin; the cross at Calvary is your guarantee. You must simply accept this redemption and grace. Then you will be at peace *with* God and that is the entrance to peace *in* God.

> *Do not be anxious about anything, but*
> *in everything, by prayer and thanksgiving,*
> *present your requests to God.*
> *And the peace of God, which transcends all understanding, will guard you hearts and your minds in Christ Jesus.*
> PHIL 4:6-7

Trust in God is also essential for peace and is the result of an intimate relationship with him. Our God would have nothing to do with hearsay. He demands a first-hand experience with him. If we don't know him personally we shall seek peace in vain.

God's peace is available to all people. Without it we shall lead a life of turmoil. Therefore, remember these words: God the Father will always love us and will grant us his peace; God the Son will always be merciful to us and strengthen us; God the Holy Spirit will always comfort us and guide us in his truth.

L oving God of peace, help your struggling child to savour your perfect peace amidst all the turmoil in this world.

Within our minds, within our entire being we receive that peace which trancends all understanding, the peace of reconciliation and justification at the very moment when the soul, responding to all God has done for us, drawing a deep breath, says AMEN
— MARTIN LUTHER.

Givers and grabbers

C hristians cannot live for themselves only. We have contact with other people and influence their lives. If you live for yourself only and help nobody unless you can personally profit from it, your life becomes a mere existence which lacks that quality which makes life worth living. Then you become a "grabber"!

The secret of an exciting life is rooted in that which you can *give* life. If you wish to be loved by others, you must give yourself and your love unconditionally. If you wish to be blessed, you must be a blessing to others. Then you are a "giver"! This is what Christ taught us – he gave himself: even unto death.

> *I am the good shepherd. The good shepherd lays down his life for the sheep.*
> JN 10:11

Begin small. Just for one day try to live in such a way that your life will be a source of unselfish blessings for all those with whom you come into contact. Be willing to listen and to be friendly. Show interest in others, foster a spirit of goodwill, sympathy and thoughtfulness. Allow the joy of the Spirit of Christ to flow through you to others, thereby enriching their lives and making them happy. You will experience that this joy flows back to you in a mighty stream.

H eavenly Father, help me to be a blessing to others. Keep me from being selfish and callous. Grant me the attitude of Jesus Christ, the great Giver!

I find life an exciting experience, and it is all the more exciting when I live it for others – HELEN KELLER.

Read DANIEL 6:7-15

My mind wanders

D aniel was well disciplined with regard to his prayer life and therefore his mind did not wander when he prayed to God. He went to pray in a specific spot – his upstairs room – although he knew that he could pray anywhere. He also had fixed times for prayer. Everybody knew that he made time for God three times every day in spite of knowing that he could talk to God at any time.

> *. . . he went home to his upstairs room where the windows opened towards Jerusalem. Three times a day he got down on his knees and prayed, giving thanks to his God, just as he had done before.*
> DAN 6:10

Daniel focussed his mind on God. His windows were open towards Jerusalem, the city of God. It is never difficult to focus on someone whom you love, therefore if you love God, your prayers will be effective. Your mind will not wander if you talk to God in faith, for faith and love complement each other.

Someone once said, "Prayer is the simplest form of speech uttered by childish lips." It is true that the sincerity of children's faith and their unconditional love make it easy for them to pray. All God's children should have this childlike faith when they address God in prayer.

F ather, you know how easily my mind begins to wander when I try to pray. I pray that your Holy Spirit will focus my mind, so that I may be blessed in my prayer life – as you had intended me to be.

If you don't feel like praying, it is a sure sign that you should immediately start praying – BILLY GRAHAM.

Liberation through belief in God

I n times of suffering you really have only three options: you can think only of yourself, you can become trapped in your circumstances, or you can focus on God.

If you focus only on yourself, you reproach yourself for your mistakes and failures. If you become obsessed with your circumstances, you realise how incapable you are of changing things and you become desperate. However, if you turn to God, you will see him as the One who is master of your circumstances and your faith wil be strengthened.

> *I know that my Redeemer lives, and that in the end he will stand upon the earth.*
> JOB 19:25

Faith is to know and trust the God who holds your future in his hands. A person who believes in God does not necessarily have all the answers, but he knows the Person who has all the answers. Through his grace you realise how righteous God is, and you will know that all the unrighteousness and suffering of this world racked by sin are only temporary. Permanent peace will reign in God's kingdom where he will give complete comfort.

If you trust in God he will nourish your soul even in the desert of suffering and you will find the strength to survive. Faith relieves the bitterness of suffering and helps you to overcome your fear of grief. Through faith you see the hand of God in all things and you will find inner strength and joy.

*H*eavenly Father, I believe in you and put all my trust in you.
Reveal yourself to me in the midst of this storm
through Christ, my Redeemer.

Faith means simply to accept God's Word – *DAVID WATSON.*

The test of true Christian love

T he test of true Christianity is love. Our world is sorely lacking in love. There is so much jealousy that we can easily be swept along – unless we are continually on our guard.

To counteract this spirit of lovelessness we must experience the Holy Spirit as a reality in our lives. We must develop such a love for Christ that it becomes a positive driving-force in our lives. We shall then be able to dress wounds rather than inflict wounds; we shall serve each other in humbleness instead of trying to dominate them.

> *By this all men will know that you are my disciples, if you love one another.*
> JN 13:35

Love is the trademark which should be visible in our everyday lives. As Christ is the source of all true love, we must open up our lives to the Spirit and allow him to love others through us. The world will know beyond any doubt whose children we are and we shall pass the test of true Christian faith.

After the example of Christ, we shall even be able to demonstrate true Chrsitian love to those who hate us. Christ demonstrated this love to us when he prayed for those who had nailed him to the cross.

L oving Father, help me to share love abundantly and never to ask whether it is deserved. From you I deserve only punishment and yet, because of the atoning death of your Son, you bless me with abundant love from day to day.

I have decided to stick to love. Hate is indeed far too heavy a burden to bear – MARTIN LUTHER KING (JR).

Sustained prayer

I nnumerable books have been written about prayer, many of them suggesting steps which should help to counteract the negative effects of a wandering mind. These guidelines have helped some people; others found them frustrating because they could not apply them effectively.

Whatever method you are using to develop a meaningful and fruitful prayer life, make sure that it does not break down the communication shared between you and God. Prayer must never be a dreary obligation

> *Pray continually.*
> 1 THESS 5:17

where you say, "I must go and pray again!" Your prayers will then reflect no joy and kindle no inspiration.

Effective prayer is determined by your attitude towards God. Make a habit of talking to God in a natural tone of voice, as you would with a true friend. Share your life with him: your joy and grief; your successes and failures. Continually ask for his help and guidance and prayer will become an integral and natural part of your life.

/ thank you Lord, that you are not restricted to time or place. It
is an indescribable privilege to be able to pray, simply
because Jesus Christ had made it possible for me.

---

*If you cannot pray about what you are doing, it would be best
not to do it – ABRAHAM LINCOLN.*

Notes

NOVEMBER

PRAYER

❖❖❖❖❖❖❖❖❖❖❖❖❖❖❖❖❖❖❖❖❖❖❖❖❖

*H*eavenly Teacher

This month we worship you as being the beginning and the end of all true wisdom and knowledge.

It's time for thousands of scholars and students to write
  exams to account for their work over the past year
  – but there are also those who have to account for their lives.

Grant me your peace
  which surpasses all understanding.

Strengthen me and make me calm
  when I am under pressure.

Live within my heart so that I shall remain calm and collected
  when I have to account for my deeds.

Be my eyes so that I shall have
  good judgment and understanding
  when I read and learn.

Be in my thoughts so that I may
  be able to think logically and clearly.

Take my hands and make them strong and firm
  and help me to reproduce my knowledge and be able to
  express the facts clearly in writing.

Thank you for all those who lovingly think about
  and pray for me.

During this time – each day – be for me
  the Way along which I must walk;
  the Truth about which I should be informed;
  the Life which I must live.

In the name of the loving Teacher,
  Jesus Christ.

*A*men

Read PSALM 30

Night gives way to the morning

The Bible often describes death as "sleep". This implies that we shall wake up to a new morning. The night comes to an end and the eternal day dawns! After that day there will be no more sleep, tears or sorrow. 1 Thessalonians 4:13 offers us a rich consolation, "Brothers, we do not want you to be ignorant about those who fall asleep, or to grieve like the rest of men, who have no hope."

When a loved one dies, we mourn and find it difficult to believe in a "dawn" and a "sunrise". The children of God, however, have the assurance that the night will pass. In Revelation Christ declared that he is the bright morning star and that there will be no night!

> . . . *weeping may remain for a night,*
> *but rejoicing comes in the morning.*
> PS 30:5

Do not despair during your night of sorrow. Focus on the horizon where God, the loving Creator, will allow a new day to break for you.

Lord Jesus, thank you for the steadfast assurance that the sun will shine again and that my loved ones and I will eternally be with you in a happy reunion.

This is the secret of joy: not to battle to have things your way, but to simply surrender completely to God's will and find your peace that way — *EVELYN UNDERHILL.*

2 NOVEMBER

Read EPHESIANS 5:6-20

With a song in your heart

Singing and thankfulness go hand in hand. Thankfulness spills over in song, regardless of circumstances. If we sing, we prove that God is in our hearts; moreover, our song will prove to the world that he is King of our lives.

All of us who care to listen, will hear song and music all over in God's creation: the wind sighing through the trees, the waves breaking rhythmically onto the sand, the undulating cornfields. When Christ was born, the jubilant song of angels could be heard. Before Jesus was arrested and crucified he sang hymns of praise with his disciples. In heaven the unceasing song of the redeemed will be heard. Let us make sure that we rehearse for it in the meantime!

> *Instead, be filled with the Spirit.*
> *Speak to one another with psalms,*
> *hymns and spiritual songs.*
> *Sing and*
> *make music in your heart to the Lord.*
> EPH 5:18-19

Singing gives us courage. Like Paul and Silas we must be able to sing in affliction. We are witnesses of the cross, but also of the glory of Christ's triumphant procession through the ages.

May your song serve as an encouragement to other believers and strengthen them.

Holy God, and in Jesus Christ my heavenly Father, make me faithful in the ministry of encouragement. Grant that the song within me will never be silent.

A new creature, a new song and the New Testament all form part of the same kingdom – *ST AUGUSTINE.*

Man's cry from the heart

M an has an inborn desire to pray and we are disappointed if this need is not satisfied.

When man implores in his distress, "Lord, teach me to pray," he asks God to open a door to a fuller en richer life for him. Nobody can utter this cry of distress and remain bitter or petty. The desire to pray is the desire to reach out, to search for and find God's hand and tackle life with God at your side. He shows you the way to a meaningful existence. He will lead you on the road to your goal if you constantly depend on him.

There will be times when you are tired and have little desire to pray. Keep a check on your emotions. Don't think you need not pray, because you don't feel like it. In fact, that is exactly the time to put more effort into your prayers. When your spiritual life is barren and unfruitful,

> *Lord, teach us to pray. . .*
> LK 11:1

it is time to persevere in prayer until God's love begins to shine upon you again.

Pray at all times, because that is the only way in which you can sustain a productive prayer life. Let these words be the desire of your heart, "Lord, teach me to pray. . ."

G od of grace and love, sometimes I despair about my prayer life. I implore you to enable me to pray to you in truth.

The person who has learnt to pray is no longer alone on earth. He lives in his Father's house – WILLIAM ADAMS BROWN.

Read PSALM 126

Songs of joy follow dark moments

Our omniscient God varies our experiences in life like the changing seasons. Sometimes we imagine our grief to last for ever; however, God will allow you times of joy and song again. No matter how improbable this might seem at this moment, don't harden your heart. If you don't keep on wallowing in your grief, God will temper it through his love and grace and allow it to pass.

> *Those who sow in tears will reap with songs of joy.*
> PS 126:5

In Psalm 126 the psalmist sings praises to the miraculous and renewing grace of God. Unless we refuse to be comforted, our grief will always be turned into joy and happiness in God's own good time. The darkest night is always followed by a clear daybreak. For the Christian joy and heavenly happiness always follows suffering and pain in this world.

While we are comforted by God, a song of praise will spring from our hearts. The melody will become richer, deeper and more convincing. Through God's gracious consolation we shall experience an exuberant joy. When we have passed through the training-school of grief, we have grown in spiritual strength. Praise the Lord!

Loving Lord, free me from the prison of depression and grief. Change my grief into joy and my tears into a song to your glory.

Teach me, my God and King, in all things Thee to see, and what I do in any thing, to do it as for Thee – *GEORGE HERBERT.*

You are God's child

Are you dismally alone and without comfort? Does the future look bleak and has your self-confidence suffered a blow? Is depression threatening to overcome you? Remember: You are God's child! If you have first-hand experience of being a child of God, you will find life to be dynamic, you will experience a sparkling joy and your negative attitude will change completely.

Through Jesus Christ you may call God your Father and because he loves you and yearns for your love and obedience, you are called to be the person God wants you to be. He wants you to reflect his glory and that can only be accomplished if you surrender to him completely.

> *How great is the love the Father has lavished on us, that we should be called children of God! And that is what we are!*
> 1 JN 3:1

The more his will is realised in your life, the stronger you will be bound to him. The blessed assurance that he is truly your Father and that you are irrevocably his child will be part of your life. You will never be alone again; new horizons will continually be opened up to you; self-confidence will develop in your life again and when you reflect on your Father's great love for you, you will experience true joy instead of depression.

I thank you, dear Father, for your immeasurable love which surrounds me. I am speechless at the privilege of being your child.

We do not belong to ourselves . . . We did not create ourselves . . . We cannot be our own masters. On account of our creation, redemption and rebirth we belong to God
— *JOHN HENRY KEWMAS.*

Rejoice!

Rejoicing in the Lord is an outstanding Christian virtue. In his letter to the Philippians Paul said that they should rejoice in the Lord (3:1) and in chapter 4:4 he repeated this command, "Rejoice in the Lord always. I will say it again: Rejoice!"

We need to remind one another of the duty as Christians to rejoice, simply because our religion and our faith in the Lord provide sufficient reasons for rejoicing in the Lord. What is more, the Gospel is the Word of God which brings us glad tidings.

> *Finally, my brothers, rejoice in the Lord!*
> PHIL 3:1

So many people, for some or other reason, have lost the exuberance of their Christian joy. A little more joy will make this world a better place to live and to work in. However, our eyes must be opened to the difference between the joy which is rooted in God and the joy of this world. The joy of this world resembles that of the prodigal son in a far country. It is transient. The joy which comes from God is the permanent joy of the feast in the house of our Father where we belong.

I thank you, Lord, that I can rejoice because you have saved me and have opened the gates of heaven to me. Allow my joy to originate in you always so that nobody will be able to take it away from me.

Seeing our Father in everything makes life one long thanksgiving and gives a rest of heart, and, more than that, a gaiety of spirit that is unspeakable – HANNAH WHITALL SMITH.

Love one another

Love is no idle, meaningless word, but a practical way of life. When you are disappointed, bitter or cross about something somebody has said to you or has done to you, you can only come to terms with it by identifying yourself with the love of Christ.

For Christ love was the all-important characteristic. He even loved his enemies and prayed for them when they nailed him to the cross. Only a sanctified love of this kind can obliterate feelings of revenge or bitterness.

If the love of Christ lives in us, it enables us to be patient, friendly and tolerant, irrespective of the degree of the provocation. It enables us to see the good in every person; to see the image of Christ in all people and to become aware of our unity in Christ.

> *A new command I give you: Love one another. As I have loved you, so you must love one another.*
>
> JN 13:34

This love forms part of the fruit of the Holy Spirit in our lives. The more we accept the religious truths of the Spirit of God, the more this godly love will control our lives.

Father, fill us with this heavenly gift – love – to such an extent that no room will be left for hate or bitterness.

Only three things are needed to make us happy: something to do; something to hope for; and someone to love – CONFUCIUS.

Yearning for God

Life moves at a terrific speed and when at times we come to a standstill, a strange nostalgia gets the better of us – a yearning which we cannot really define.

This yearning can sometimes turn into a burning desire for a long-lost, peaceful past; for times gone by and for people we used to know.

> *When anxiety was great within me, your consolation brought joy to my soul.*
>
> PS 94:19

This type of longing, however much as you may revel in it, should not paralyse you or hamper your actions. You must not become an idle dreamer and thereby neglect your obligations towards the realities of life.

God has an answer to the yearning for him, just as he provides answers when we are faced by stumbling-blocks in life. In the end his undying love leaves us with only one yearning: the yearning for God himself.

This yearning is satisfied in our communion with him which is our defence against the erosion caused by nostalgia, a defence which is rooted in a prayer life full of vitality and an existence which is founded in the eternal Word of God.

Heavenly Father, I thank you that you always offer me your favour; that even in the midst of my nostalgia I can sing your praise and can pray to you, the God of my life.

Daily prayer is the gymnasiun of the soul – *C E COWMAN.*

Read JOHN 11:17-32

He who believes in God will live

Many people are shortsighted and have a distorted attitude towards eternity. All tasks which have a bearing on this life are performed with the utmost conscientiousness and they wear themselves out for a worldly existence. But they display a deplorable shortsightedness as far as spiritual matters are concerned. The eternal, the only security in our unstable existence, is neglected, even ignored.

Jesus Christ, however, promised a glorious life in the hereafter for those who love him and look forward to his coming. He himself prepares our place in heaven and promises his children things that the eyes have not seen, that the ears have not heard, nor which the heart can ever imagine.

> *He who believes in me will live,*
> *even though he dies;*
> *and whoever*
> *believes in me will never die.*
> JN 11:25-26

Your life becomes meaningful only when you have a sound perspective on eternity. Then you will know that this life does not end in the grave, but that death is only the gateway through which you enter into the illuminating glory of heaven. This knowledge makes life open up like a flower. It becomes a mere apprenticeship for eternity and you can joyfully sing praises to the Lord for your redemption.

Eternal God, thank you that the gates of paradise which closed behind Adam and Eve were opened again through the death and resurrection of Christ, my Saviour.

The tragedy of life is that man can die while he is still alive
— ALBERT SCHWEITZER.

Read JAMES 4:1-10

Draw near to God

These words in James 4:8 are a wonderful encouragement to all of us. However, it also spells out a warning.

We gather from this verse that we ourselves are to be blamed when we have the impression that God is far from us and unreal – it is our fault and not that of our heavenly Father. It is our disobedience or pride which makes us turn our backs on God; we refuse to confess our dependence on him and thereby cut ourselves off from communion with the Lord.

If we realise that God is the source of all that is worthwhile in life, that outside him we cannot find true rest, no peace or joy, that love and redemption are only to be found in him, we also realise how essential it is to stay near God.

> *Come near to God and he will come near to you.*
> JAS 4:8

To be near God, is no heavy burden, but an unspeakable privilege. If we live near him, we will find a richness and depth in life which we would never have deemed possible. Drawing near to God is to experience fulness of life which is to be found nowhere else.

*H*eavenly Father, forgive me that through sin I continually stray from you. Help me to stay near you and to be filled with your love and grace.

If you find no joy in your religion there must be a leakage somewhere in your Christian life – W A SUNDAY.

Read ROMANS 15:7-13

Sharing your faith and joy

L et us meet this day with joy in our hearts and let us share the glory of this joy with all those whom we may encounter today. If your faith makes you a happy person, you will not be able to keep this experience to yourself.

Sharing your joy with others is a wonderful privilege. An expression of appreciation; a friendly gesture; a word of encouragement to someone who is dejected; time spent with someone who is grief-stricken – all these things speak of a heartfelt and profound joy.

> *Therefore I will praise you among the Gentiles; I will sing hymns to your name.*
> ROM 15:9

To share joy freely is a way of life which makes our existence worth-while. It builds friendships and makes us sensitive to the needs of others. It helps us to see the positive side of life and makes us cheerful in whatever we do.

To be happy and have joy in our hearts is a gift of God to his children. After all, he is the source of all true and permanent joy. Thank him for it and sing praises in his honour.

*H*oly Lord, help me through your love and grace always to be a cheerful person. Grant me the will to share my joy **with others.**

The surest sign that someone is a Christian is not the faith or love that he reflects, but the joy which he shares
– SAMUEL M SCHOEMACHER.

Read PSALM 27

Safe in the light

Whenever we think of God, we instinctively think of a bright light which expels the dark. Christ declared that he is the Light of the world and the Word tells us that heaven is the place where God himself is the light.

However, we are mistaken if we think that God is not present in the darkness of this life. In Psalm 23:4 we read, "Even though I walk through the valley of the shadow of death, I will fear no evil, for you are with me; your rod and your staff, they comfort me."

We may take hold of the encouraging truth that God comes to us in our darkest moments and even when we despair of life. However dark your life may seem, God is there. In his own good time he will turn the darkness into light.

> *The LORD is my light and my salvation – whom shall I fear?*
> PS 27:1

Are you surrounded by the darkness of your own sinfulness? Are you confused, undecided, stricken by illness? God is there! He wants to take your hand and guide you out of this darkness into his wonderful light!

God of love and light, thank you that in my darkest hour I may know that it will never be too dark for you to be there; that even in the most sorrowful of moments your light will cast out the dark.

God is never conquered. He can be opposed, attacked and queried, but there will be no doubt as to the outcome of it all
– BROTHER ANDREW.

You are never alone

L oneliness is a painful reality. There is the loneliness of the bed-ridden who feel completely cut off from life; there is the loneliness within a family, of family members who miss each other with aching hearts; there is the loneliness of old age when physical strength decline; there is social isolation, when you feel isolated amidst bustling crowds; there is the loneliness of drug addiction, of alcohol abuse, dishonesty and immorality; and also the loneliness in death.

> *And surely I am with you always,*
> *to the very end of the age.*
> MT 28:20

However, our Guide is aware of our loneliness, therefore there is so much comfort in his promise that he will be with us always. In Gethsemane he was completely alone when he wrestled with God. Because even God had forsaken him on the cross, we can have complete faith in his promise. When we, therefore, pass through the valley of the shadow of death, our joyful song of victory can still resound to the glory of God, in spite of all our fears and our loneliness.

/ praise you, Lord Jesus, and I worship you as the One who can lift us out of loneliness and isolation. Thank you that you remain with me always. Help me to remain in you always.

The stronger and tougher your faith in God, the more abundantly you will receive whatever you ask of God in faith
— ALBERT THE GREAT.

Praise the Lord

The words of Psalm 103:2 can serve as a banner under which we can meet each new day.

Thankfulness is a wonderful remedy. Whenever you feel depressed and lonely; when you ask yourself whether life still has any purpose or meaning, just look around and you are sure to find something for which you can thank God.

If you come to the conclusion that there is nothing for which you can thank God, you have forgotten that you are his child and that he loves you very much. Convince yourself again that this is an unsurpassable truth; repeat it to yourself with conviction: God loves me; I am his child! Subsequently thank him for his love – you will be surprised what a positive effect it will have on your state of mind.

> *Praise the LORD, O my soul; and forget not all his benefits.*
> PS 103:2

Praise God and thank him every day. This is the surest cure for worry and self-pity. It will improve your view on life and you will be a blessing to others.

*H*oly and loving Father, fill my heart with joy, praise and thankfulness so that there will be no room for depression or self-pity.

The degree of a person's happiness depends on how profound his thankfulness is – *JOHN MILLER.*

Read GENESIS 1:26-31

In God's image

All of us lose our self-confidence at some time or other. Perhaps it has been happening gradually and imperceptibly, but it can reach such alarming proportions that you become desperate. When this happens to you, it is a good idea to remember the words of Genesis 1:27.

Maintain your dignity. You are God's creation, you have been created in his image. You can make a list of all you shortcomings, and take an unhealthy delight in meditating on it and in pitying yourself. But if you want to be sensible, don't succumb to judging yourself and others, both of which may drive you to despair.

> *So God created man in his own image,*
> *in the image of God he created him . . .*
> GEN 1:27

Pray to your heavenly Father and remember that he sees great potential in you and has great expectations for you. In his mercy God will assist you and you will become who he has destined you to be.

Live for God and not as others think you should live. However humble your task may be, do everything to the glory of God and that task will also bear the stamp of dignity.

Father, I thank you that you have a loving plan for my life. Protect me against despair and inspire me with your holy ideals.

What helps us to triumph over most problems? Patience and courage — *WALDO RALPH EMERSON.*

God blesses us

God made the special promise in Genesis 12:2-3 to Abraham when he instructed him to leave his country and embark on a journey of faith to an unknown, promised land.

Through Abraham's faith God's blessings would extend to all the people he encountered along the way. By means of intercession Abraham passed on his God-given blessing to others; he dug wells where those who were thirsty could freely quench their thirst; as a servant he was a blessing to his environment and as a priest he was a blessing to his family. And from his descendants, Christ would one day be born.

> *I will bless you . . . and all peoples on earth will be blessed through you.*
>
> GEN 12:2-3

We may never keep God's blessings to ourselves. Although we don't know what others need to live a blessed life, the almighty God knows. It is our duty to pray that God will enable us to become channels through whom his blessings can flow to others in this world.

If we reflect the disposition of Jesus Christ in this world; if we show appreciation and praise the work of others; if we have faith in our fellow-men; if we encourage others and pray for them, we can be a rich blessing in the world where God has placed us, to the glory of his name.

I worship you as the source of all blessings, Father. Thank you for blessing me so abundantly that I can not help but be a blessing to others.

The greatest deed a human being can perform for his heavenly Father is to show compassion towards his other children
— HENRY DRUMMOND.

Jesus Christ, the Unchangeable

L ife moves on and sometimes we have to adapt to changes that can be quite painful. One of the most difficult adjustments is to accept a changed world in which your circle of friends and loved ones grows smaller.

When your life is influenced by this truth, guard against morbidity and bitterness or self-pity. Adapting to your loneliness will require much patience on your part. The new generation may be difficult to understand, but don't begrudge them the opportunity to improve the world which they have inherited from your

> *Generations come and generations go, but the earth remains for ever.*
> ECCLES 1:4

generation. Show appreciation for their purposefulness, their honest intentions and their effort with regard to the things they believe in.

Reconcile yourself to the fact that what has been, belongs to the past and is only valuable in as far as it can serve as an inspiration for the future. Cherish pleasant memories, but don't allow them to chain you to the past. Hold onto the truths which will never change: faith, hope and love, but above all, hold on to Jesus Christ. Then you will see beauty in this changing world and a song of praise will resound in your heart.

U nchangeable God, I thank you for all the wonderful memories life has given me. I put my trust in you for the unknown future.

Hope is patience which has lit its lamp from God's light
— TERTULLIAN.

18 NOVEMBER

Read ISAIAH 45:1-7

Treasures of darkness

These remarkable words in Isaiah 45 strengthen and encourage all those who suffer. None of us can claim that it never gets dark along life's way.

However, when we read these words, they seem to contain conflicting ideas and sound impossible. What treasures can possibly be in store for us during the dark moments in our lives? Yet it is one of the secrets of life: it is especially in the dark hours of our lives that God desires to bestow on us the gift of his most valuable treasures. It is then that he desires to be near us.

> *I will give you the treasures of darkness,*
> *riches stored*
> *in secret places,*
> *so that you may know that I am the LORD,*
> *the God of Israel,*
> *who summons you*
> *by name.*
>
> IS 45:3

In our hour of suffering he wishes to assure us that he is our Father and we are his children. He desires to strengthen our faith. He wants to share the unutterable treasure of his love and comfort during our dark hour.

What more could we desire?

Thank you, heavenly Father, that the wonder of your love and comfort, the certainty that I am your child, are revealed to me during the dark moments in my life.

Faith is deaf to doubt, numb to discouragement, blind to impossibilities and knows of nothing else than success
— CHEYNE BRADY.

Do good to others

N ever hesitate to express honest appreciation and gratitude. We so easily take work or sacrifices for granted and assume them as a right. Appreciation not only brings joy to the person to whom it is expressed, but it also lightens the hearts of those who express it.

Guard against being self-centred and trying to get more out of life than you are prepared to put into it. Be sensitively aware of everything for which you can be thankful and you will realise that there are so many wonderful things which you simply take for granted in your own life.

> *Therefore, as we have opportunity, let us do good to all people, especially to those who belong to the family of believers.*
>
> GAL 6:10

Love, loyalty and a spirit of sacrifice are all attractive characteristics which you experience and see in the lives of people you encounter every day. Regain the ability to appreciate the everyday deeds of love that come your way and try to reciprocate with your own unselfish deeds of love.

Never forget God's goodness to you. Nobody can possibly stand before God in praise and thankfulness and be depressed at the same time. Let your thankfulness towards God culminate in deeds of love towards others and you will be a rich source of blessings to all those around you.

/ thank you, Lord, for all your blessings. Thank you for all the love and help I receive from so many people around me, but particularly from you, dear Lord.

There is no purer religion than serving others. To work to the benefit of the community for the love of God, is the highest confession of faith.

Be alert to the needs of others

The book of Job touches us because so many of us share Job's experiences to a larger or smaller extent. In addition so many of the Lord's surprising messages are conveyed to us in this book of the Bible.

When you are in trouble of any kind you easily lose your perspective on life. Without realising it, you may be lapsing into self-pity. You see only the dark side of your life and consequently lose your positive outlook.

> *After Job had prayed for his friends, the LORD made him prosperous again and gave him twice as much as he had before.*
>
> JOB 42:10

God uses Job's life story to teach us to look away from ourselves for a change and to see the needs of others as well. Somewhere there is someone who is in greater distress than we are and who needs our prayers. The reality of our suffering will not disappear, but it will be tempered, because around us we shall see suffering and distress far greater than our own. We shall then discover how much we have in life for which we can be grateful.

When I look away from you, dear Lord, I see only my own distress. Help me to look away from myself, to pray for others and to use my energy to their benefit, just as you have taught us.

I complained because I did not have any shoes, until I saw somebody without feet – ANONYMOUS.

Death is only the beginning

At some time or other all of us are faced with death. Throughout our lives death is our companion. We sense its presence whenever we see the signs of death invading our bodies; and then we fear death.

This world has an undeniable enchantment for all of us. We cringe at the thought of death and we see the grave as a cruel, bottomless pit, although in actual fact it is a doorway through which we can enter into the shining glory of God, into heaven where we shall share in God's immortality.

When we die in Jesus Christ, death is a new beginning. For all of us who love him, God has preprared a place with him. However final death may seem to us, Christ

> *As for man, his days*
> *are like grass,*
> *he flourishes like*
> *a flower of the field;*
> *the wind blows over it*
> *and it is gone,*
> *and its place remembers it*
> *no more.*
>
> PS 103:15-16

assured us, "I am the resurrection and the life. He who believes in me will live, even though he dies" (Jn 11:25).

Whenever we lose a loved one, we can cling to this comfort: Jesus has gone to prepare a place for us and we shall meet again. We can put all our trust in Christ, even when we walk through the valley of death. When we die in Christ we shall be liberated from the last overwhelming fear and we shall sing songs of victory.

Thank you, dear Saviour, that you have conquered death and have opened up eternity for me. Thank you that in faith I can claim the consolation of immortality for myself.

We only begin to have some understanding of death when it lays its hand on someone whom we love – ANNE L DE STAEL.

Read PHILIPPIANS 4:2-9

Speak to God in prayer

There is nothing on this earth about which you cannot pray to God. However, you must remember that prayer involves much more than presenting God with a long list of requests. True prayer involves sharing your entire life in all its dimensions and at all levels with your heavenly Father.

Have you come to a dead end in your prayer life? Perhaps you believe your faith to be weak. You are confused and don't know to whom you can turn for help. Under these circumstances you may be tempted to stop praying because you believe that God is no longer listening to you.

Right then, when you feel overcome by this darkness of uncertainty, the time is right for you to make time to be alone with God and to talk to him. It may not sound so easy, but if you talk to God about your spiritual slump, as you would to a trusted friend, you will experience renewed spiritual strength.

> *Do not be anxious about anything,*
> *but in everything, by prayer and petition,*
> *with thanksgiving,*
> *present your requests to God.*
>
> PHIL 4:6

Thank you, Lord Jesus, that you are a faithful friend in whom I can confide at all times and about all things. May I remain on my knees before you so that I can stand steadfast in this world.

When you pray, it is far better to have a heart without words than words without a heart – *JOHN BUNYAN.*

Love drives out fear

The unfailing Word of God tells us that fear and love cannot live to-gether, yet fear forms part of our everyday life.

The intensity of fear varies in our lives. However, the most destructive fear in one's life is that of a persistent problem. We also worry about many small, sometimes quite insignificant things, often without even being aware of it. These worries obscures the sunshine of God's love for us and robs us of so many spiritual riches.

A loving attitude destroys fear and triumphs over worry. How can you ever be anxious or worried if you truly love God and understand something of his love for you? To fear, is to doubt God; to love God, is to conquer fear. You will even be able to say, "Even though I walk through the valley of the shadow of death, I will fear no evil, for you are with me; your rod and your staff, they comfort me" (Ps 23:4).

> *There is no fear in love. But perfect love drives out fear, because fear has to do with punishment. The one who fears is not made perfect in love.*
>
> 1 JN 4:18

If your hand is firmly in God's hand, fear will never rule your life, even if fear attacked you in a thousand different shapes, because God's love will protect you against all forms of fear.

*H*eavenly Father, thank you that you understand my fear. Thank you that love is the remedy for all my fears and worries. Help me to manifest the law of love in my life.

Let me assert my firm belief that the only thing we have to fear is fear itself — FRANKLIN D ROOSEVELT.

Christ will never let you go

In his omniscience God made the book of Job available to us as an instruction manual to help us cope in crisis situations. The pressures we are subjected to in life, the demands at work and in our relationships often cause tension to mount and we may find it extremely difficult to cope. We might even feel that our values are threatened. It is then that we feel like repeating after Job, "My days are swifter than a weaver's shuttle, and they come to an end without hope. Remember, O God, that my life is but a breath; my eyes will never see happiness again" (7:6-7).

> *I know that you can do all things;*
> *no plan of yours can be thwarted.*
> JOB 42:2

Stress makes us feel depressed, frustrated and leaves us without any drive or will to face life. We begin to question the meaning of life, to doubt God's existence and his purpose with us.

All these signs signify but one thing: our prayer lives have deteriorated. A positive, prayer life full of vitality is our guarantee against losing our faith in life and in God's existence. It is our assurance against despair. A meaningful prayer life will give us a firm grip on life and will strengthen the knowledge that *Christ will never let me go.*

Father, because I know that you are there, I am able to live a more purposeful life through your mercy, power and love.

For today only I shall look twelve hours ahead and not try to solve all my problems all at once – ANONYMOUS.

Reach out towards your opportunities

Many of us are burdened by feelings of guilt and self-reproach about the past. We can therefore identify with Paul's words to the Philippians in chapter 3:1-14.

We carry so many unnecessary burdens. If only we would leave them behind, we shall be able to walk with a lighter step and experience far more joy.

> *I press on towards the goal to win the prize for which God has called me heavenwards in Christ Jesus.*
> PHIL 3:14

Therefore, forget about your disappointments and reach out towards the new opportunities which God is offering you. Forget about your bitterness and hatred and reach out to avail yourself of God's love.

Forget about irrevocable failures and follow Jesus Christ on the road to victory. Forget about sins of the past and reach out towards the forgiveness which your Saviour offers you. Forget whatever is behind and focus upon the author and perfecter of your faith – Jesus Christ.

Lord Jesus, I thank you that with you tomorrow will always be better than yesterday; thank you that I need not worry about yesterday or the day before, as long as you are in control of my life today and tomorrow.

It is right and good that you should begin each day anew. There is no better way of enriching your spiritual life than to begin each day anew without thinking that you have done enough
— *FRANCIS DE SALIS.*

Why?

Most people find if difficult not to ask the question "Why?" when they are confronted with sickness and suffering. When you ask this question, it is a wonderful grace to hear God saying that all will end well. Inspired by the Spirit of God, Paul, who himself had his own share of sickness, suffering and problems, tells us this in Romans 8.

Believe that the trials which have come to change your life, will be for your own good. No parent will ever intentionally allow something unpleasant to happen to his or her child. This applies so much more to God who will not allow anything to happen to us without a purpose. Everything that happens to us will complete God's blueprint for our lives and will work out for our own good.

> *And we know that*
> *in all things*
> *God works for the good*
> *of those who love him,*
> *who have been called*
> *according to his purpose.*
> ROM 8:28

What is good for us? Who will be able to judge this? The suffering of the crippled man in the Bible did not look "good", but when his friends brought him to Jesus, even the suffering proved to be for his own good. Not only did he regain his health, but he also received life everlasting.

Our prayer should be that God grants us the grace to view our suffering and grief in this light and that as a result we may experience peace in our hearts.

Father, help me to be thankful even in sickness and grief. I know that all things will work for the good in my life, because you love me.

Sickness of the body forms part of the kingdom of Satan and Christ has come to destroy it – FRANCIS MACNUTT.

God himself will comfort you

No man is above the need of being comforted. That is why the words of Isaiah 51:12 are universally comforting, but they are particularly comforting to those who believe in God.

There is much sorrow in this world torn apart by sin. Grief and depression form part of everyone's lives at some stage or other. It is our Christian duty not to succumb under the pressure of these emotions. In the same way as light drives out darkness, God's comfort banishes our grief.

In Isaiah 66:13 we read, "As a mother comforts her child, so will I comfort you." That is why there is a song in our hearts, even in the darkest night.

> *I, even I, am he who comforts you.*
> *Who are you that you fear mortal men,*
> *the sons of men, who are but grass . . .?*
>
> IS 51:12

God regards our peace of mind as so important that he desires to give it to us himself. He does not delegate this duty to someone else, but comforts us himself. Let us rejoice in this wonderful and lasting comfort which God gives us time after time!

Holy God, fill my heart with joy through the comfort which you grant me. I desire to remain in your love. Thank you for the promise that you yourself will wipe every tear from my eyes.

Let us trust God! He alone knows what is beneficial for our temporary and eternal joy and good
— WOLFGANG AMADEUS MOZART.

28 NOVEMBER

Read 1 PETER 5:5-11

Cast your anxiety on the Lord

The course of our lives never exactly follows the path that we would like. The burdens which rest upon our shoulders sometimes threaten to break and overwhelm us. At times like these it is easy to become depressed, to give up and despair of ever living a victorious life.

The mistake we make, is that we try to solve our problems ourselves; we want to resist the setbacks in our own power. This is the point where our burden becomes too heavy to carry. We become spiritually and intellectually exhausted.

> Cast all your anxiety on him because he cares for you.
>
> 1 PET 5:7

Under such circumstances we need a true experience with God, an experience so real that we surrender to him completely without being afraid. He, the source of power and strength, will touch our lives and enable us to remain steadfast, even when it feels as if our foundations are shaken.

The wonder remains that God does indeed care for us. All our burdens and worries can become new opportunities to enhance our experience with the Lord, and to increase and deepen our knowledge of him.

*H*eavenly Father, thank you that I may come to you with all my worries and burdens in the steadfast faith that you will care for me. Help me always to hold on to this truth.

What doesn't destroy me, makes me strong – JOHN PERKINS.

Read JOHN 14:1-14

Do not let your hearts be troubled

Problems and worry form an essential part of our lives on earth. All of us have to contend with them at some stage or other. Sometimes our own careless conduct is to blame, but at other times they come our way for no reason at all.

In John 14:1 Jesus commands us not to be anxious. In the same breath he commands us to have faith.

Your attitude towards the problems you experience in life is of the utmost importance. You can allow panic to overwhelm you and everything will just get worse, or you can consider your position calmly before God and do something constructive about it. The choice is yours. Be assured of the help and assistance of the Almighty and be positive. Believe in God and trust in him. Always put God first in your life and know that you can go to him with all your problems.

> *Do not let your hearts be troubled. Trust in God; trust also in me.*
> JN 14:1

In his presence you will be able to see your problems in the right perspective and through God's grace and omnipotence you will know for sure that there is a solution.

Almighty Redeemer, I place my problems before you in prayer in the knowledge that you will grant me wisdom to deal with them.

To love God is something far greater than merely knowing him
— *THOMAS AQUINAS.*

30 NOVEMBER

God arms you with strength

Life can be very confusing and unpredictable. For a while everything runs smoothly and you feel strong and full of confidence. Suddenly the unexpected happens; friends disappoint you; problems overwhelm you; grief descends on your life; your faith loses its purpose and meaning. At times like these the words of Psalm 18:33 can be a wonderful encouragement.

In your darkest moments you must remember that God has a perfect plan with your life, but he expects you to fulfil that purpose through obedience. Never lower your spiritual standards to adapt to the world around you. If you do this, you will live an artificial life and you will deny God's power in your life.

> *It is God who arms me with strength
> and makes my path perfect.*
> PS 18:32

We all know that God expects us to walk in his ways and power, but at the same time we know that on our own it is impossible to do this. That is why we often start making compromises with the world.

The time has come for God to realise his perfect will in your life. Believe in him. Trust that he can and wants to do it. Blinded by God's holiness and omnipotence, Paul asked God on the road to Damascus, "Lord, what do you want me to do?" *You* must ask God that same question. Now, get up from your knees and live according to the will of God.

Saviour, thank you that my life finds it highest fulfilment in you. Help me to become what you have intended me to be through the power of Jesus Christ.

Man – our neighbour – becomes a holy object only when we understand that he is the property of God and that Jesus Christ has died for him – HELMUTH THIELICKE.

DECEMBER

PRAYER

❖❖❖❖❖❖❖❖❖❖❖❖❖❖❖❖❖❖❖❖❖❖❖❖

*I*mmanuel, God with us
Lord Jesus, Child of Bethlehem, we worship you.
We look forward to celebrating your birth at Christmas.
Grant that we shall enter this Christmastide
　　with an attitude of sincerity.
Cleanse us from a spirit of bitterness and hatred,
　　and free us from sin.
Let us give each gift in a spirit of love
　　and may each greetings card be a confession of our faith in
　　you, our Redeemer.
May your Spirit add a new meaning to
　　well-known Christmas carols.
Grant that Christmas will bring renewed reconciliation
　　between God and man, so that each and everyone will call
　　you Father.
Also bring about reconciliation between man and man.
May the peace of which the angels sang
　　not only be an idle dream or an unattainable ideal,
　　but may it become a reality through our faith.
Grant that the wonder of Christmas will bring joy
　　into our hearts, not only for a short while,
　　but that it will remain with us when we have to resume our
　　duties,
　　when we have to face the worries and responsibilities that
　　each day brings.
This we ask in the name of Jesus who came
　　to save man from his sins
　　and to be Immanuel – God with us for the entire world.

*A*men

A shoot has come up

The house of David stood like a strong tree in die middle of the field, but then all this splendour was chopped down and the house of David fell into decay. The only one left was Mary, but she was not held in high esteem and consequently she could not believe that God was calling her to become the mother of his Son. Yet, through God's omnipotence a shoot came up and heralded a wonderful new era – the birth of Jesus Christ.

> *A shoot will come up from the stump of Jesse; from his roots a Branch will bear fruit.*
>
> IS 11:1

Although a shoot often looks insignificant, it contains life and the potential to grow into an independent and mighty tree. The tender shoot which Isaiah foretold came up from a felled stump, grew into an indestructible tree which extends its branches all the way to the ends of the earth. The child in the crib became the way, the truth and the life and his reign will have no end.

With Christmas right around the corner we must evaluate our personal relationship with Christ. First of all we must confess our spiritual decay so that God can revitalise our faith like new shoots on a stump.

Lord, you are mighty and able to create new life from a partly withered stump. Take my weak faith in your hand and let my life also be renewed.

Jesus' coming in the flesh is the final and unshakeable proof that God cares – WILLIAM BARCLAY.

God with us

The Son of God came to us in the form of a man. This is joyfully proclaimed on Christmas Eve. The Light which was the light of the world long before Christ came to earth, became "flesh". As a human he was without the glory of his original heavenly image. In everything he became our equal, yet he was without sin. The wonder of Christmas is this: Immanuel – God with us! God, exalted into the highest heavens, so far removed from sinful earthlings, came down from above. In the person of his Son he paved the way in order for us to share in the favour of the Father once more.

> *But now in Christ you who once were far away have been brought near through the blood of Christ.*
> EPH 2:13

Jesus Christ became flesh to restore the relationship between us and God, he came as mediator to reconcile us with God, he became our Saviour.

God above us; God far from us; and now: God with us!

This is the secret of the divine Christmas Eve and the reason for our indescribable joy during this festive season.

Father, I marvel at the mystery of your Son becoming flesh. In faith I accept this miracle and rejoice in the assurance that he came to the world for the sake of my sins.

Remove Christ from Christmas and December will be the most miserable and dreary month of the year – A F WELLS.

Read ISAIAH 62:6-12

Celebrating our redemption

At Christmas we celebrate Christ's coming to the earth. However, we may never forget that he came to live in our hearts and souls. We may not merely confess with words that he came to the world as the Lamb of God to take the sins of the world upon him. It is a wonderful confession, but it will serve no purpose if we do not personally share Christ's redeeming power in our hearts. Christmas will be around us but the true joy of Christmas will not fill our hearts.

If we truly want to experience the joy of Christmas, we must allow Christ to enter our hearts with his redeeming peace. Thank God that he came to seek and save what was lost. Moreover, to all who receive him, to those who believe in his name, he gives the right to become children of God (Jn 1:12). Do you believe this? Do you believe that he will relieve you of your worry and despair about your own sins?

> The LORD has made proclamation to the ends of the earth: "Say to the daughter of Zion, 'See, your Saviour comes.'"
>
> IS 62:11

Christ comes to you with his hands full of mercy, forgiveness and blessing. He comes to change your grief into joy. It is Christmas – a time to rejoice about your redemption. Immanuel – God in the flesh with us, God with us in spirit!

Holy Father, thank you that you want to grant us the unmatched joy and happiness of faith and redemption through Jesus Christ.

Even if Christ had been born in Bethlehem a thousand times, unless he was reborn in my own heart, I shall be lost
— MARTIN LUTHER.

---

4 DECEMBER

Read ISAIAH 62:10-12

Christ with us in our hour of death

Although God's children all long to share in the coming of the Lord, not everyone will witness it. However, the coming of the Lord arrives for each of us the very moment we die. In this poignant moment we meet the Lord: it is an encounter which heralds either life everlasting or eternal darkness.

In the weeks preceding Christmas we are again faced by the following questions: Shall we be able to welcome him with joy when he comes to us on our death beds? Do we see the even greater majesty of eternity behind the magnitude of death?

> See, his reward is with him, and his recompense accompanies him.
>
> IS 62:11

Death pervades the last days of the year as we hear reports of numerous lives lost in road accidents. It is the time to find an answer to the question: Is death the great Advent for us? Shall we be able to meet Christ with a shout of joy that the bridegroom has come and go out to meet him? If we really testify to this joy, death will hold no fear for us and we shall enter into the eternal wedding feast and share an eternal Christmas in heaven.

Father, during Christmas we always experience something of death. Give us insight into the majesty of life in Christ, so that death will hold no fear for us.

The last heartbeat of the Christian is not the misterious end to a meaningless existence. It is the glorious beginning of a life which will never end – JAMES DOBSON.

Behold, He is coming soon!

Jesus descended from his heavenly splendour to the humbleness of the manger and the stable. His entire life on earth would be a road of sorrows, so that he would be able to save a lost world from sin and make all men children of God.

Christmas reminds us that Christ, the great Sower, shed tears as he sowed the seeds. His work, commenced in humiliation, will be completed when he comes again in splendour to reap the harvest: the rich harvest of human souls who have found peace at the manger and at the foot of the cross. It will be a triumphant coming. The Son of man will appear, the heavenly host will surround him, the last call of the trumpet will sound and the dead will be raised. That will be the day of the great Advent, for which the congregation of Christ is waiting.

> *"Behold, I am coming soon!"*
> REV 22:7

During the Christmas season we hear the voice saying again, "Behold, I am coming soon!" We reply with sighs of longing, "Amen. Come, Lord Jesus!" Thus all these days preceding Christmas become rich in comfort. In these days we initially see Christ in his manger and Christ on his cross; but then our eyes are opened to his grace, his victory and at any moment, his second coming in splendour!

Thank you, holy Lord, for the great blessing of Christmas. Grant that my prayer will always remain:
Come, Lord Jesus!

The Son is the image of the invisible God. Everything that belongs to the Father is glorified when Christ's majesty is revealed to us – ST AMBROSE.

6 DECEMBER

Read MATTHEW 2:1-12

Do not despair

The Magi, wise men from the east, persevered in their search for the Child. Initially a star guided them. God wanted those who were far removed, to come nearer to him, therefore he made himself known to them through something that was within their frame of reference: he made a star appear. After all, they were star-gazers. Their home country was Mesopotamia, but they followed the star all the way to find Jesus, the Messiah, and to worship him.

The star signified the beginning of the Light for them, because they were still children of the darkness. The star was the signpost to Christmas, but it was not Christmas itself! Obediently they followed the star in their search for the Child. God still seeks and calls men just as he called the wise men: he called the wise men by means of a star

> *After Jesus was born in Bethlehem in Judea . . . Magi from the east came to Jerusalem . . .*
>
> MT 2:1

which guided them; he called the shepherds with angels singing God's praises; he calls each of us in his or her unique way.

God's love also provides stars to guide us and we thank him for them. However, we may not remain standing where the star is, for the star is only the beginning of the way to redemption. From the star we must proceed to the Word which has become flesh.

*H*oly God, thank you for the stars in my life which guide me to you. Help me to persevere on the road you have mapped out for me according to your holy will.

Courage does not mean turning a blind eye to dangers. It means observing it and in conquering it in the name of Christ
— JEAN PAUL RICHTER.

The light for our path

There was a great upheaval in Jerusalem. Everybody was expecting a king, but nobody knew where to find him. The scribes had to ponder the question: what does the Word of God say? The Magi probably looked upon this as taking a step backwards: why leave the shining star just to be sent back to the musty books?

However, the Word speaks with indisputable authority. The relevant prophecy was proclaimed by Micah, "But you, Bethlehem Ephrathah, though you are small among the clans of Judah, out of you will come for me one who will be ruler over Israel" (5:2). So, in obedience to the Word of God, the Magi went to Bethlehem.

It is clear, therefore, that the star is subject to the Word. When the gilding is gone: the truth remains. When emotion and romanticism disappear; the Word of God triumphs. We might love the stars, but we need the Word. If we only have the

> *Your word is a lamp to my feet and a light for my path.*
> PS 119:105

stars without the Word of God, we are left without the address of our King. The Word guides us to Bethlehem, to the stable, to the manger, but above all, to the King!

God of the eternal Word, keep me from being so fascinated by the stars and the bright lights of Christmas that I shall not seek your Word and consequently not find you.

Meditate daily about the words of your Creator. Become acquainted with the heart of God through the Word of God so that a burning desire for the joys of heaven will set your soul aflame – POPE GREGORY.

8 DECEMBER

Read JOHN 1:1-18

The Word became flesh

The Magi regarded the star as their guide, but in Jerusalem they discovered the Word which would lead them to Bethlehem and to the King. The Christmas drama reached its climax when they bowed down and worshipped the Child. For the first time they understood the mystery of God in the flesh. The fascination of the stars had gone – the Light of God was breaking through, touching their hearts. Now the child became the star – the bright Morning Star.

> *The Word became flesh and made his dwelling among us.*
> *We have seen his glory...*
> JN 1:14

From the star we must proceed to the Word. On our way to Christmas we must look up as the Magi did: after all, the stars are around us . . . But the stars lead us to the Word and the Word guides us to the stable where we bow down in unconditional worship and in full surrender. We offer our gifts: the gold of our love, the incense of our prayers, the myrrh of our sacrifice. In the stable we are taught what the stars could never convey to us: that the earth became the centre of the universe on Christmas Day. The fading stars allow the eternal day of God to dawn. No longer will God speak to us through stars, but eternally through the Scriptures, the Word which has become flesh, Jesus, Immanuel!

God Almighty, guide me past the stars, through the holy Word of God to the Child in the manger, this Christmas – so that I can worship in spirit and in truth the Word which became flesh.

To know Christ is not to speculate on the manner of his coming in the flesh, but to have first-hand knowledge of his redeeming grace – PHILIP MELANCHTON.

Christ – born for all!

Simeon was in the temple when he had the most wonderful experience of his life. Just imagine: the grey old man taking the Child in his arms, thereby receiving Christ as a gift. At the same time he accepted God's redeeming love. In this way he proclaimed the message of the gospel.

Simeon confessed, "Sovereign Lord, as you have promised, you now dismiss your servant in peace. For my eyes have seen your salvation, which you have prepared . . ." (Lk 2:29-31). That is what faith means: seeing the invisible. Simeon rejoiced and sang that Christ is "a light for revelation to the Gentiles" (32). Christ came for Simeon, but also for all nations, as well as for you and me.

> *Moved by the Spirit, he went into the temple courts. When the parents brought in the child Jesus . . . Simeon took him in his arms and praised God . . .*
>
> LK 2:27-28

This is God's Christmas deed: he lays the Child of his love in your arms and with this child he offers you his love, his blood, his body, yes, everything which you need in order to be saved. However, we also need to perform a Christmas deed: we must embrace the Child and accept him, for Christmas not only involves God coming to man, but also a deed of man coming to God.

Help me, Lord, to take Christ in my arms and the message of your love on my lips, for then it will be truly Christmas in my heart.

You can never truly enjoy the Christmas blessing unless you have looked into the Father's face telling him that you have accepted his Christmas gift – JOHN R RICE.

Read MICAH 5:1-4

The Bread of Life

M icah prophesied that Christ would be born in Bethlehem – also called Ephrathah – a little town thirteen kilometres south of Jerusalem. The word Bethlehem means "house of bread", a most appropriate name since it is situated in a fertile area.

Bethlehem was the town where David, the great king, grew up. He longed for the water of the well at the gate of Bethlehem when he was a refugee in the mountains. From this lineage of David God allowed his son to be born as the Saviour of the world. He was the one who would become the bread of life to millions of people; the fountain of living water which would for ever quench the thirst of mankind.

> *But you, Bethlehem Ephrathah, though you are small among the clans of Judah, out of you will come for me one who will be ruler over Israel, whose origins are of old, from ancient times.*
>
> MICAH 5:1

Today, when a pilgrim enters into the church erected on the spot where Christ was born, he must bow low to be able to enter through the opening which serves as the door. During this month, but also for the rest of our lives, we must also bow down low before the Child who was born in Bethlehem.

F ather, I thank you that I have discovered the bread of life and have found the living water and that the grace of our Redeemer who was born in Bethlehem will satisfy all my needs for ever.

I feel a great need for Christ; I have a great Christ to satisfy my needs – CHARLES H SPURGEON.

Examine your attitude

Herod hid his dislike of God behind hypocrisy. He pretended a desire to worship the child, but all he really wanted to do was make sure that he would remain king. To people like Herod Christmas says: Only people with the right attitude in their hearts and who worship in sincerity will be able to find Christ.

The scribes knew all about the Messiah whom they were expecting, but it was only book knowledge. They themselves never made contact with the Child himself. Christmas demands a personal testimony from us about the Child who was born.

The Magi persevered in their search for the Child. They made contact with him because they had the right attitude and they were sincere when they honoured him with their gifts. If we persevere in our search for Christ we shall find him and we shall experience great joy. Moreover, God will bless our sincerity of heart with all the blessings he has in store for us during the Christmas season.

> *Then Herod called the Magi secretly and found out from them the exact time the star had appeared. He sent them to Bethlehem and said, "As soon as you find him, report to me, so that I too may go and worship him."*
>
> MT 2:7-8

*H*oly Spirit of God, my guide, help me during this Christmastide to find the Child anew and through him, life eternal.

Christmas was created in the heart of God. It is fulfilled only when it reaches the heart of man – *JOHN RAY.*

Read LUKE 2:8-14

Christic in the centre

For many people Christmas has become a feast without Christ. He had to make room for worldly superficiality. As Christians it is our duty to restore Christ to his rightful place in this most wonderful of all holy days.

We must keep our eyes open for all the signs of the commercialisation of Christmas. We should not allow ourselves to become so caught up in the mad rush of Christmas that we arrive at church on Christmas day in such a state of exhaustion that we can barely manage to sing praises to the love of God.

> *Do not be afraid. I bring you good news of great joy that will be for all the people. Today in the town of David a Saviour has been born to you; he is Christ the Lord.*
> LK 2:10-11

It is our duty to put the Christ back in Christmas. We have more than enough reasons for celebrating, but if Christ is not the centre of our celebrations we cannot experience true Christmas cheer. We need to experience the true glory of Christmas in our own hearts. During Christmas the world should undeniably see who we are: through our Christmas cards; through our Christmas trees which point to the cross, through our prayers, through our gifts and all we wish to sacrifice to God – the gold of our love, the incense of our prayer, the myrrh of our sacrifices – all should breathe the spirit of a truly holy day.

Holy God, guide me past all the superficialities of Christmas to the true inner joy which can only be found in your Son, Jesus Christ.

The Lord of heaven: born of a girl from an obscure little town; a carpenter's Son; yet wonderful – Prince of Peace, almighty God!

Read MATTHEW 18:1-5

A family celebration

hristmas is a celebration for the entire family. As Christmas day approaches, children beam, full of expectation for the special day. If only adults could also beam with expectation, Christmas could be a renewing power in their lives.

Christmas is the time to rediscover the lost glory of our faith; to realise that God can renew the experience of Christ in our lives. This is the time when life can begin to have a new meaning for us; it is a time to surrender ourselves to God with renewed dedication and to rejoice in his Spirit who desires to live within us.

> *And he said, "I tell you the truth, unless you change and become like little children, you will never enter the kingdom of heaven."*
>
> MT 18:3

Christmas Day tells us that the child should be the centre of the family. It tells us about the love of parents, their interest in and their care for their children. This brings us back to the secret of true happiness and joy: the family – mother, father, child and God! May you experience the joy of true family unity during this Christmas. May this lead you to renewed resolutions to preserve the sacredness of the family, for then Christmas will bring you happiness within the family and true peace.

oly Father, we worship you as the God of Christmas and we thank you that the family acquired a new, special meaning through your Son, Jesus Christ.

Sometimes it is good to become like a child again, and there is no better time than at Christmas, because that was the time when the Friend of Children became a child himself.

14 DECEMBER

Read LUKE 1:26-38

A mother's love

Christmas and the birth of Christ gave a new status to all women and mothers. This renewed status was accompanied by an added appreciation of the religious faith of women. If our appreciation of women is dwindling, may God grant that our respect for them will be rekindled during this Christmas season.

> But the angel said to her, "Do not be afraid, Mary, you have found favour with God."
>
> LK 1:30

Christmas wishes to proclaim to us: woman and mother, you are privileged. You must assert your nobility as a woman and be a heroine for faith. When you feel like succumbing to the demands of motherhood and womanhood, when worry and burdens oppress you, heed the message from heaven saying: Do not be afraid, you have found favour with God.

Mary's cup of happiness was overflowing because of the wonder of motherhood. And like thousands of women throughout the ages she said in faith, "I am the Lord's servant. May it be to me as you have said" (38).

May the hearts of children go out to the hearts of their believing mothers and therefore also to God during this Christmas. May they reflect a love that cannot be put into words.

Thank you, my Father in heaven, for the love and the loyalty of a mother. May all mothers be blessed during this time of Christmas cheer for the sake of the Child Jesus.

God could not be everywhere, that is why he created mothers
— *JEWISH SAYING.*

A family belongs together

T rue to the message of Christmas, families have the desire to be together on Christmas day.

Joseph was just where God expected him to be: with his wife and Child. He knew he had to be with his wife Mary in the miraculous moment in the life of a family – the birth of a baby.

Christmas once more proclaims the truth we find in Genesis: man and wife belong together. There are times when a husband's family may claim his attention above all other things and he may not try to escape this responsibility. Joseph's presence gave Mary courage during the unfamiliar experience of giving birth to a baby. It strengthened her self-confidence and relieved her anxiety.

> *So they hurried off and found Mary and Joseph, and the baby, who was lying in the manger.*
>
> LK 2:16

May Christmas teach us once more that marital bliss must be earned through our sacrifices; that it requires hard work to enrich our marriage; that we can only experience true happiness if we give our utmost, because, "If I speak in the tongues of men and of angels, but have not love, I am only a resounding gong or a clanging cymbal" (1 Cor 13:1).

W e thank you, holy Child of Bethlehem, that the love which only you can instill in family members, inspires them with a renewed awareness of each other.

A successful marriage always forms a triangle which comprises man, wife and God! – CECIL MYERS.

God is already there, waiting

It is wonderful to find that when you turn to God in your need, he is already there, waiting to meet you in your extremity. He does this unconditionally but for us to benefit from his presence, we must be quiet before him and long to be with him. Even in the midst of our rushed existence it is possible to feel the touch of his healing presence.

> *My soul glorifies the Lord and my spirit rejoices in God my Saviour, for he has been mindful of the humble state of his servant.*
>
> LK 1:47-48

The most important point stressed in the gospel is that the almighty God became flesh and lived among men, thereafter to live in the hearts of those who loved and served him.

Although Christ lived and worked in a specific period of history, he is eternal. Therefore, wherever you may be, he will be there with you. Many people choose to ignore this glorious truth, but to those who really accept it, a whole new dimension is added to their lives. They share their problems and fears with him; they are strengthened and inspired so that they can fulfil their ideals and they develop a deep and rich relationship with the living Christ. In this way we do not merely exist but we have a rich, full and abundant life.

Loving Lord, make me always truly aware of your living presence and grant that my relationship with you will continue to improve in depth and quality.

Without God time is meaningless – STELLA SEYFFERT.

DECEMBER 17

Read PSALM 94:16-23

God the comforter

Christmas is normally a time of joy and good cheer but we know that during this time there are many who are grieving, lonely and homesick.

For many people the past year has been very painful and whilst others sing Christmas carols and rejoice, their lives are darkened by anxieties. There are those people who are anxious about their physical condition, their approaching old age. Many will never again be able to celebrate Christmas as in the past because the family circle has been broken. There are parents who will miss their children who are far away

> *When anxiety was great within me, your consolation brought joy to my soul.*
> PS 94:19

or estranged from them. Worst of all, there are those people who have lost a loved one this year. It is impossible to describe the anguish and longing of such a person.

The Child of Bethlehem also had to walk along this road of suffering. That is why he can identify with us in our grief and suffering. Persevere in his strength and you will enjoy the victory which is part of the pilgrim's reward when he or she reaches the goal after a worthy pilgrimage. Then take comfort from the words of Psalm 94:19.

God of the lonely and grieving, thank you that we can rejoice in the knowledge that in Jesus Christ you took our weaknesses and sorrows upon your shoulders.

You can be assured of comfort in affliction only if you have a steadfast faith based on the Scriptures and the teachings of Christ — THOMAS MOORE.

18 DECEMBER

Read LUKE 2:8-20

The decision is ours

God speaks to us in various ways, through nature, through the Scriptures and also through trials, sickness and loss.

However, during Christmas God speaks to us through a Child in a manger. God himself became a Child to speak to us in a language that can be universally understood. That is why we have to have a heartfelt longing, a joyous anticipation to hear God speak to us through his Son during these days of celebration.

> *This will be a sign to you: You will find a baby wrapped in cloths and lying in a manger.*
>
> LK 2:12

The Child of Bethlehem speaks of God's unfathomable love for us. Should this love not spur us on to love our own children more and to pray earnestly for their salvation? Christmas is the ultimate family festival. It is a time of celebration when parents and children renew their bonds of love and respect for each other.

Our children always represent a choice; either we love them and care for them or we neglect them and make them sad. God loves us and therefore gave us his Child. Bethlehem's Child confronts us with the same choice; shall we love him of make him sad? The choice is yours.

Eternal Father, give me the capacity to love more.

Jesus Christ is God's complete and encompassing answer to mankind's total needs.

Christ came to us

The Lord God chose Israel as the nation with whom he wanted to enter into a covenant. He blessed them and prepared them for the coming of Christ. The prophets foretold that a Messias would be born who would free them from all injustice and establish an eternal realm of peace. Therefore, when this King was finally born he came to a people who, in a special sense, belonged to him. So what happened?

One would expect that he would find welcoming hearts, but what a bitter reception awaited him. He had come to claim his own . . . but they did not accept him! How tragic that the King had come to his own people to bless them and offer them forgiveness, justification by faith, sanctification and eternal life – only to find the door to his own palace locked. This is why Christmas is the

> *He came to that which was his own,
> but his own did not receive him.*
>
> JN 1:11

start of the passion of Christ. Behind the wooden manger we already see the shadow of the wooden cross.

When the Son of man came to claim his own he was faced with people who refused to believe and accept him.

If he came back today would anything be different?

*C*hrist Jesus, once again I ask that you dwell in my heart and my life forever.

To love as Christ loved, is to make of our love a practical reality, instead of a sentimental flight of fancy – CHARLES STANFORD.

20 DECEMBER

Read JOHN 1:9-18

Have you accepted Christ in faith?

The words in John 1:11 were spoken to the people of Israel, but they also apply to you and me. The Lord has also included us in his covenant of grace and comes to us as our Saviour. His work of redemption gives him ownership over our lives and he can rightly say: You are mine! I have a right to your love and life. I have come to reconcile you with God, to redeem and free you from your sin and to make you an heir to life eternal.

On the first Christmas Christ came to those who belong to him and since then in his grace he has come to us countless times. This year he again stands and knocks at the door of your heart. Will you receive him with joyful Hosannas or does your life crucify him?

> *He came to that which was his own,*
> *but his own did not receive him.*
>
> JN 1:11

Out of his own free will and love Christ came to you. Have you accepted him in faith? Receive him for what he is and wants to be in your life – Immanuel – God with you; Intercessor between you and the Father; Guarantor who pays all your debts with God; High Priest who sacrificed himself for you; King and shepherd of his flock.

As children joyfully meet their King with "hosannas" and Sion
greets its Messiah with jubilation – so I sing about
your peace, your sovereignty and in my prayers
of praise and gratitude I honour you in exultation.

If Christ lives in us and is in control of our lives, we shall leave a blessed imprint on the lives which touch our lives. Not because of our wonderful characters but because of his
– EUGENIA PRICE.

Make room for God and his Son

If the people of Bethlehem only knew Who it was who were looking for a place to stay that night, they might have made room for Mary and Joseph. However, they were not to know that the Messiah would be born there, because God did not come to the world in glory. He came as a servant and was born in a stable.

Will there again be no room in our lives for him this Christmas? Then we are far more guilty than the people of Bethlehem, for we at least know that he is Christ, the King of kings. But we don't honour him as such because our lives are so crammed with self-interest that there is no room for him.

> *In my father's house are many rooms;*
> *if it were not so I would have told you.*
> *I am going there to prepare a place for you.*
>
> JN 14:2

The wonder of God's grace is that he does not repay us according to our deeds. In spite of the fact that there was no room for him on earth, he goes ahead to prepare a place for us with his Father in heaven. There we shall never find a sign that says "Full house". Let our deed this Christmas be to make room in our lives for God and his Son. After all, we know that a place has been prepared for us with the Father in his eternal home, by our Lord, Jesus Christ.

Lord, this Christmas I want to open the door to my life to you. Thank you for the place which you have prepared for me in heaven.

God accepts you – not because you have deserved it or because of your hard work for him, but because Christ died for you
– COLIN URQUHART.

Love triumphant

Although the people did not want to accept Christ, he gave everyone who believed in him the right to become children of God. At his birth there was no room for him in the inn, yet he guarantees a place in his Father's house for every person who loves him. People despised him. Nevertheless he promises that he will never leave us. On the cross he was challenged to prove that he was the Son of God by coming down and saving himself. Yet he chose to die on that cross for our sake. There is no greater love than this.

There is so much hatred in the world which obscures the relationship between God and man and between people. However the message of Christmas is that love triumphs over everything because God so loved us that he gave us his Son. If this is the way in which God loves us, we can't help but love one another.

> *And they will call him Immanuel –*
> *which means God with us.*
> MT 1:23

Let us tell each other about that love during this Christmas time. Tell your husband or wife, your parents – and watch the tension disappear. Tell those who do not believe – and see how their attitude towards Christ changes. Tell God that you love him and Christ will be born anew in your heart. Immanuel – God with you, but also Hallelujah – you with God.

*H*eavenly Father, I want to thank you again that your Son saved me and that through this deed your love for me was so clearly demonstrated. Grant me more love for others.

God does not love us because we are precious. We are precious because God loves us – FULTON J SHEEN.

Christ banishes the darkness

Hundreds of people stumble on in unbelief, superstition and ignorance. The non-believer, the church-estranged person and the atheist have lost their way in the dark passages of sin. Many have been broken and disillusioned by injustices. Like Judas, because of their evil deeds, they are often driven to suicide or they lead a meaningless existence. This is so unnecessary and in the process God is dishonoured.

Christmas fulfils Isaiah's prophesy, "The people walking in darkness have seen a great light . . ." This is a liberating message to each and everyone who fears the darkness of death. The

> *The people walking in darkness have seen a great light; on those living in the land of the shadow of death, a light has dawned.*
>
> IS 9:2

Child of Bethlehem came to conquer death; to ensure that the grave would not be the end, but merely a brilliant portal to a wonderful heaven.

Even though I walk through the valley of the shadow of death . . . Immanuel – God is with me. On that first Christmas Day, he, the Light of the world, came to transform the darkness in our lives into rays of heavenly light, banishing the darkness forever!

Christ, guide me through this earthly darkness. Thank you that we know that you are at our side guiding us as we take every step along this dark road.

Darkness offers us no choices. It is only the light which enables us to see the difference between right and wrong and Christ gives us that light – C T WHITMELL.

Don't be afraid

Christmas proclaims that God is with us and he replaces our fear with rejoicing. On that first Christmas Eve the angel said, "Do not be afraid, I bring you good news of great joy . . ." (Lk 2:10).

However, the world is filled with fear because fear is a product of our sinfulness. We fear that the world will end; we fear the unknown like a child fears the dark; we fear for our health, our marriages, our children; our jobs; we fear loneliness, old age and death.

> *But the angel said to her, "Don't be afraid, Mary, you have found favour with God."*
>
> LK 1:30

However, on Christmas Day God sends us his messenger to say to us: Don't be afraid, for God is with you! This is a joyful tiding, because God's love has banished fear from our lives. It has been replaced by great joy, because the Redeemer conquered the origin of that fear: sin, Satan and death.

In the storms of life the Redeemder tells you not to be afraid. God is with you. With this motto on your lips your heart can rejoice in Christ, your Redeemer.

Immanuel, thank you that in the most dire of circumstances I can say: Though I pass through the darkest depths I will not be afraid, because you are with me. That is possible because of that first Christmas.

Any concern too small to be turned into a prayer is too small to be made into a burden – CORRIE TEN BOOM.

The saving grace of God

On Christmas Day "the grace of God that brings salvation" was brought to us in the form of Jesus Christ. On that day God descended from heaven and appeared to us on earth in his love and grace. He revealed himself to us as the Father who blesses, protects and comforts us.

God also reveals himself on Christmas Day as the Son who came to take the curse of sin on himself; to redeem us from all unrighteousness and to claim us as his purified own. He came to give us the resurrection and the victory and everlasting joy.

> *For the grace of God that brings salvation has appeared to all men.*
>
> TIT 2:11

God's presence on Christmas Day in the human body of Jesus Christ already embodied the promise of the Holy Spirit who would come to gird us with power; to equip us for our life of service; to teach us, to guide and comfort us; to give us understanding, warm our hearts and to lift our souls in adoration.

A blessed Christmas Day to you – the day on which God's saving grace was given to us! God is with us and in us. May that be true for you today and every day.

My Father, thank you that your incomprehensible saving grace was brought to us in the person of your Son. Thank you that you live in us through the Spirit. Fill our hearts with love for others and for you.

One day peace will reign over the entire world and in the hearts of man. One day it will be Christmas for ever.

26 DECEMBER

Read REVELATION 3:15-21

Have you opened the door?

At the end of the year we are tired in body and mind. But Christmas renews our faith, hope, love and our ideals. Christmas brings our will in harmony with God's will and reminds us again of Christ's love for us. It is then that we understand that Jesus was born so that we could be reborn children of God, and that we could have a new heart, a new understanding and a new attitude to life.

> *Here I am! I stand at the door and knock.*
> *If anyone hears my voice and opens the door,*
> *I will come in and eat with him, and he with me.*
>
> REV 3:20

If we truly understand the message of Christmas, we shall know that in the same way as God showed his love on that first Christmas Day by giving us his Son, he will continue to give of his love, grace, forgiveness and eternal life to all who want to accept it. The love which God revealed on Christmas Day is eternal and unchanging.

If we interpret the message of Christmas correctly, we shall know that even though we might shut God out of our life, he nevertheless keeps the door to heaven wide open for us.

The message of Christmas is clear. We know that God seeks us. Every day he says, "Here I am. I stand at the door and knock."

Thank you, Lord, that you come to us at Christmas. Thank you that you continue to knock at the door of our hearts.
Come in, Lord Jesus!

Christ is the secret, the source, the content, the centre and the circumference of all true and lasting joy – *C COWMAN.*

Christ is the way

M any people have the type of faith which is never applied on a practical level. Christ is never allowed to move from the manger into our everyday lives. We must thank God that Christ did not remain a little child. Then he would never have spoken the sermon on the mount with its wonderful beatitudes to prop up our needy hearts.

He would not have been able to carry the cross to Calvary. He had to leave the manger and become a man in order to carry out God's will.

> *"I will set out and go back to my father. . ."*
> LK 15:18

In our faith we cannot remain at the romantic scene in Bethlehem. Manger love is not enough; we must move forward to faith in the cross, in the resurrection and ascension into heaven. Then God can send us into the world to do his work.

If we have met the Child at Bethlehem during Christmas, he will show us the way to the House of our Father. Like the prodigal son, our sins have caused us to stray from the Father. The prodigal son was lost in sin. But in his deepest need he finds that there is a way back to the Father's heart and love. That is the guarantee which Christmas brings us. The Child became a man who proclaimed, I am the way . . . We must embark on that journey from the manger to the cross to the Father's heart.

H oly Father, I dearly want to move on beyond the manger. Help me, this year, to become stronger in spirit because I have been privileged to enjoy another Christmas.

He who merely provides for this life without being concerned about eternity is clever for one short moment, but foolish for ever – JOHN TILLOTSEN.

Keep the spirit of Christmas alive

Every year we experience something of the wonderful events of that first Christmas Eve, but what will remain in our hearts once Christmas has passed? Will the Christmas glow fade as we bid farewell to the old year? Or will an inspiring afterglow remain which, even in the cold of June, will warm our hearts with memories of Christmas?

A Christmas conviction which, together with the withered Christmas tree, is thrown onto the refuse heap, is useless and makes a farce of Christmas. Christmas brings out the best in people. How wonderful it would be if one could bottle the Christmas spirit so that you could open one every week of the year!

> The shepherds returned glorifying
> and praising God, for all the things they had heard and seen.
> LK 2:20

If we celebrated Christmas and in the spirit knelt down in the stable in Bethlehem, if we met the Christ Child this year, then that meeting should leave an after-glow in our hearts. When Christmas has passed, that glow of love in our hearts must encourage us to help find those who are lost, help the sick, feed the hungry, be compassionate with those in prison, help rebuild the world, bring peace and fill the world with love.

You, O Lord, who are God of Christmas and also of the whole year, help me through your Son, Jesus Christ, to sing the song of Christmas unceasingly, only to honour you.

Even though Christ is no longer with us in the flesh, we have our neighbours who, for the purposes of love and service, might just as well be the Lord himself — TERESA OF AVILA.

The value of self-examination

If you ask God to search your heart you are stripped of all hypocrisy. You see yourself through God's eyes. This self-examination is necessary so that we can be useful to God. Under the tutelage of the Holy Spirit we become useful instruments in his hand and are able to work to his honour. If our self-evaluation brings us to a realisation of our sinfulness, let us then cling more firmly to God, the unchanging and eternal. Then the truth of the words of Marie Louise Haskins is proved in our lives,

"I said to the man at the gateway of the year, 'Give me a light so that I may safely step out into the unknown darkness.' He answered, 'Go forth into the darkness and place your hand in the almighty hand of God. That will be better for you than a light and safer than a familiar path.'

> *Search me, O God, and know my heart;*
> *test me and know my anxious thoughts.*
> *See if there is any offensive way in me*
> *and lead me in the way everlasting.*
> PS 139:23-24

"And so, with my hand in God's hand I joyfully ventured forth into the darkness and he led me to the mountains and the dawning of a new day in the East."

*H*oly Father, may I never refuse to be examined by your Spirit. Go to the core of my being and know me, mould me so that I may become a fruitful labourer in your service.

A humble and modest knowledge of yourself is a surer way to the Father's heart than the ardent searching of science
— THOMAS À KEMPIS.

30 DECEMBER

Read MARK 7:31-37

He has done everything well

God's most direct way of speaking to us is through his Son from his eternal Word. In the light of that Word we must review the road along which we have come and beg for God's friendly light to guide us along the way ahead. What we have done with the year which lies behind us is far more important than its duration.

> People were overwhelmed with amazement.
> "He has done everything well," they said.
> MK 7:37

In the past year God has exposed us to many experiences in our life to give it substance. He has crowned our efforts with success this year and has bestowed his grace on us. We enjoy life and health, a happy family life, free access to his Word. We do not deserve all these blessings and we humbly confess: You have done everything well!

Not all our experiences during this year necessarily brought us joy, but they were good for us. His pierced, loving hands were compassionate enough to heal our wounds and even in our pain we can confess: Everything you do is good!

When we reach the end of our pilgrimage and enter into the eternal glory we shall lift our hands in amazement and confess prayerfully: Everything you do is good!

Heavenly Father, I worship you as the one who guides the pilgrim and I rejoice because I know that, in spite of everything that has happened along the way, everything you do is good.

God is the God of promises. He honours his word, even when to us it seems impossible to do so; even when circumstances seem to indicate the opposite – COLIN URQUHART.

Thank God

At the end of the year there is much about which we feel ashamed; so many lost opportunities for which we blame ourselves. But there is also so much grace which we have received from God. The year was filled with joy and sorrow, victory and defeat, and still we can call God our Father. Perhaps we have lost much, but we have gained so much.

Today you are richer if you smiled often, forgave others, if you made new friends and used the obstacles along your path as steps to climb higher; if you thought more in terms of "you" than of "I".

You have been enriched today if you made time to admire God's handiwork; if you learnt to distinguish the things which are really important; if you were patient with the faults of others.

> *"I am the Alpha and the Omega,"* says the Lord God, *"who is, and who was, and who is to come, the Almighty."*
> REV 1:8

You are wealthy beyond measure if a little child smiled at you; if you searched to bring out the best in others and gave your best to them. Then you would not complain about the year which has passed. On the contrary, you will thank God for this year and start the new year, safe in the love and grace of Jesus Christ.

Thank you for your grace and love which carried me through another year. Thank you that I can embark on a new year in the sure knowledge that you will never forsake or abandon me.

May the road come up to meet you, may the wind be behind you and the sun caress your face; may the rain fall softly on your fields and until we meet again, may God keep you in the hollow of his hand! – *IRISH BLESSING*

Notes

_____
_____
_____
_____
_____
_____
_____
_____
_____
_____
_____
_____
_____
_____
_____
_____
_____
_____
_____
_____
_____
_____
_____
_____
_____
_____
_____
_____
_____
_____
_____
_____
_____
_____
_____